HUMAN RESOURCE MANAGEMENT AND CHANGE

This exciting new book has grow   need to provide practical advice to managers who deal with contem   uman resource and change issues. A crucial role of a manager is to respond   the best interests of the organization and at the same time retain talent. Skill shortag   and ageing populations in developed economies and the need for emerging ec   omies to develop their workforce coincide to present managers with unique challenges.

Human Resource Management and Change: A practising manager's guide offers a timely overview of recent environmental and economic changes as depicted by the Delta forces of change. These include demographic, environmental, legal, technical and attitudinal changes that are in part the product of globalization and the Global Financial Crisis (GFC). The fundamental strategies for managing change and implementing human resource practices are clearly explained. End-of-chapter study guides further explain the topics of the chapters by providing case studies, ethical dilemmas and review and discussion questions as well as further reading.

The text reflects the everyday challenge managers face in a turbulent environment and focuses on providing practical guidelines to managers who may not have higher academic qualifications to help them manage people and change.

Lanny Entrekin is Emeritus Professor at Murdoch University, Australia.

Brenda D. Scott-Ladd is Associate Professor of Human Resource Management at Curtin University, Australia.

HUMAN RESOURCE MANAGEMENT AND CHANGE

A practising manager's guide

Lanny Entrekin and
Brenda D. Scott-Ladd

Routledge
Taylor & Francis Group

LONDON AND NEW YORK

First published 2014
by Routledge
2 Park Square, Milton Park, Abingdon, Oxon OX14 4RN

and by Routledge
711 Third Avenue, New York, NY 10017

Routledge is an imprint of the Taylor & Francis Group, an informa business

British Library Cataloguing in Publication Data
A catalogue record for this book is available from the British Library.

Library of Congress Cataloging in Publication Data
Entrekin, Lanny
Human resource management and change : a practising manager's guide /
Lanny Entrekin and Brenda D. Scott-Ladd.
pages cm
Includes bibliographical references and index.
1. Personnel management. 2. Organizational change.
3. Organizational effectiveness. I. Scott-Ladd, Brenda D. II. Title.
HF5549.E734 2014
658.3--dc23   2013006158

ISBN: 978-0-415-82404-0 (hbk)
ISBN: 978-0-415-82405-7 (pbk)
ISBN: 978-0-203-68401-6 (ebk)

Typeset in Bembo and ITCStoneSans
by Cenveo Publisher Services

100722026X

Printed and bound in Great Britain by
TJ International Ltd, Padstow, Cornwall

CONTENTS

FIGURES

TABLES AND EXHIBITS

Tables

Exhibits

1

INTRODUCTION

HRM in a changing environment

Since 2008, the worldwide economy has experienced the worst recession since the great depression of 1929–1933. This has resulted in massive downsizing of labour forces around the world and the demise of major institutions such as Bear Stearns, General Motors and Chrysler, among many others. The ILO's worst-case estimate was that 50 million people would be out of work worldwide by the end of 2009. Economists and other financial analysts varied considerably in their opinions about when a recovery would take place, with opinions ranging between late 2009 to 2012, but at the end of 2011 ILO (2012a) figures showed that 29 million more were still unemployed by comparison with the situation prior to the crisis. Some countries have fared better than others have, but the economic crises in Spain, Greece, Italy and the United States have seen rising unemployment through to the end of 2012, suggesting the recovery will be slower than expected.

Assuming that a recovery will occur, and history tells us it will, the question for human resource management (HRM) is: what will be the major issues and implications for HR practice and policies in the intervening period between contraction and recovery? One view, and probably the predominant one, is simply to survive, in which case we will likely see the current carnage of workforces continue. Another, perhaps more considered, view is the need to protect investments in human resources built up over a considerable period at very substantial costs. Considerable research into what creates 'sustainable competitive advantage' in an organization clearly indicates effective human resources are at the heart of an organization's intellectual capital and that, in turn, accounts for about 80 per cent of profits.

Retaining knowledge and sustainable competitive advantage, therefore, is essential for organizations to position themselves for the recovery period and beyond. We call into question whether many aspects have changed! We have written considerably about skill shortages while acknowledging the vast number of job losses and unemployment. Yet there is little evidence of investment in up-skilling and skill shortages still remain, even though those skills may not be required during the downturn and will pose an ongoing problem as economies improve. When the recovery does come, there will still be a need to have a reliable workforce in place and ready to go. Those organizations that recklessly downsize and lose valuable intellectual capital and organizational memory will recover more slowly with reduced capability, market share and profits.

Thus, this book has several aims. First, we wish to explore the issues that are driving change in the current environment and explain the concepts of human resource management and how these can help an organization to manage change. The aim is to provide a practical framework that organizations can use to assist them in achieving quality outcomes for all stakeholders. To survive, organizations do need to turn a profit, but they need to do this in a way that balances the needs of all stakeholders, including employees. Providing quality customer service is one aspect of this, but they also need to recognize their responsibility to the communities they exist within and the employees they hire.

For this reason, we focus on the roles adopted by managers and decision-makers and provide guidance on how to integrate the job, the technology and, more importantly, the people that work in tandem to achieve strategic objectives. The central tenet is that strategic choices are driven by where the organization wants to position itself and what it needs to do to achieve the outcomes it desires. While managers coordinate and integrate these activities, it is motivated individuals who help achieve an organization's goals and they need to be recognized and valued for doing so.

This book is an update and expansion of an ILO publication in 2001 entitled *Human Resource Management: Adaptation and change in an age of globalization*. The major focus of that publication was to examine whether traditional HR practices were still relevant, in their current form, in a vastly accelerated operating environment characterized by globalization practices. The interim period witnessed a booming stock market as part of a bull market cycle and the downturn of the global financial crisis. Some major issues for HRM still remain: these are skill shortages, retention of key staff, recruitment of new, high-quality workers and the remuneration issues pursuant to a tight labour market for skilled workers, and a loose labour market for unskilled workers.

A tipping point proposition

It is generally acknowledged that globalization started sometime in the early to mid-1980s. This period was characterized by the practice of downsizing the workforce with the objective of doing more with less staff. It is a fact that this practice will reduce costs and, to a point, increase productivity. This practice is typically followed by outsourcing all but core activities and competencies. These actions are then followed by a reorganization or reengineering of organizational structures and production processes to reconfigure the organization to fit the new competitive environment. This sequence is illustrated in Exhibit 1.1 below.

Exhibit 1.1   A likely chain of events and their consequences

- External market pressures lead to internal pressures to do things faster, better, cheaper
- Benchmarking takes place to get an external comparison on where an organization stands in comparison to best practice
- Core and non-core processes and competencies are identified
- Non-core processes are outsourced
- The workforce is downsized to reflect the need for fewer people due to outsourced activities
- Functions and processes are reengineered to create a leaner, flatter, more adaptive organization
- An organization is now seen as a process-based supply chain

---

The above practices are primarily employed to achieve the twin objectives of reducing costs and increasing productivity and have been widely practised over the past twenty-plus years. The critical question is – do they work? It is our proposition that these practices do work – up to a point, which we refer to as the *tipping point*. Beyond this, the negative consequences may outweigh the positives. Some well-documented negative consequences are considered below and these will be discussed throughout the book:

- the loss of job security
- the loss of loyalty to the organization
- a 'me first – organization second' attitude
- excessive workloads
- excessive turnover and absenteeism
- stress-related illnesses
- poor morale
- poor job satisfaction
- increased accidents
- increased occupational and health costs
- increased staffing costs
- increased training and replacement costs
- reduced productivity.

It is not our intention to suggest that cost saving and efficiency measures should not be practised and continuously explored, but rather that these are structural measures that have limitations if not balanced by social-psychological measures and management of a workforce. Social-psychological measures are characterized by human-oriented practices that are embodied in HRM processes and systems and are designed to enhance the quality of working life and contribute equally to the bottom line.

What we do argue is that well-designed HR processes and systems can reduce many of the negative consequences noted above while working in concert with structural measures to reduce costs and increase productivity and profitability. Effective HR practices help the organization to manage the risk involved in employing and managing people, and at the same time can help reduce the risks employees are faced with in the work environment. The key here is to implement HR practices that align and work in concert with the strategic objectives of the organization.

Thus, the tipping point proposition is about balance; it is about reaching equilibrium between structural and human systems. The above points are usefully illustrated in the following discussion about the SAS Institute in Exhibit 1.2; this company has sustained its position as one of the best Fortune 500 American companies to work for since 1998.

Exhibit 1.2   SAS institute – a Fortune 500 best company to work for

In 2002, Rogovsky and Sims wrote about the American company SAS Institute and its commitment to its employees. SAS is a world leader in software analytics, is regularly listed as a Fortune 500 company and regularly appears as one of the best companies to work for. In 2001, SAS was ranked as the top company to work for; eleven years later in 2012 it was ranked third, after Google and the Boston Consulting Group. The SAS CSR report (2009) showed that 40 per cent of SAS employees have been with the company 10 years or more. The average turnover in the software sector was 22 per cent, whereas at SAS it was 2 per cent, which is even lower than the 3 per cent cited by Rogovsky and Sims in 2002, when they wrote:

> *All people at SAS Institute are treated fairly and equally. SAS emphasizes egalitarianism. It has a very flat organizational structure; depending on the particular division, there are only three or four levels in the company. Everybody at SAS (including assistants) has a private office, not a cubicle. Nobody, including SAS co-founder, Dr. James Goodnight, has a reserved parking space. There is no executive dining room. Everybody has the same health plan. ... SAS believes in and relies on intrinsic, internal motivation. Management trusts people, treats them like responsible adults and relies on them to do a good job. SAS has no formal sick days or sick leave policy; if people are sick, they simply stay at home. Performance appraisal forms have*

been eliminated. Instead of formal appraisals, managers spend time talking to their people and providing feedback on a regular basis (at least three times a year)

(Rogovsky and Sims, 2002)

The SAS company started in 1976 in the United States of America and the name is a derivative of Statistical Analysis System. It is now a worldwide company that operates 400 offices in 135 countries and employs over 13,000 staff. It services in excess of 60,000 other businesses and 90 of the top companies listed on the Fortune 500 list. In 1978 revenue was $1.2 million, by 2000 it reached $1.12 billion, and in 2012, worldwide revenue was $2.725 billion. Twenty-four per cent of revenue is committed to research and development. Customer loyalty and service are important and the company also invests heavily in its people.

SAS has been consistently listed as one of the top companies to work for in the USA since 1998 and is earning the same reputation in other countries. Quite apart from the working arrangements described above, employees have the opportunity to ask any questions they have of senior management through informal meetings over coffee. Staff have access to a wide range of benefits to support work–life balance. Apart from the employee assistance programme that gives access to counselling support, the company provides support for adoptions, health care, childcare, retirement benefits and recreational facilities. Employees also get help with the purchase of their homes.

Employees stay at SAS because of the company's values and ethics and, clearly, looking after employees is good for business. The 20 per cent difference multiplied by the size of the workforce means that SAS loses about 2,600 fewer employees per year than if it were an average competitor. Considering that replacement costs per annum can be one and a half to two times the annual salary, even using an entry-level salary of $80,000 per annum, suggests the saving from the lower turnover is in excess of $208 million. As Rogovsky and Sims (2002) point out: "*SAS shows that even in an era of relentless pressure, a company can differentiate itself from the competition and succeed just by being nice to its people.*" The other side of the coin for intrinsic motivation is that the work is also challenging and interesting, as Forbes quotes one employee as saying: "*I haven't felt so intellectually alive in any other place I have worked.*"

References for this case include:

SAS (2013) About Us: Corporate statistics. http://www.sas.com/company/about/statistics.html; http://www.sas.com/company/about/index.html.

Forbes(2013)http://money.cnn.com/magazines/fortune/best-companies/2012/snapshots/3.html.

Rogovsky, N. and Sims, E. (2002) Corporate success through people: Making international labour standards work for you. Geneva. Switzerland: ILO.

Historical background

Human resource management is currently being evaluated in terms of its role in the context of globalization and other trends. Although HRM has undergone quite dramatic change in the last 20 years or so, that change was associated with the long overdue recognition of HRM as an important strategic consideration. The current evaluation, while still strategic, has more immediacy and is broader in concept than the traditional focus on managing people at work.

HRM, and personnel management before it, are products of the bureaucratic age of large, self-contained entities in which their roles were fairly clearly specified and often organized by function, such as recruitment, remuneration, industrial relations, occupational health and safety, and so on. That type of organizational structure and operating environment is fast becoming history and HRM is faced with redefining its role in a rapidly changing landscape. The environment has become a permanent feature of business today and it is dramatically different from the stable conditions of the 1960s and 1970s. Many of our current HRM practices evolved in this stable context, which makes it necessary to question some of the premises and assumptions on which they are based.

This section briefly traces the historical development of personnel management and HRM, considers the forces driving change, and then looks at contemporary practices and the strategies pursued by companies to gain a competitive advantage. It also tracks the evolution of the human resource movement from the human relations movement, the personnel department and the change to human resource management. The emergence of new pressures of globalization have led to the human resource function evolving to a more strategic and holistic role as strategic human resource management. Finally, we look at specific HRM practices in relation to these changed conditions and suggest where human resource management may need to change.

During the twentieth century, growing emphasis was placed on the importance of managing people to build a flexible, competitive and productive organization. Managers learned to pay a lot more attention to the role that employees play in achieving the company's strategic goals. A focus on the workforce is emerging as one of the most important means to ensure the success of a business. In the past, personnel administration dealt with workers' concerns. Because of changes in the environment, the scope of action became broader and HRM appeared as an expanded function for managing employees. A brief historical review will show where the field has come from and how it has changed.

The terms Taylorism and Fordism are used in the management literature to refer to the influence of Frederick Taylor and Henry Ford on management practice in the early part of the 20th century. Taylor emphasized simplified work practices based on efficiency, while Ford used these concepts to establish the economies of scale resulting from assembly line practice.

At the beginning of the twentieth century, the organizational concepts of Taylorism and Fordism prevailed. Scientific management was used to organize, utilize and manage the workforce for mass production (Downie and Coates, 1994). Assembly lines required a large number of workers with low skills to perform repetitive tasks. Workers needed to be interchangeable and expendable. Organization hierarchy was vertical with a precise definition of the different tasks to be performed and little or no possibility for workers to participate in decision-making. Work was coordinated through the hierarchy, by maintaining close supervision on workers. Rules and procedures made bureaucracy a key feature of company management and the business world was relatively stable and certain. An example of this was the concept of a manager's span of control – the maximum number of subordinates a manager or supervisor should control. Even into the 1960s, personnel management classes in universities taught that a manager's span of control should not exceed 8–10 people. The logic behind this was that a manager needed to oversee the work of subordinates and could not do this beyond 8–10 subordinates. This, in part, resulted in tall hierarchies of authority with many levels of managers and supervisors. The message this sent to subordinates was "We don't trust you to make decisions and act responsibly of your own volition"!

In this environment, the personnel role was administrative. Important decisions were the responsibility of line managers. The personnel role was a maintenance function of which record-keeping was a major component. Personnel officers were also involved in screening applicants, conducting orientation for new employees, planning the company picnic and circulating memos (Cascio, 2006). In other words, the role of the personnel administrator was basic and limited, focusing on administrative tasks and processes.

Human relations

The new concept of the human relations movement emerged from the famous Hawthorne plant surveys carried out from 1924 to 1932, although, in reality, some humanists existed long before then. These studies explored how changes in the work environment could affect productivity through better lighting in the workplace. Elton Mayo, the father of the human relations movement, discovered that productivity increases were linked to the amount of attention paid to employees, rather than the improvement in lighting (Losey, 1998). As a result, managers were encouraged to care about their employees' attitudes, and motivation became an important feature in running a company.

The personnel department

The role of the personnel administrator began to change as the importance of the social dimension emerged and labour relations became a prominent issue. Personnel policies and programmes were developed to enhance negotiation and the implementation of collective agreements. The personnel department assumed a more important place in the organization's strategy. It began to deal with recruiting, testing, mediating and overseeing employee morale and production efficiency (Losey, 1998).

As a consequence of environmental changes and new pressures in the workplace, the role of the personnel department changed so that it was no longer an administrative and maintenance function. At this stage, the term 'human resource management' appeared as a more appropriate description of this aspect of running an organization.

Emergence of new pressures

The population in the United States and elsewhere increased considerably in the post-war baby boom. However, the economy deteriorated in the mid-1970s following the oil shocks (something that has reappeared in 2008), and companies were forced to downsize. Governments were then focusing on the way companies lay off their employees to protect them from discrimination. During the 1980s, temporary employment was booming. Companies saw this as a way to employ people only when they needed them, and thus as a way to reduce costs. In addition, management decisions had to be taken more and more quickly as the environment become more turbulent and the pace of business increased.

From an economic point of view, foreign competition was putting pressure on companies to boost production and become more competitive. A survey was conducted in the early 1960s by *Dun's Review* and *Modern Industry* among companies whose products were being challenged by foreign goods. Company presidents estimated that imports were taking an average of 7 per cent of their market; they believed the percentage would double by 1965 (cited by Delden, 1998). Internationalization was an important feature of this emerging environment. The opening to the world market forced innovations in marketing, and new products emerged as well as more efficient production processes. The pace of business was accelerating and bringing rapid industrial obsolescence. New technologies appeared and robots started to replace human workers. As a consequence, consumption patterns changed; workers wanted a higher quality of life and more leisure time.

In this context, managers had to become socially responsible towards their workforce, and the human dimension gained importance. Although the earlier Hawthorne studies demonstrated that employees reacted positively to recognition, this emerging need was largely paid 'lip service' with superficial gestures from managers. The need for a more genuine approach to employee development is well illustrated by this example from a large, divisionalized company in the United States with a new CEO.

The new CEO kept a low profile for a couple of months, moving around the various divisions to try to understand the dynamics. He discovered that line managers were largely ignoring a well-qualified HRM department that was in place. He called a meeting of senior executives and managers and, among other things, announced that in the future, in addition to their existing performance criteria, they would be assessed on how many promotable subordinates they produced. This powerful statement conveyed to managers that employee development was an important part of their job and would affect their rewards. This had the immediate effect of causing a 'run' on the HRM department by managers seeking assistance on how to develop their subordinates, which was what the CEO wanted to happen. It also illustrates the validity of the notions by the famous Harvard professor B.F. Skinner, the originator of research into operant conditioning, that "behavior is a function of its consequences".

Employees were beginning to ask for more interesting jobs and to act more like stakeholders in their company than like hired hands. In this quest for social consideration, there was a shift in emphasis from groups to individuals. Even though group welfare was still important, job satisfaction was shown to be a personal matter. Managers became aware of this and began to acknowledge responsibility for the personal development of their employees. They believed that employees could contribute to company success if the possibility was given to them. The greatest progress was to be made through maximum participation (Delden, 1998).

The human resource function

While government controls and labour organizations intensified their pressure, the HRM function needed to adapt constantly to the changing environment. The human resource manager had to understand this environment and its workforce expectations. Workers' rights were placed at the forefront. Emphasis started to be placed on women and their efficiency at work. As more and more women entered the workforce, gender became a social issue. Childcare and paid maternity leave also appeared as issues. If parents worried about their children's welfare during work hours, this would affect their efficiency and productivity on the job.

Moreover, at the beginning of the 1990s, smoke-free workplaces appeared. A Strategic Human Resource Management/Bureau of National Affairs (SHRM/BNA) survey revealed that the percentage of companies that restricted smoking had jumped from 54 in 1987 to 85 per cent in 1991 and the percentage of totally smoke-free workplaces had more than tripled, from seven to 34 per cent in the same period (HR News, 1998). Protecting employees against unsafe jobs and discrimination, pension rights, civil rights, and health and safety in general were all emphasized in legislation at this time. Most recently, work–life balance and diversity management have gained greater prominence as organizations struggle to maintain skilled workers as baby boomers are increasingly retiring and leaving the workforce.

These changes meant the human resource manager had become a key player in a successful organization. HRM acted like a social partner, representing management in its dealings with employees and caring for workers' personal development. HRM began to emphasize corporate contribution, proactive management and the initiation of change (Dessler, 2008).

Effectively, HRM had evolved from personnel administration to a key strategic function in the company. As the business environment became much more unstable and turbulent, HRM moved to a new role: strategic human resource management (SHRM). These changes are not only shifts in definition; they are also a consequence of changes in the environment and their effects on the workplace. They show the need for managers to respond and adapt to ever-changing environmental pressures.

Organizations have recognized the importance of valuable human resources and are optimizing their assets. Human resource managers have to promote gender, race, age, national origin, diversity and religious equality and they have to reward their workers to maintain their motivation. HR staff have to be generalists with an understanding of economics, politics, social and cultural trends, technological innovations, changing work values, skill shortages, labour law, health care management, privacy concerns, international trends and many other issues (Losey, 1998). The forces of change are important factors in the new human resource model that is being built.

The relationship between the external and internal environments, and the multiplicity of factors that influence an organization's ability to respond, including its internal and external stakeholders and internal operations and systems, all need to be taken into account. The reality is that an organization needs to respond to what is happening in its environment and may have a limited choice in how it does this because of the situational factors and competing demands of different stakeholders. Nonetheless, its choice of response influences its internal capacity. In many situations, the organization can manage the challenges it faces; however, there are times when it does need assistance.

Using consultants

The need to deliver what is best for the organization is one of the reasons many organizations engage consultants to help with diagnosing and guiding the change process. The advantages of consultants are that they provide additional resources and expertise that the organization does not have and, as outsiders, they are more objective about the organization's needs as they are not caught up in its culture and politics. The consultants need to be aware of political behaviour, coalitions, power plays and the organization's culture and subcultures so they can manage around these; but they also need to remain outside them. The disadvantages are that they are not as familiar with the organization and they may be expensive. If hiring consultants is a feasible option, then it is important to clarify the expectations of both the organization and the consultants and establish clear ground rules early in the engagement.

Regardless of whether you use internal or external consultants, ground rules are useful as they establish who has responsibility for what. Clarify who the client really is! The person who hires a consultant is quite often not the person who owns the problem, and the owner may not welcome outside intervention. Is it a manager, is it the work team, or is it the customer? Who has the power and decision-making authority in the organization? The demarcation between the organization's power and authority and the consultants' needs to be discussed to avoid any misunderstandings. The ground rules can be re-negotiated when and if necessary, but are important in helping to manage the expectations of both parties.

Ground rules should address the consultants' role in terms of their interaction with the organization; for example, what level of access to staff, plant and equipment and other stakeholders such as the union, community or customers is expected. Other issues include confidentiality, how frequently they need to report to the organization, the cost of the service, the time it will take, the outcomes and deliverables to be provided and how these will be measured. It is also critical that the consultants have the necessary knowledge, skills and ability to perform their role professionally. Mishandling the change process will aggravate the negative side effects; for example, the change consultant who runs a discussion on dealing with problems and doesn't get to solutions can in fact undermine people's confidence in the organization's and the management's ability to solve these problems.

Consultants can take on a range of roles. At one extreme, the consultant can be an expert who makes decisions on what needs to happen within the organization, as usually occurs when an organization faces a severe financial crisis and attempts are being made to save it from bankruptcy. At the other end of the spectrum, the consultants can facilitate and provide support and guidance to the organization. For example, the process consultant focuses on how to change and this is more effective in engendering long-term change because it engages employees in the process. Other roles might be to provide training, coaching and mentoring, which can occur at the senior management level to improve leadership skills or can be extended to all managers, or key stakeholders, or the whole of the organization.

Study guide

Review questions

1. Compare and contrast Taylorism and the human relations movement.
2. Explain how globalization has affected the five key forces that drive change.
3. Explain the changes that have occurred within the human resource function when comparing the 1980s to 2010 onwards.
4. Explain the meaning of strategic human resource management.

Discussion questions

1. Explain some of the key factors that have lead to changes in managers roles and a change in the human resource management function?
2. Do you agree with the tipping point proposition? Draw on examples from your own experience to identify situations where you think a tipping point has been reached, and explain why this occurred.

Research activity

Undertake some further research to understand the origins and key functions of Taylorism. Do you agree that there are strong elements of Taylorism still present in many modern jobs? For example, are there Taylorist elements in the work that you do?

Case study: Palmer's growing pains!

Jim Palmer sat at his desk gazing out of the window that gave a view across the plant, contemplating the events that had led to the meeting scheduled for later this afternoon with a human resource management consultant. He had founded this electronics company shortly after graduating from university with first-class honours in electrical engineering. The ideas for his unique range of testing instruments had been developed with the help of his research project supervisor, Prof. George Smith. In the early days it had been frustrating finding financial backers and appropriate facilities for the design and manufacture of the instruments they had designed. However, ten years later, his products were selling well since they had first taken off in the mining support sector, and he was now also manufacturing for medical technology. Currently, both the mining and medical plants employed three shifts, with each having approximately 50 skilled tradespersons and assemblers per plant, to make up a total of approximately 360 full-time employees.

Rapid growth saw the company double in size in the early years, which had resulted in little time for formal planning. The focus had to be on meeting market demand, growing the business and designing a second generation of instruments. It had been an all-consuming task! A chance meeting with a friend from his university days, who had recently completed an MBA, convinced him that he needed to pay more attention to the management and people side of his business. He pulled a copy of the organizational chart, shown in Figure 1.1, towards him, quickly checking that it did indeed reflect the current structure.

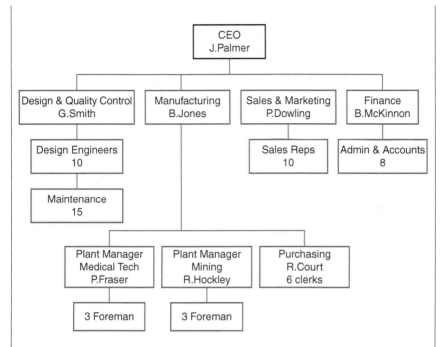

FIGURE 1.1 The organizational chart

Thinking about his meeting, Jim reflected that the company had been successful so far. Profits had grown quickly and sometimes doubled annually in the early days, but growth had slowed more recently, in part because of the high cost of funding further expansion. Nonetheless, there were a number of issues that concerned him and he made the following quick notes about these, as follows:

- Initial growth had been rapid. The company had successfully recruited by using a 'word of mouth' approach in which employees recommended others who could work for the company. Recently they have encountered problems in attracting high-quality people that are needed. A number of recent recruits have been unsuccessful, and turnover among the established workforce reached 20 per cent in the last year. This means recruitment and employment costs have risen substantially.
- The company pays higher than average salaries, which should be an effective strategy for keeping turnover costs low.
- Despite that the measures for productivity are relatively crude, when measured by machine utilization, assembly rates and total output, productivity has declined.

- There is a pending case in the Equal Employment Opportunity Commission for an unfair dismissal claim by a former employee. The company lawyer thinks it is unlikely the company will win this case.
- Recently, two very promising design engineers quit to take up positions in competitor firms. Their reasons for leaving work were vague, but generally their concerns related to their career prospects if they remained with the company.
- The workplace is non-unionized, which Jim believes is related to the higher wages in good working conditions. However, some employees are talking to several relevant unions for the first time. Jim has heard indirectly that employees are uncertain about future pay and conditions and are seeking the security union membership could offer.
- Recent discussions with some key employees indicate uneasiness about their personal future with the company. Jim has tried to reassure them that they are valuable and he could not afford to lose this group of people at this time.
- The board of directors, which includes some of the company's major backers, have expressed some concern that the human resource side of the business is considerably less well managed than the technical aspects of the business (which are still highly regarded).

Looking at his notes, Jim conceded that although there was no need to panic, some timely steps needed to be taken.

Questions

Assuming you were the consultant,

1. Provide an overview of how you would advise Jim Palmer to proceed.
2. What specific steps would you recommend, and in what order should they be taken?
3. How, if at all, would you involve Jim and his senior executive team?
4. What kind of intervention would you want and how would you go about obtaining it?
5. Given the current workforce population of 360, how many people would not need to be replaced if a 10 per cent reduction in turnover could be achieved?

Ethical Dilemma – The risk of non-disclosure

The concept of golden rice sounds like a great idea. This genetically modified rice is yellow in colour, hence the name golden, because it has much higher levels of beta-carotene. The beta-carotene is claimed to help increase vitamin A levels and the makers of golden rice claim it has potential health benefits that will save many lives, particularly in developing countries where many, and particularly children, die of malnutrition annually.

Problems, however, arose when the rice was fed to children in the Chinese province of Hunan as part of a trial. Although the study was led by a nutritionist from Tufts University in Boston and partly funded by two US institutions; the Department of Agriculture and the National Institute of Diabetes and Digestive and Kidney Diseases, it was implemented in China through the Chinese Center for Disease Control and Prevention (CDC).

The aim of the trial was to identify whether the rice did in fact increase vitamin A levels. Children aged between six and eight were given the rice daily over a three-week period. Although the parents were aware that the children were taking part in a trial and had signed consent forms for this, they were not aware that the trial involved genetically modified rice. There was no attempt to highlight the uncertainty around genetically modified foods or potential risks of harm.

It subsequently emerged that the Chinese officials who had approved the trial had omitted to identify the rice as 'golden rice' because of the connotations of risk associated with it being genetically modified. Subsequently the families of children who took part in the study have been offered compensation, though some have refused compensation because of uncertainty over the long-term health risks to the children. It is little consolation to the parents that the CDC has sacked the three officials involved.

Questions

1. What ethical issues does this case raise?
2. Should the Golden Rice project be held responsible for the breach that occurred in China?
3. What other business issues arise from this case?

Source: Qui, J. (2012) China sacks officials over Golden Rice controversy. *Nature*, 10 December. http://www.nature.com/news/china-sacks-officials-over-golden-rice-controversy-1.11998. Accessed 31.12.2012.

Further reading

Armitage, A. and Keeble-Ramsay, D. (2009) High performance working – what are the perceptions as a new form of employer–worker relationship? *International Journal of Employment Studies*, April, 17(1): 57(33).

Hellqvist, N. (2011) Global performance management: A research agenda. *Management Research Review*, 34(8): 927–946.

Lähteenmäki, S. and Laiho, M. (2011) Global HRM and the dilemma of competing stakeholder interests. *Social Responsibility Journal*, 7(2): 166–180.

Lengnick-Hall, M.L., Lengnick-Hall, C.A., Andrade, L.S. and Drake, B. (2009) Strategic human resource management: The evolution of the field. *Human Resource Management Review*, 19(2): 64–85.

2

THE FORCES OF CHANGE

Executives, managers, consultants and academics spend a good deal of time thinking and talking about change. The notion of change is ubiquitous and arises in many different ways. We tend to think in terms of planned change, which is often incremental, where the need for change is perceived, adopted, implemented and resourced (Daft, 2007). However, deliberate, controlled change is more and more often accompanied by unplanned events and developments that require almost continuous adaptation. The idea that "change has changed" is exemplified in a statement attributed to a consultant: "I can remember when change was an event".

Organizations operate within both a macro- and a micro-environment. These days change is often ongoing, with numerous events occurring simultaneously. They need to grasp opportunities as they arise to either enter new markets or develop new products and services. Consider, for instance, the rapid growth of micro-entrepreneurs. For example, West Australian-based coffee wholesaler, Five-Senses, has been able to contain its costs through internet sales while at the same time rapidly expanding its market. Of course, in our rapidly changing world not everything can be predicted, so there are also times when organizations need to respond to external events and take advantage of opportunities as they present themselves. Examples of this need to grow can be seen in the expansion of Australian, American and European businesses into China, India and South East Asia.

The advantage of doing business in China and other emerging economies, such as Indonesia, India and the Philippines, is not just the low wage costs, although these are likely to increase over time, but it is also about accessing a large potential market. A good example of this is the experience of the former employees of the failed Australian airline company Ansett, who, after the company was bankrupted, turned their job losses into an opportunity by setting up a company to audit airlines in China (Harcourt, 2008). There was little opportunity for them to set up business in Australia's small and relatively saturated market, but the large Chinese market provided a chance to develop a successful business. Of course, the third scenario is when events that cannot be predicted happen and organizations have to react to ensure their own survival.

Some extreme examples of this were the attack on the twin towers in New York, the sub-acute respiratory syndrome (SARS) epidemic and the global financial crisis (GFC) – combined, these two led to a massive downturn in airline travel worldwide. Because organizations need to respond and adapt to their external environment, they are referred to as open systems. An organization that is closed to its external environment can easily become out of touch with its market and competitors. To be able to respond quickly, it needs to monitor the external environment for changes, or likely changes, and be flexible and adaptive internally. The key elements affecting both the internal and external environment of the open organization are shown in Figure 2.1.

The inter-relationship between the internal and external environments is apparent in the open systems model. This model demonstrates how external factors provide inputs in the form of raw materials, resources and information. The organization uses these materials and resources to generate outputs in the form of goods, services and ideas, and these in turn influence the external environment's perception of the organization. This feedback loop influences inputs and outputs, cyclically and over time. Of course, an organization is more than the sum of its parts and the coordination of the various elements is equally as important as individual components.

Organizations need to take a contingency approach to managing change, and the open systems model provides both a pragmatic and a practical framework for formulating change strategies or responses. The contingency view encourages analysis of the cause and effect relationship between actions and their reactions. It is a case of asking "if this happens, then what happens next?" so the various possibilities

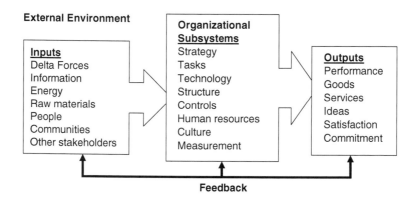

FIGURE 2.1 The organization as an open system

can be interrogated. The five key internal systems to consider are the strategy, structure, people (HR and culture), technology and measurement systems. Therefore, once the strategy is clear the focus of the change is on adapting the structure, technology or employees' behaviour and should consider both the formal and informal activities affected.

How an organization deals with inputs is influenced by the complexity of the business, as in whether it has many products and services, and the rate or pace of change and the opportunities in the marketplace that will allow it to adapt or expand. In fact, it could be said that organizations, and even non-profit organizations, exist because their external environment allows them to exist by virtue of a demand or niche for the services they provide. The inputs and outputs influence the internal choice, and precipitate internal changes, which in their turn often have a ripple effect across the organization. Managers need to be mindful of these flow-on effects across the wider organization and to take steps to identify and manage responses in an integrated, holistic manner. Because organizations are in constant interaction with the external environment, they need to respond proactively where they can.

The open systems model demonstrates how changing societal expectations in terms of the Delta forces (demographics, economics, legal and regulatory, technology, attitudes and values) and the task environment (competitors, suppliers, labour forces, customers and community) that organizations operate within. The acronym Delta was devised by Kraut and Korman (1999) to represent the symbol delta that represents change in mathematics. The Delta forces are, essentially, an environmental scanning mechanism that allow organizations to monitor changes and shifts in their operating environment that are largely outside of their control.

We know that this analysis is not formally done in many, if not most, organizations, although it would be done, in part, in larger organizations through a strategic planning exercise. This analysis should be carried out as a separate exercise on a semi-annual basis by either internal or external people who have some expert knowledge of the various forces. The Delphi consensus-seeking exercise, to be discussed in a later section on human resource planning, would lend itself to this exercise. These forces are constantly changing and evolving and can catch organizations and industries out if they are not monitoring critical variables.

Apart from the external factors such as the Delta forces that are discussed in this section, the organization also needs to take in resources in the form of information, energy and people to be able to perform its functions. Once it has taken in the raw materials, then it needs systems to be able to utilize those materials effectively so it can produce goods and services or ideas based on the interaction between both the internal and external environment. Organizations expand and grow because there are opportunities in the external environment. A good example of this is the expansion of manufacturing into developing countries, where companies want to reduce the costs of manufacturing in order to reduce the cost of products.

The choices open to an organization are of course affected by the level of complexity of the business, the bounty or opportunities to expand and grow a market and the dynamism, or rate and pace of change. Complexity refers to how many elements the organization has to manage; for example, a company that has many different products in different markets has greater complexity to deal with. The English-based supermarket chain Tesco, which is the largest supermarket chain in the world, operates across Asia, from India to China, in North America and across Europe as well as the United Kingdom. The company prides itself on providing local products to local communities and this adds to the complexity of its products and services. Further complexity is added by the expansion of the company into finance, clothing and homewares. It is complex in terms of goods and services and administration. While some of Tesco's markets change rapidly, the rate and pace of change is still considerably lower than would be seen in high-technology industries. Of course, such an expansion can take place only where there is the opportunity, or bounty, in the market to grow. Also, the rate of change in these markets is lower than, for example, in technology markets, where new products and new trends emerge much more rapidly.

Some examples of how quickly things can change can be seen in the following examples. In 2007 and 2008 there was a skill shortage in the mining industry in Australia, an event that could have been at least partially predictable, if someone had been watching! The demand for minerals by China and India put a premium on skilled and semi-skilled labour in the mineral extractive industries which distorted wage rates, housing prices, university enrolments and immigration policies. The mining sector was attracting workers from other areas, further exacerbating shortages of teachers and police, among others, who incidentally were able to return to their former jobs when the downturn hit. In this environment school leavers appeared to reason "Why should I go to university and go into debt to become a teacher when I can drive a truck in the mining industry and earn a 40 per cent higher salary?".

By mid-2009, the global economic crisis saw a dramatic slowing in the mining sector and the loss of many jobs. The events of late 2008 and 2009 illustrate how quickly the employment environment went from skill shortages to massive layoffs and how quickly things can change. Even though Australia weathered the economic crisis better than most countries, uncertainty about the future of China's growth means the mining sector is still slower in 2012, and the extent of high-paying jobs has not returned.

Demographic forces

Demographics refers to the composition of the workforce in terms of age distribution, gender, education level, participation rates, migration, immigration and birth rates in different periods. These data are important in HR planning because they can point to gaps and potential shortages in the future, and help to build a profile of the workforce.

For example, the 1930s produced a relatively small cohort of workers (the silent generation) who entered the labour force in the 1950s and 1960s and, in the

United States and other developed countries, enjoyed the advantages of a long period of growth, development and stability that will probably not be repeated. Most of these workers are near retirement now, although a number still hold very senior positions in business and government.

The baby-boom generation, people born between 1946 and 1964, are the largest group of workers today. The end of the Second World War saw returning war veterans starting families and the rebuilding of Europe and Japan. The boomers, aged from 44 to 62 in the year 2008, started entering the workforce in the mid-1960s. They are experiencing completely different issues from their parents, being the first cohort to face large-scale downsizing, plant closures, lack of job security and shrinking advancement opportunities due to flatter organization structures that provide fewer rungs on the corporate ladder. Having seen many of their parents fired or rushed into early retirement, this group feels somewhat betrayed by big business and is concerned with mid-career issues, medical benefits, retirement planning and fears about shrinking social security benefits. In addition, the events of late 2008 and early 2009 have decimated retirement savings and exacerbated these trends.

The challenge to HRM is to provide a measure of job security yet retain sufficient flexibility to cope with rapidly changing markets and skill sets. Due to acute skill shortages and the smaller cohorts of workers that follow in the next generation, many developed countries are stressing the need to keep the 'boomers' in the workforce beyond the traditional retirement ages of 55–65. Because of this a number of countries around the world, including the UK, the USA, Japan, Australia, Germany, Denmark and Turkey, have increased their retirement ages (OECD, 2012; http://www.guardian.co.uk/news/datablog/2010/jun/24/retirement-ages-oecd-countries). This in turn presents challenges to HRM in terms of the physical arrangements of work as well as the attitudes of younger managers towards older subordinates.

The 'baby bust' or Generation X cohort, as it is more conventionally referred to, was born between 1965 and 1976 and is considerably smaller than the boomer cohort. The shortage of entry-level workers in the early 1990s was a consequence of the lower birth rates in the 1970s (Kraut and Korman, 1999). Cascio (2006) notes that this group is clearly divided between those with knowledge skills who have a future and those without knowledge skills who have little hope for the future. These people, who entered the workforce in an unprecedented period of downsizing, business closures, mergers and takeovers, have little sense of loyalty to business organizations and represent a challenge to companies who profess that their greatest assets are their human resources.

Coupland (1996) was one of the first to describe Generation X as a cohort that felt no connection to the cultural icons of the baby boom generation. They are a category of people who wanted to hop off the merry-go-round of status, money and social climbing that often frames modern existence. A Time Magazine feature article in the late 1980s summarized Gen X as possessing only a hazy sense of their own identity but a monumental preoccupation with all the problems the preceding generation (baby boomers) will leave for them to fix. A general consensus is that post-baby boom generations will never have it quite as good as their parents' generations. An economic study by Pew Charitable Trusts, the American Enterprise Institute, the Brookings Institute, the Heritage Foundation and the Urban Institute published results that made headlines in PR Newswire in the US in May 2007. In essence, the study demonstrated that in real dollar terms, Gen X made 12 per cent less than their parents' cohort at the same age in 1974.

Generation Y are primarily the children of the baby boomers and a succession from Gen X. This generation has been shaped considerably by information and communication technology. A survey of business owners in Australia (2007) sums up the general impression of Gen Y employees. They found Gen Ys to be demanding, impatient and bad at communicating, with poor spelling and grammar skills and no understanding of appropriate corporate behaviours. But they praised Gen Ys in terms of their energy and charisma. Access to technology is part of the reason for this; for example, Junco and Mastrodicasa (2007) found in a survey of 7,705 university/college students in the United States that:

- 97% own a computer
- 94% own a cell phone
- 76% use instant messaging
- 34% use websites as their primary source of news
- 28% own a blog and 44% read blogs
- 75% have a Facebook account.

In essence, this generation is the first to have lived their entire lives immersed in digital technologies. In contrast, Prensky (2006) labelled the various generations as:

1. Digital Aliens (The Silent Generation, 1925–1945)
2. Digital Immigrants (Baby Boomers, 1946–1964)
3. Digital Adaptives (Generation X, 1965–1987)
4. Digital Natives (Generation Y, 1988–2000).

An interesting point about Generation Y is that they have a very different approach to work from their parents. They want involvement and will walk away if they don't get it (Woodward, 2009). This has practically led to an industry that has developed around keeping Generation Y happy in the workplace. He points out that Gen Y have grown up in a time of prosperity and, until very recently, have never experienced a recession. By contrast, Gen X grew up in a time of recession and have experienced both the ups and downs of economic cycles. Another point is that so many of the characteristics ascribed to Gen Y are really the characteristics of any educated worker in buoyant economic times and that this generation may experience a hard reality when faced with the recessionary times of the GFC and ongoing high levels of youth unemployment.

Each generation is shaped and influenced by different phenomena at different points in time, such as: wars, depression, recessions, boom times and dramatic increases in technology. In addition, this is the first time in history that four generations have been in the workforce at the same time. This will continue as the Silent Generation exits and Generation Z enters. This raises serious issues about how to attract, manage, motivate, reward and retain talent from the various cohorts who have different needs, expectations, values and timeframes in which to satisfy these requirements. It follows that a demographic profile (particularly of age) of one's workforce is essential. Age profiles by essential work categories can expose gaps in succession time lines and fit nicely into succession planning (to be discussed in some detail later).

This company experience illustrates the point. The company discovered during a succession planning exercise that they had an age gap between the ages of 32 to 45 in their middle to senior management structure. The company was a very desirable place to work and had experienced little turnover of senior management and executive staff. This exercise revealed that, with impending retirements in the near future, there were not enough younger managers qualified to step up to more senior positions. The puzzle was to determine why the gap existed. They carried out an analysis of managers aged 28–32 who were promising and who had resigned in the past few years. They were able to contact a number of these former employees who still held the company in high regard, and who agreed to a post-exit interview.

The post-exit interviews revealed that the majority of reasons for resigning were the perception that the path to promotion was blocked by senior management and executives who still had some years to go before retirement, so they looked elsewhere for more promising promotion opportunities. The strategy that the company employed to address this problem was quite innovative. They approached a number of senior managers and executives who had about five years to go before retirement, who were seen to have reached a plateau and were still valuable, but not likely to go any further. They asked these people to consider a new role of mentoring younger managers to replace themselves without loss of status or remuneration and benefits; alternatively, to serve as trouble shooters in roles where they had expertise, or as special project leaders. This initiative was well received by managers and executives who saw these new roles as less stressful and without loss of face, self-esteem or rewards.

The issues arising for HRM from this analysis are, broadly, how to invest wisely in human capital while retaining flexibility in an ever-changing environment. This has serious implications for employment security, training and development, employment stability and the ability to attract and retain top talent.

There is a world-wide shortage of skilled workers that is exacerbated by ageing populations in the developed countries and in many developing countries, as is illustrated below. On the one hand, all the populations will place a heavier economic burden on economies and workers as they will need to be supported.

For example, in the UK the percentage of people aged 65 years and over increased by 1.7 million between 1985 and 2010, and is projected to reach 23 per cent of the total population by 2035, although this is less than the average across the European Union (Office for National Statistics, 2012). Although the events following the Global Financial Crisis belie the view of skill shortages, because of the over-supply of labour and high levels of underemployment, in the longer term, when the economic cycle is reversed, the skill shortages that existed prior to the down-turn will still be evident. These shortages place an absolute premium on HRM policies and programmes designed to attract, develop, maintain and retain key employees.

The ILO (2012a) report on global employment trends suggests that although some countries are better off than others, worldwide problems are not abating. There are 200 million unemployed, which is 29 million more than before the crisis. Another major concern is that, particularly in the poorer areas such as sub-Saharan Africa and South Asia, poor working conditions and low remuneration mean many workers are classified as working poor. The daily wage for 910 million workers is less than $2 per day, with 456 million of these workers earning less than $1.25 a day. A further 400 million jobs will be needed in the next decade. Unemployment among younger workers aged from 15 to 24 years has reached close to 75 million, which is of particular concern, particularly as, since the GFC, older workers are remaining in the workforce longer. This means the younger workers are not get-ting the opportunity to develop the skills and take on positions of leadership or responsibility in the future.

Economic inequality increases the risk of social unrest. Evidence of this has been seen in the riots in Greece, Spain and the United Kingdom, which lends credence to Standing's (2009) concerns about a *precariat*, where those who are unemployed are not only detached from the workforce but also from society. Coupled with this, the volatility of the environment and uncertainty of work means that anyone can fall into a precarious state where security, health and livelihood are threatened.

Unemployment is highest in some of the poorer regions, and in 2011 the ILO (2012a) estimated unemployment rates of 10.9 per cent in North Africa, 8.2 per cent in sub-Saharan Africa, 8.6 per cent in the central and south-eastern non-European countries, 7.2 per cent in Latin America and the Caribbean, 4.1 per cent in East Asia, 10.2 per cent in the Middle East, 3.8 per cent in South Asia and 4.7 per cent in South East Asia and the Pacific. These areas remain very vulnerable to further job losses. History has shown that financial changes and their impact on labour markets are cyclical; however, the difficulty with the current crisis is that it is more far-reaching than previous downturns because of globalization, and its duration is hard to predict.

While many developing countries have younger populations, they still suffer from skill shortages due to a lack of educational and training facilities and resources to up-skill their workers. Consider Indonesia. The country has a population of 248.6 million and an estimated workforce of 117.4 million, and 12.5 per cent of the population lives below the poverty line; half the population is under the age of 28.5 years and unemployment between the ages of 15 and 24 years is 22 per cent as opposed to 6.6 per cent as the national average (CIA Factbook, 2012).

Even though the GFC has led to job losses in the short term, the implications for attracting skilled workers remain a longer-term problem. For example, the Australian Productivity Commission findings of 2006 suggested a shortfall of 270,000 technically qualified workers by 2016 (Graduate Careers Australia, 2006). One of the main results of these skill shortage phenomena is the sourcing of talent from outside one's own company or country. However, to some extent, this is a zero-sum game. If companies and countries are all poaching human resources from each other, these being the same static pool of skilled workers, then this is sort of a closed loop where nobody wins. An example of this is the nursing profession, where there is a worldwide shortage and everyone is poaching from everybody else, which usually means these skilled workers are taken from the developing economies to fill gaps in developed countries.

Given that the demographics predict that these phenomena are likely to con-tinue regardless of buoyant or depressed economic cycles, it makes sense to pursue other strategies such as: grow and retain your own talent. Voluntary turnover is costly not only in terms of replacement costs, but also in terms of the loss of tacit knowledge (that knowledge which is unique to an organization and represents a competitive advantage) as well as lower productivity, morale, motivation and, ulti-mately, profitability. The benefits of a stable, loyal workforce were well illustrated with the SAS Institute in the tipping point proposition at the beginning of this book. This scenario suggests it would seem sensible to look for segments of a com-pany's or country's workforce that have not been fully utilized. Working women fit this picture more than any other group.

The number of women in the workforce has grown over the last several dec-ades. In the United States, for example, the number of women in paid employment increased from 18 million in 1950 (Kraut and Korman, 1999) to 63.5 million in 2010 (US Census Bureau, 2010, Table 605). This trend has continued even during economic downturns, as women are employed in a variety of jobs and professions formerly dominated by men, and women have overtaken men as university and professional graduates. For example, in 2009 nearly 59 per cent of all graduates in higher education were females (US Census Bureau, 2012, Table 299) and there is a similar pattern in New Zealand, the UK, Canada and Australia, where, for exam-ple, 40 per cent of women between the ages of 25 and 64 are tertiary qualified as compared to 34 per cent of males (Australian Bureau of Statistics, 2012, Cat. 4102). Although this is not true of all countries – for example, Japan and Korea both have slightly higher numbers of male graduates than females – the picture is similar in many emerging economies; for example, the ILO identified that in 2003 women's enrolment in tertiary education in sub-Saharan Africa and South Asia was also considerably higher than men's (ILO, 2007). However, there is no doubt that edu-cation outcomes for emerging economies still need to grow.

Despite predictions that, as organizations moved increasingly to flatter, team-based structures, the 'glass ceilings' that frustrated women's mobility in traditional hierarchies would disappear so women would play a more prominent role in future, this ideal has not been realized. The dual-career, dual-income families, which are here to stay, present a number of challenges to HRM. Among them is the need for more flexible working arrangements such as flexible scheduling, flextime, telecommuting, job sharing and so on (Cascio, 2006). Unfortunately, this advancement has not been realized, as a few examples will illustrate.

Although the participation rate of women has increased in virtually all countries, their conditions of remuneration, status and access to leadership roles have not. ILO research suggests that 2004 female labour force participation rates were only 3.5 per cent behind those of males, with growth being highest in Latin America, the Caribbean, the EU and South Asia (ILO, 2007). Despite women's higher participation rates in tertiary education, their remuneration still lags behind their male counterparts. For example, the ILO has identified that, at a broad level, a 15 per cent gap in gender wages in the EU and a 10 per cent gap in Latin America exists (ILO, 2007). In 2012, women had gained marginally but not because their wages had improved but because in some areas men's wages and job security had declined (ILO, 2012b).

In 2012, the World Economic Forum's (WEF) Global Gender Gap Report identified that the countries that ranked among the best out of 135 countries for moving to close the gender pay gap were Sweden, Finland, Iceland and Norway. Countries closest to the bottom ranking were Morocco, Turkey, Egypt, Iran, Chad, Pakistan and Yemen. Countries that ranked just over 100 were Malaysia, Japan, Cambodia and India. The United Kingdom was ranked at 18, Canada 21, USA 22, and Brazil 62. One of the problems is that even in the developed world women tend to be over-represented in lower-paid occupations such as sales, catering, cleaning, hair and beauty and in the 'care' professions such as health, education and family support.

There is also 'vertical' segregation where women are under-represented in higher level, better paid managerial and senior positions in organizational hierarchies and occupational career ladders. Interestingly, even though Australia has both a female Prime Minister and Governor General, the country's ranking has slipped from 15 to 25 in 2012. Even though Australia is a country of great prosperity, women in full-time work still earn 16 per cent less than men: they are concentrated in the lower-paid care and service industries and are under-represented in managerial and executive positions (Barnes and Preston, 2008).

The employment position for women in Asia is more mixed and less easy to generalize about. A report from the ILO's 14th Asian regional meeting in South Korea (2006) focused on the migration patterns of Asian workers to more developed countries. The jobs people migrated for are said to be either at the top end for skilled professionals, or at the bottom end of the labour market, and referred to as "dirty, dangerous and difficult" (ILO, 2007), and included jobs locals did not wish to do. The remittances from migrant workers back to their home countries do a lot towards reducing poverty, increasing standards of living and increasing opportunities for education. Remittance amounts continue to grow and The

World Bank (2012) estimates $406 billion was remitted to developing countries from overseas workers, but suggests the real figure could be larger as money moving between countries is not always recorded. The largest recipients of remittances are India ($70 billion), followed by China ($66 billion), the Philippines ($24 billion), Mexico ($24 billion) and Nigeria ($21 billion).

The thrust of this analysis about demographics is to emphasize that an organization needs to understand a force that it cannot control but must be able to cope with. It suggests that an organization should place a very large premium on its ability to source, develop and retain its key resources and these capabilities are largely embodied in human resource management systems.

Economic forces

A quote from Peter Drucker, the distinguished management consultant and writer, illustrates the importance of understanding economic trends:

> The proper social responsibility of business is to tame the dragon – that is, to turn a social problem into economic opportunity and economic benefit, into productive capacity, into human competence, into well-paid jobs, and into wealth.
>
> (1968: 323)

Economic forces are probably the least predictable of the Delta forces of change. Demographics, legal, regulatory, technological, attitudes and values as forces of change are more predictable. These can be drawn from internal and external databases such as Human Resource Information Systems (HRIS) and national databases (such as bureaus of statistics), although they do take time to develop. For example, age cohorts are known through internal age profiles and national and international statistical analyses. Attitudes and values are fairly well known to change between generational groups such as Generation Y and baby boomers.

Economic forces can change fairly rapidly, as is evidenced by the recessions affecting many countries around the globe following the GFC that started following the property market collapse in 2007–8. The collapse of the Greek economy necessitated a European Union bailout; a prolonged recession in Spain led to a bailout of the banks to try to stabilize the economy, but there is still much uncertainty about the country's economic future. Unemployment has reached 25 per cent, with youth unemployment above 50 per cent (Aljazeera, 2012). The American economy is in serious trouble and, at the beginning of 2013, narrowly averted another recession when the American Congress negotiated amendments to taxes and spending, but the deal brokered is an uneasy one (NBC, 2013).

In a globalized environment, a slowdown in growth in one nation can have quite serious impacts for others, as is seen in the concern that a slowdown in the Chinese economy, in particular, could slow growth across the Asian region and Australia, which so far have not been as affected as Europe and America. Economic forces can be broadly classified as 'less predictable' and 'more predictable'. Examples of less and more predictable forces in recent times are listed below:

- Natural disasters: The tsunami of 26 December 2004 devastated coastal regions in parts of Indonesia, India, Malaysia, Myanmar, the Maldives, Sri Lanka, Somalia and Thailand, killing over 225,000 people and causing widespread dislocation of populations and industrial activity. The hurricane that devastated regions of Myanmar, the earthquake which devastated regions of China and the hurricanes that severely disrupted oil production in the Gulf region of the United States and Mexico in 2008, hurricane Katrina which devastated large parts of New Orleans in 2005, and more recently the tsunami that devastated Japan in 2011 are but a few of largely unpredictable events that can severely disrupt economic activity.
- More predictable economic forces would include: global warming, the exponential rise in the cost of oil and energy costs generally, the sub-prime loan crisis in the United States which has created chaos in financial markets globally and in the housing and real-estate markets in the US in particular. Other better-known factors affecting economic activity are global skill shortages, ageing populations in developed countries, wars in the Middle East and Africa and widespread political unrest in many parts of the world.
- Although natural disasters are largely unpredictable in any longer term sense, others are somewhat more predictable and may represent opportunities. Global warming is an example that has been predicted for quite a long time and yet has only been taken seriously in recent times. Alternative sources of 'green' power such as wind, solar and wave were seen to be uneconomical until the polluting effects of conventional fuel sources and their costs made the new sources economically viable. Hybrid motor vehicles which are far more fuel efficient are replacing 'gas guzzling' sports utility vehicles (SUVs) as the vehicle of choice as gas prices rise to unprecedented levels. The hybrid Toyota Prius is selling as fast as it can be produced in place of larger, less fuel-efficient cars and SUVs. Some recent reports suggest that the extent of climate change has been underestimated and changes are likely to occur more rapidly and be more extensive than has been expected, and this is likely to either increase demand for cars like the Prius or increase competition through the development of improved models from other manufacturers.

The purpose of the analysis above is to emphasize the need to monitor the economic forces that can be somewhat predictable and to have contingency plans for those that are less predictable, together with an environmental scanning mechanism to help you to do this.

Globalization

The most pronounced trend in economic terms is the intense competition brought about by globalization in the last 25 years or so. In the years following the Second World War, the United States produced about three-quarters of all the world's goods and services, but this had fallen to approximately 21 per cent in 2008 (The World Bank, 2008). By 2011, China had taken the lead as the largest exporter, followed by Germany and then the USA (The World Bank, 2012).

The period 1946 to the mid-1960s (the baby boom era) saw unprecedented growth in the United States and the appearance of large business bureaucracies. In the 1950s and 1960s, barriers to international trade fell substantially as a result of the GATT (General Agreement on Tariffs and Trade), thus accelerating the international flow of goods and services. By the 1970s, the European and Japanese industrial infrastructure that was damaged during the Second World War had been rebuilt and globalization had begun in earnest. 'Globalization' is a term that means different things to different people; it has proponents as well as opponents, as witnessed by opposition to the World Trade Organization meetings in Seattle and Prague in 2008, and Geneva in 2009. Globalization is defined by Oman (1999) as "the accelerated growth of economic activity over national and political boundaries". This has largely been driven by multinational corporations (MNCs) from Europe, Japan and the United States and more recently by China, India, Brazil and South Korea.

Many companies have changed from colonialist international firms expanding overseas from a domestic base, to multinational corporations duplicating themselves in other countries or becoming truly global in that products are made by global teams for global markets.

Globalization has been enabled by new organizational forms and dramatic advances in information and communication technology (ICT). For example, the Wellcome Trust Sanger Institute is based in Cambridge, UK, but brings together researchers from all around the world to collaborate and integrate research into various diseases (Sanger Institute, 2013). Research projects from around the world work together to share information and increase the speed of response times. These new organizational forms and ICT applications are discussed in more detail in a later section. Some obvious challenges for HRM that arise from globalization are to design team-based work systems and associated performance management and remuneration systems appropriate for this organizational form.

Cost of labour

Intensified global competitiveness has led to a never-ending search for ways to cut costs by applying high technology and finding cheaper sources of labour. This is exemplified in the apparel and footwear industries where leading brand name MNCs outsource much or all of their production to developing countries in Asia and Latin America through the use of suppliers and contractors who own the sources of production.

In the 1970s, the United States lost much of its competitive edge, partly because of the high cost of labour relative to Japan and Europe. By the 1990s, the USA had regained labour cost competitiveness due to wage stagnation that saw weekly earnings drop by 19 per cent by 1995 (Kraut and Korman, 1999). At this time many Japanese and German companies opened major manufacturing facilities in the United States to take advantage of wages that were lower than in their own countries.

Because of globalization and the search for lower labour costs, many new players have appeared, which presents a number of challenges to HRM. These include increased interaction between staff from different countries with different cultural values and management styles, issues of equity in remuneration, the preparation of more people for international assignments and the appropriateness of Western styles of management in non-Western cultural settings. The global financial crisis that emerged in 2008 has already led to many job losses worldwide, with an estimated 2.55 million job losses in America alone (Rampell, 2009). The worsening of global trade has caused closure of many Chinese factories, and the Chinese government estimates that 20 million rural workers alone have lost their jobs (Anderlini and Dyer, 2009).

The situation in 2012–13 is still grim in many countries, with continuing job losses and uncertainty. In 2012, in the month of November alone, the American Bureau of Labor Statistics reported 1,759 mass layoff actions, which affected 173,558 workers (Bureau of Labor Statistics, 2012). A recent advertisement for 340 teachers in Pakistan attracted 150,000 applicants for the vacancies (Right Vision News, 2012). In the UK, 80,000 applied for 18,000 pre-Christmas sorting jobs with the Royal Mail (Milmo, 2011). The ILO does not expect any improvement in the global employment situation for some years to come, and predicts a slight rise in unemployment for 2013, particularly for younger workers (ILO, 2012a).

Another response is for countries and companies to seek wage freezes to stave off further retrenchments; this can be seen happening all around the globe. One of the first actions of the newly elected US president, Barack Obama, was to freeze wages for senior White House staff. He also moved to cap salaries of executives of companies getting financial assistance to $500,000 per annum. Obama continues to speak of his antipathy towards excessive earnings for executives in the existing financial climate. Another concern with the loss of jobs worldwide is the mass return of some migrant workers and the loss of income that may have been remitted to their home country, although the continually growing amount of money being returned suggests there has not been a downturn, or alternatively the tracking mechanisms are more accurate.

Service economy

The nature of employment has also changed significantly in the last half century. In the United States and other industrialized countries, between 1950 and 1995, the goods-producing sector fell from 41 per cent to 21 per cent of total employment, while the service sector rose to 79 per cent of all jobs (Kraut and Korman, 1999). In 2011, the CIA Factbook identified that services make up about 79 per cent of the American and French economies, and the figures are similar at 78 per cent in the UK, 70 per cent in Germany and Japan, and 67 per cent in Brazil. In contrast, growing service sectors made up 43 per cent per cent of China's GDP, 58 per cent in Russia, 56 per cent in India, 55 per cent in Zimbabwe, 53 per cent in Pakistan, 38 per cent in Indonesia and 37 per cent in Vietnam.

This shift has greatly reduced the number of lower skilled jobs and dramatically increased the number of knowledge workers with high-level technological skills. This gap, sometimes referred to as 'the digital divide', is occurring within developed countries as well as between developed and developing countries. Accompanying the trend towards service sector work has been the loss of numbers and power of unionized workers.

A major challenge for HRM will be to attract and retain highly skilled workers in light of the projected longer-term skill shortages. As the skill base of workers increases, so does their mobility. Concurrently, as organizations seek to become more flexible, job security declines, changing the nature of the employment relationship from loyalty and security to contractual. This can be observed in the computer/information technology industry where large 'sign-on bonuses' are used instead of job security to attract talent. This in turn causes problems of wage compression from existing employees with more experience who see less experienced new hires getting a better deal than they did.

Shifts in geographical location can be significant both within and across national boundaries. Such a shift took place in the United States with the long-term decline in manufacturing. This caused a large-scale relocation of workers and industries from the 'rust belts' of the Northeast and Midwest to the 'sun belts' of the West and South. These relocations changed the availability of skills and employment rates in different areas. For example, Silicon Valley in California became a haven for people in the computing/information technology industry.

Globalization has also fostered the large-scale movement of jobs across national boundaries, particularly from developed to developing countries. This is largely to do with finding cheaper sources of labour to reduce costs for labour-intensive, low-skilled jobs, such as in the apparel and footwear industries mentioned previously as well as many other industries. This movement has fuelled much debate about the exploitation of cheap labour in 'sweatshop' conditions, causing many MNCs, accused of these practices, to institute 'codes of conduct' and 'labelling schemes' to combat the criticisms (OECD, 2000). These schemes are of some value as they focus attention on practices such as the use of child labour, but are limited in reach and scope as they mainly apply to image companies with brand name products (Entrekin, 2000). In an attempt to redress these problems the United Nations implemented the Global Compact, where companies are asked to sign up to and voluntarily maintain ten core principles that relate to the protection of human rights, labour management, environmental protection and anticorruption activities (UN Global Compact, 2013). By the end of 2011, over 10,000 corporations or other stakeholders, from over 130 countries, had signed up to uphold these principles.

More recently, call centres have been outsourced by companies in industrialized countries to countries, such as India, where reasonable standards of English are available and lower wage costs prevail. These are usually customer service and back office jobs that offer workers higher than local wage rates but are less costly than performing those services at home. This has been extended in recent times, for example in India and the Philippines, to more highly skilled jobs, such as programming and software development, for companies such as Microsoft.

There is a flip side to the practice of outsourcing that is being referred to as 'back sourcing' or 'reverse outsourcing'. These terms refer to the practice of bringing outsourced activities back in house due to dissatisfaction with the quality of the performance of outsourced services or with the failure to attain the cost savings and efficiencies envisaged. These practices will be further elaborated in a subsequent section on consolidating around core functions and outsourcing.

Generally, the choice of location and business partner has not been a decision for HRM. However, with the sometimes devastating effects of plant closure on a one-employer town and evidence of labour exploitation in developing countries by business partners, HRM will be increasingly involved in determining what is fair.

Legal and regulatory issues

The daily practice of HRM and its strategic input are greatly influenced by a nation's laws, particularly those governing the treatment of employees. These include conditions of employment, minimum age, minimum wages, payment of overtime, hours of work, freedom of association, the right to organize and occupational health and safety (OHS). Most developed countries have such laws, although they are not uniform across countries and the degree of enforcement may vary. Developing countries vary considerably in terms of coverage and standards, which are generally less stringent than developed countries' standards and laws (Liuibic, 1998). To illustrate the importance of having appropriate HR systems in place that comply with legislation we can review the case of Stanton that took place in the Midwest in the United States.

The case involved a 56-year-old laboratory technician in a Midwest manufacturing company. He claimed that he was discharged because of his age. His employer stated that even though the man had been employed for a long time, the quality of his work was consistently poor and his attitude and attendance had been unsatisfactory. The company further claimed that the employee had been advised repeatedly of the company's dissatisfaction with his work before his employment was finally terminated. The employee responded by stating that his work was in fact acceptable, that his attitude was good, and that he had never been advised that the company was not pleased with his work. He further stated that he had received regular pay increases. The court ruled in favour of the employee. It ordered the company to give him back his job and to pay back wages and legal costs, because the company could not offer sufficient written documentation that the employee's work performance had been bad enough to warrant discharge.

It may be that Stanton's performance was everything the company said it was, but because the company could not produce substantial documentation through an appropriate performance appraisal system and because he had received regular pay increases, the court had no choice but to find in favour of the employee.

This is by no means a unique example. In a similar case in Australia, a manager, who had falsified his past work history and credentials, successfully made a claim for unfair dismissal when his employment was terminated after ongoing performance problems. The fact that he had maintained his employment over a period of time and been promoted early in his career with the company was deemed as evidence that he was able to perform in the job. Also critical in this case was the fact that the organization did not have sufficient documentation of poor performance and evidence to demonstrate the steps they had taken to address this. The total cost of this case was approximately half a million Australian dollars in legal fees, compensation for lost earnings and to pay out the stress claim lodged by the employee.

Legislation

Anti-discrimination laws are fairly common in developed countries and were originally intended to protect minority groups. Today, however, with the focus extending to women, people with disabilities and older workers, the legislation typically covers a broader spectrum of workers in developed countries. HRM has to ensure compliance with legislation and it has to keep a company up-to-date on new legislation and enforcement issues. These may relate to safety and health, medical benefits, retirement funding, educating employees, recommending and formulating new practices and so on. In addition to monitoring and administering these programmes, HRM is responsible for keeping detailed records for company files, as well as external reporting to government agencies. Newer laws are continually being enacted on such matters as employee privacy, genetic screening and illnesses such as AIDS or other viruses that affect occupational health and safety in the workplace, work–life balance and employee rights such as maternity and paternity leave.

This is the maintenance function of HRM. It is important in protecting both the employer's and employees' rights and ensuring that a company avoids expensive lawsuits as in the case of Stanton mentioned above. The challenges for HRM are to have in place good information systems and environmental scanning mechanisms that keep an organization well informed and ready to anticipate and respond to major changes.

Deregulation

The deregulation of protected industries and state-owned enterprises has played a significant role in the globalization of business. One of the most common examples is that of telecommunication companies. Countries have been particularly reluctant in the past to deregulate their telecommunications companies, as they were a source of protected revenue. Following the break-up of AT&T in the United States, many countries have deregulated this industry or, as in Australia, partly privatized the company, giving rise to greater competition and much lower prices for services. In another example, the deregulation of financial services has changed the nature of the entire industry, giving rise to new organizations offering banking, stockbroking and insurance. There are now combined full-service organizations where there were formerly separate industries.

These activities have spawned entirely new entities, many created by merger. Such mergers even transcend traditional sector boundaries, e.g. mass media and entertainment, transport and travel. The acceleration of mergers, acquisitions and strategic alliances will present some serious challenges for HRM. It will not be easy to reconcile different organizational structures, cultures and managerial styles, or to integrate them with established HRM systems and practices. For example, deregulation has increased the competitive forces in the airline industry to such an extent that profit margins are reduced. An influx of low-cost carriers, financial uncertainty that has reduced passenger numbers, increases in fuel costs and uncertainty of costs into the future, plus the high cost of maintaining a competitive modern fleet, are factors that are forcing new alliances or threats to survival. This can be seen in the partnership agreement planned in 2012 between the Emirates and Qantas airlines (Australian Financial Review, 2012), and the threatened survival of American Airlines (McIntyre, 2012).

Technology

Advances in information and communication technology (ICT) have radically changed the way we work in today's digitized world. They have also enabled types of organizational structure that were not possible even five years ago. The magnitude and profundity of these changes in ICT are illustrated by a few examples.

While it was 38 years before 50 million people listened to radio, the same number were navigating the internet within four years of its introduction. In the early 1990s traffic on the internet doubled about every 100 days. As recently as 1997 it doubled annually (ILO, 2001), and a recent estimate is that it is still doubling about every year (Odlyzko, 2008). Keep in mind that this doubling has accommodated huge increases in volume annually. Since the invention of the integrated circuit by Texas Instruments in 1958, and the microchip by Intel in 1971, computing power has increased dramatically, resulting in a 10,000-fold increase in computing power over a twenty-year period (ILO, 2001).

The advent of the web 2.0 platform has made the internet interactive, giving a lot more power to consumers and other stakeholders. This also led to the evolution of social media, where communication about an organization can flow through channels outside of the organization's control, as occurs on product review sites. This holds organizations to account, but it also allows for communication directly between the organization and all their stakeholders. The latest figures from Internet World suggest that half the world's population (3.6 billion) are internet users and traffic has increased 566 per cent between 2000 and 2012 (http://www.internetworldstats.com/stats.htm). The rapid expansion of ICT is aided by falls in cost due to competition, economies of scale in production, and the emergence of common standards in both hardware and software.

Internet sales through online purchasing of goods is another growing phenomenon that is affecting many businesses. Clothing, pharmaceuticals and toiletries, groceries, books and electrical goods are just some of the products that are enjoying a huge migration to sales through online purchasing. One of the first casualties of this shift in purchasing was the bookstore Borders that finalized closing its stores in 2011 (Sanburn, 2011). Whereas Borders outsourced its online sales to Amazon and lost out on this, Borders' competitor Barnes and Noble developed their own online bookstore and an e-book reader so they could compete more effectively.

A second, concurrent, development in telecommunications was the advent of fibre-optic cable, replacing copper wire. A fibre thinner than a single hair can transmit a laser signal carrying many thousands of telephone conversations, so that the cost per voice circuit becomes infinitesimal. In addition to improvements in fixed-wire telecommunications, wireless technology is making substantial gains in capacity and there has been a rapid growth in mobile technology for computers, smart phones and tablets with the introduction of 3G and 4G networks. The International Data Corporation ranks China, the United States, India, Brazil and the UK as the areas of fastest growth in smart phone use (IDC, 2012).

The convergence of these technologies has a number of implications for the way in which information is shared and who has access to it. In the past there was a trade-off between richness and reach of information. If you wanted to reach many people, information quality (richness) declined, whereas conveying high-quality information meant the sacrifice of reach. These days, information is readily available from anywhere in the world at the stroke of a keyboard or smart phone screen; richness and reach can go together as distance is independent of cost. This has created new possibilities for the structure of organizations, as discussed below.

Organizational architecture

Before the advances in ICT, organizations handled information through various layers of middle managers who summarized, synthesized and otherwise filtered the information that passed up and down the hierarchy. With 10 to 15 layers between the CEO and first-line supervisors in many large bureaucracies, there was considerable scope for message distortion and misinterpretation. The fact that rich information could not be widely shared imposed a departmentalized structure where function-specific information could be shared among a more limited group of people. Because people tended to hoard knowledge rather than share it, information became a source of power that sustained many departments.

With computer-based networks now doing much of this type of work, the need for middle managers has declined substantially, resulting in flatter organizations with senior management much closer to the actual work setting. The fact that rich information can now be shared quickly and widely has enabled unconventional organizational structures and the adaptation of conventional structures.

The advantage is that virtual organizations can exist in a meaningful way as individuals across the organization can communicate easily in real time regardless of where they are; the disadvantage is that work can be extended to 24 hours a day, seven days a week, so there is no getting away from it!

In the recent past, cost and quality were the common mantras and they are still important. However, globalization has led to the compression of time and space and created new imperatives that guide the way business is conducted. Competitive pressures can come from anywhere in the world, and do so without warning. Think of the cycle time as the amount of time it takes to create and produce a new product or service, and then bring in the impact of globalization; those who are first to market with a new product or service usually have a first-mover advantage. This has led to cases where manufacturing has been brought closer to home to improve the turnaround time; for example, companies like Top Shop and Zara want to have the latest style of clothing in their shops within weeks of the clothes appearing on the Paris runways.

In order to decrease cycle time, organizations are closely examining the way they conduct business. This has emerged as a concept known as reengineering, which is basically a method of examining processes and how they fit together to accomplish the desired end result, rather than just accepting the traditional collection of jobs required to do the work (Hammer and Champy, 1993), which worked well for a while. However, the increasing speed and pressure of change has led to a greater focus on customers and their needs. Bundling, where several human resource practices are combined, helps build capacity and motivate employees and leads to high-performance work practices (HPWS) and systems that recognize human capability as a great source of competitive advantage (Messersmith and Guthrie, 2010). In a study of 215 organizations across the United States, Messersmith and Guthrie (2010) identified that using a high-performance approach significantly related to higher levels of innovation and sales growth in young firms. Although this was a relatively small study, other studies have found similar results.

In the traditional departmentalized structures, sometimes referred to as 'functional silos', departmental boundaries were obstacles to the smooth flow of information and processes. They also created barriers between people who needed to interact. As a result, reengineering has led to a much wider use of 'team-based' structures, such as cross-functional teams, which effectively replace rigid structures with more flexible ones. Teams cut across narrow specialities to focus on better ways to create value among the various activities and are inherent in HPWS (Messersmith and Guthrie, 2010).

An obvious result of these activities is that many jobs have changed substantially. This has affected a major HRM activity known as job analysis. Instead of job analysis, which defines what a worker does, work process analysis may be more appropriate for defining activities. Another variation is competency profiling, which defines the competencies that will be required of staff at future points in time and will, in turn, influence training and development as well as staffing programmes. Thus, it can be seen that HRM itself is adapting and developing new tools.

A major challenge that organizations and their HRM functions will have to face in this changed work environment is a trade-off between achieving flexibility and investing in human capital. Articles on HR architecture identify this trade-off (Palpacuer, 1997; Lepak and Snell, 1999), in which organizations classify employees in terms of whether to invest in their development or to purchase and discard labour as a commodity. The evidence of valuing employees is borne out in a number of studies on the benefits of high-performance work systems over the last 10 years.

Attitudes and values

Attitudes to work and worker–employer relationships have changed dramatically in the last two decades. We will consider several trends that involve attitudinal shifts between employees and employers. Perhaps the most striking change is in the nature of the employment relationship.

The period from 1946 to the early 1980s was characterized by long-term, stable employment relationships, where workers could expect continuous employment with one or a few employers, with gradual advancement up the corporate hierarchy over the course of their working life. In return for this job security, the employee gave loyalty and commitment to the employer and made sacrifices if required for the good of the company.

In this environment companies invested in the training and development of their employees as they expected them to stay long enough to recoup the investment. Beginning in the early 1980s, massive downsizings changed that relationship forever. As giant mainstream companies scrambled to become more flexible and agile in the face of intense competition, many sacrificed job security, and contractual relationships became the norm. Long-term employment security is no longer promised, implied or expected and mutual commitment is no longer a cornerstone of the employment relationship. The downsizing of the 1980s has been eclipsed by those made since the global financial crisis that started in 2008. Just to give one example, international coffee chain Starbucks closed 600 stores and laid off 12,000 employees in 2008 (de la Merced, 2008).

On the one hand, some skilled workers are able to move quickly and easily between companies, but the paradox for organizations is that if they shed skilled workers when they are not needed, they may not be able to attract enough workers when they are. This presents a paradox for the many companies that want to shed workers when they are not needed, but at the same time want to retain valuable employees for as long as possible. As Kraut and Korman (1999) pointed out in the late 1990s, employees without job security tend to spend their time looking for other jobs or opportunities, and both they and the companies they work for focus only on their own short-term gains.

Certainly in Australia, many small to medium-sized firms preferred to avoid laying off their workers during the worst of the global financial crisis, knowing that once these workers were lost to competitors they would have difficulty regaining appropriately skilled people. As Hewlett (2009) points out, good people can get a job regardless of how tough times are, and if they are unhappy they will leave, which means a company can easily lose the employees it most needs to keep. Hewlett cites the example of the London office of KPMG which, when the GFC recession first hit, offered employees a variety of different flexible approaches to reduced working hours as a way of cutting overheads and still retaining staff.

There is a growing body of evidence that the use of high-performance work practices can have a significant impact on the financial performance of a company (Armitage and Keeble-Ramsay, 2009; Messersmith and Guthrie, 2010; Wang et al., 2011). Many practices, such as comprehensive recruitment and selection procedures, incentive compensation, performance management systems and extensive involvement in training and development, are long-term investments in human resources that contradict the notion of contractual relationships. Hence, the prevailing attitudes towards employment relationships are out of alignment with what is known to be best practice. These relationships will be explored further in a later section.

Another attitudinal shift has occurred regarding family and non-work commitments. Higher divorce rates, more single-parent families, more dual-career and two-income families and a lack of job security have focused attention on the need for more flexible work arrangements and support for families. Many companies have responded to these needs and have seen this as a way to differentiate themselves as preferred employers. The SAS Institute, noted previously, is a good example of this. The benefits offered to workers extend to teleworking, flexible hours, assistance with sick dependents, child care and so on. Indeed, Hewlett (2009) suggests organizations can use time as currency for time-poor employees.

Attitudes and values are, to a certain extent, based on the underlying assumptions that people hold. If the assumptions about work and work practices made in an earlier era are no longer valid, then practices based on those assumptions are also probably invalid. It is possible that many of the assumptions on which HRM practices were originally based over the last century have changed fundamentally in the last two decades. As this analysis of the forces of change has shown, many of the multiple roles of HRM need to be re-thought to ensure the correct alignment between a set of changed assumptions and current practice.

Study guide

Review questions

1. Explain the relationships that are apparent within the open systems model of an organization and provide three examples of how an open systems approach explains an interaction between an organization's external and internal environment.
2. Explain some of the demographic changes that are occurring in the environment.

3. Three key economic forces that are influencing change are the cost of labour, the shift to service economies and globalization. Explain the meaning of, and give examples of, each of these.
4. Explain how legal and regulatory issues influence the choices organizations have, particularly in relation to the impact of globalization and how they are influencing change in the business environment.
5. Identify and explain three key areas where technological change has significantly influenced organizational operations over the last 10 years.
6. Why are attitudes and values important, and what are three changes in societal attitudes and values that are having an impact in the workforce?

Discussion questions

1. Compare and contrast the assumptions that underpin the new employment relationship with the assumptions that characterized employment relationships in the past.
2. Do you agree that there are differences between the generation defined as the baby boomers, generation X and generation Y? If so, do you think these differences are related to their generation or their life stage?
3. Should employees from different generations be treated equally or differently in terms of their recruitment, performance management, and their rewards for work?

Case study: Can Avon survive?

A recent internet article published in the Delaware Corporation's online news supplier 24/7 Wall St. identified 10 household brands that their financial observers expected to go out of business in 2013. Among these was cosmetics giant Avon. The Avon Corporation started up in 1886 when United States former book salesman, David McConnell, realized the potential opportunities of both selling perfumes and having women selling these to other women. The company was originally called the California Perfume Company and has always had an ethos to provide quality products and maintain a high level of corporate social responsibility, as is evident in its commitment to empower women through fair pay and a happy work environment. The Avon name was adopted in 1939, to give the company broader appeal as it became international.

Avon still rates itself as a company for women and actively supports and raises funds for initiatives such as the pink ribbon awareness for breast cancer, and combating domestic violence against women. Nonetheless, there has also been some controversy regarding the company's commitment to not testing products on animals. The company claims it was among the first cosmetic companies not to use animals for testing; however, an article published in the UK in 2012 disputes that Avon products worldwide are totally free of animal testing. In its defence, Avon claims that less than 0.3 per cent of its products are tested on animals, and testing is required by governments in some countries where they operate.

Like all companies that have been in business this long, Avon has had its share of ups and downs. Recent troubles began in 2007, as sales worldwide fell and the share price declined by 45 per cent. A new CEO was appointed and retrenchments and consolidation followed. The management structure was reduced from 15 to 8 layers, and new managers with expertise from other established companies, such as Procter & Gamble, Kraft and Gillette, were brought in to help professionalize the company. Initially it looked as if Avon would have a brighter future; however, this promise has not been borne out. In spite of the fact that the company is a global corporation that operates in over 100 countries, employing over 6 million sales representatives, and boasts a turnover of over $11 billion annually, the latest figures suggest it will be facing its toughest challenge ever.

2012 has been a tough year for the company. There are concerns as to whether the company's Chinese operations comply with the Foreign Corrupt Practices Act; concerns about communications with securities analysts that brought about the downfall of the former chief financial officer. In addition, a new CEO, who has not run a public corporation before but was responsible for successfully overhauling the pharmaceutical division at Johnson & Johnson, was employed in April 2012. Restructuring initiatives in 2011 were costly, but failed to effect a turnaround. The company has been hit by the falling American dollar, fierce competition from other cosmetic companies, and seems to be reactive rather than proactive.

The new CEO, Sherilyn McCoy, has been getting a feel for the organization before announcing what changes she will make. There are plans for expanding the business into new markets in China and Russia and the company wants to resolve a Securities and Exchange Commission investigation related to potential bribery of foreign officials. While Ms McCoy acknowledges that the company needs to make changes, she claims the problems have taken years to emerge and will not go away overnight. In the meantime she has engaged a new head of human resources to streamline the company's compensation plans. She has also been quoted as saying "Avon doesn't need yet another new strategy. We need to focus on the core of Avon's business: representatives, consumers and our people"(Martin, 2012). So far the changes have been received positively and Avon's share price has started to recover. Will it be enough to save this icon? Time will tell!

Discussion questions

1. Identify the Delta forces driving change at Avon.
2. Some examples in this case raise questions of corporate social responsibility. Do you think such transgressions compromise the company's commitment to corporate social responsibility?
3. The former CEO of Avon has been retained in an advisory role. Consider the implications of this decision and say whether you agree with this strategy.

Online activity

Conduct some research online to investigate whether Avon's current strategy has improved the company's financial position.

Consider any changes in the Delta forces and how these have affected the corporation's strategy.

Sources for this case

Avon Corporation: http://www.avoncompany.com/aboutavon/history/mcconnell. html

Macrae, F. (2012) Avon withdraws animal test claims from website after complaints. *Daily Mail*, UK, 6 March. http://www.dailymail.co.uk/femail/ article-2110787/Avon-withdraws-animal-test-claims-website-complaints. html. Accessed 31.12.2012.

Martin, A. (2012) Avon chairwoman to quit earlier than expected. *New York Times* on-line. http://www.nytimes.com/2012/. Accessed 31.12.2012.

McIntyre, D.A. (2012) Ten brands that will disappear in 2013. *FoxBusiness*, 21 June. Accessed from http://www.foxbusiness.com/industries/2012/06/21/ten-brands-that-will-disappear-in-2013/.31.12.201210/06/business/avon-chairwoman-to-step-down.html?ref=avonproductsinc&_r=0.

Exercise: Forces of change

In this exercise, the facilitator organizes the class into small groups of 4–5 people. Each group takes one of the five forces of change and discusses the implications of that force for HRM.

(Allow 20 minutes for this discussion.)

Each group then reports their findings back to the rest of the class.

(Allow 10 minutes per group.)

Ethics discussion

A company that is setting up a mining operation in New Guinea wants to pump tailings and waste from the mine into a nearby bay. Environmentalists oppose this strategy because the bay and its surrounds are a pristine marine environment. It is rich in marine life and there is an area of unique coral reefs just outside the entrance to the bay. Opinions among the local community and other stakeholders are divided. Some, like the company and the government, argue that the mine would benefit the local population and bring employment, education and, through these, increased wealth to the community and country that would allow for better health services and infrastructure. Some families, local government officials and farmers are concerned about possible negative environmental and health impacts, such as air pollution and acid rain from the mine. In addition, a large part of the local diet comes from fish in the bay.

Discussion questions

1. Discuss the forces of change that are operating in this case.
2. Discuss the ethical issues from the perspective of the different stakeholders.
3. Decide on a resolution to this dilemma.

The impact of business trends

Listed below are a number of trends which are leading to significant impact on organizations. Select the two most important trends, and complete the grid in Table 2.1. This grid helps you consider the impact of these trends on the human resource activities in the organization.

Trends

- ageing labour force
- globalization
- information technology enhancements
- shift from manufacturing to service economy
- increasing number of women in the workforce
- decreasing work security
- increasing competition.

TABLE 2.1 The impact of business trends

Manpower planning and staffing	Performance management	Organizational structure and work practices	Career planning

Further reading

Messersmith, J.G., Patel, P.C., Lepak, D.P. and Gould-Williams, J.S. (2011) Unlocking the Black Box. *Journal of Applied Psychology*, 96(6): 1105–1118.

Messersmith, J.G. and Guthrie, J.P. (2010) High-performance work systems in urgent organizations: Implications for firm performance. *Human Resource Management*, 49(2): 241– 264.

Wang, M.K., Hwang, K.P. and Lin, S.R. (2011) An empirical study of the relationships among employees' perceptions of HR practice, human capital, and department performance: A case of AT&T Subordinate telecoms company in Taiwan. *Expert Systems with Applications*, 38(4): 3777–3783.

Zhou, Y., Zhang, Y. and Liu, J. (2012) A hybridism model of differentiated human resource management effectiveness in Chinese context. *Human Resource Management Review*, 22(3): 208–219.

3

CURRENT RESPONSES TO A CHANGING ENVIRONMENT

The pace and rate of change influence managerial roles and responsibilities, choice, decision-making and leads to either intentional or emergent strategy (Wright and Dyer, 1999; Harrison and St John, 2009). Organizations need to keep control of the processes and structures, while at the same time they are increasingly devolving responsibility, decision-making and accountability to employees/operatives at the lower levels as organizations become flatter. The acceleration of change means it is increasingly difficult to predict the future, and discover how organizations can adapt to changes.

Organizational responses, in terms of increased flexibility and agility, impact on the way changes are managed. This can lead to such outcomes as:

- competitive strategies of flexibility versus stability and the need to foster innovations;
- structural change, and the need to balance the choices regarding control, as in whether to have centralization versus decentralization, core versus peripheral workforces, or outsourced and network structures as well as reengineering;
- supply-chain development – including disaggregated supply chains – MNCs, SMEs and small businesses;
- technological advancements in communication and information technology, with implications for human resources in terms of organizational development and change, cultural adaptation in the different working arrangements, such as the move to teams, greater autonomy and employee participation, which in turn affect remuneration and reward systems. The development of employees leads to increased skills and the opportunity for greater employee involvement, which, combined with the motivation strategies, increase employee morale and develop a managerial talent pool within the organization;

- matching the management style to the culture is an important aspect that is frequently overlooked.

The Build, Operate and Transfer (BOT) scheme for Indonesia Telecom infrastructure development is a good example (Pearson et al., 2004). Developing countries that may not have either the financial or the technological resources to develop infrastructure, or to carry out large-scale improvement projects, often use BOT arrangements. These arrangements promote private and foreign finance for the design, construction and operation of large projects for an agreed period of time, usually 10 to 40 years (Badawi, 2003). During the concessional period the investors are able to recover their investment plus profit. At the end of the concessional period the facility is transferred back to the owner, in this case the Indonesian government.

The first recorded BOT arrangement was a contract to build the Suez Canal for Egypt in 1869 by an international company (Levy, 1996). In the Indonesian example six regions were designated, two of which were retained by the home country and four were allocated to successful international bidders. The foreign partners were the United States, Singapore, France and the United Kingdom; all had highly regarded experience in local and global telecommunications markets (Pearson et al., 2004). The performance rating for each of the six TELKOM divisions was evaluated on four assessments as follows:

1. ratio of revenue to the number of employees
2. ratio of employee cost to operating income
3. ratio of lines in service to the number of employees
4. number of customer complaints per 100 subscribers.

Cultural relativity and organizational practices were linked by coupling information about how the six BOT divisions were structuring their operations and power-sharing in terms of formalization, involvement in decision-making, hierarchical relationships and role clarification (Pearson et al., 2004). The findings of the study suggest that divisions more similar to Indonesian culture had greater success as measured by the four assessments. Perhaps surprisingly, the Indonesians matched best with the French approach to work redesign, which translates into management practice.

French national culture is tolerant of inequalities of power and wealth; therefore, their organizations are characterized by centralized, hierarchical structures and autocratic management styles (Hofstede, 1993). The French division achieved the best revenue maximization and infrastructure development, and their employees reported the highest level of job scope. The US and UK divisions were shown to be culturally less compatible with Indonesian culture. Organizations from these cultural backgrounds tend to be more oriented to individual authority and participative management styles that the Indonesian workforce is unaccustomed to. The researchers thought it was unlikely that the French BOT division planned this strategy, but rather, culturally compatible work practices converged to achieve more favourable outcomes (Pearson et al., 2004).

Another strategy is to learn by examining organizational improvement methodologies such as benchmarking, customer focus, best practice, learning organizations and project management. We can understand the process, how to measure the methodologies and accordingly how to make informed management decisions.

The forces of change discussed above are largely beyond the control of individual companies. They represent the complex environment in which firms must operate. This section considers how organizations are responding to these forces and presents a snapshot of the situation today. The term 'snapshot' is appropriate as this is an ever-evolving scenario. Below are a number of organizational responses to the competitive environment:

- rethinking the strategy–structure nexus
- consolidating around the core processes and outsourcing
- managing the supply chain
- reengineering and cycle time
- use of teams.

The strategy–structure nexus

The thinking in traditional organizations was that strategy drives structure, i.e. that the strategy of a company should determine its structure. This thinking was developed in a classic historical study by Alfred Chandler (1962) in which he traced the origins of diversification and divisionalization at DuPont and General Motors in the 1920s. These measures were adopted later by other major companies. This approach works reasonably well in relatively stable and predictable conditions where business plans are based on environmental forecasts; plans are drawn up and approved, and attention is paid to building the organizational ability to implement them. However, this model, which takes a considerable amount of time, tends to break down in turbulent, rapidly changing environments that are increasingly unable to be forecast (Wright and Dyer, 1999; Harrison and St John, 2009).

Because of rapid change, intended plans become unsustainable. They have to be modified and sometimes there are major changes such as restructuring, reengineering and downsizing. These steps are undertaken in an effort to realign organizational capability with organizational strategy. This form of strategy and structure is known as *intentional* as opposed to *emergent strategy,* as illustrated in Figure 3.1.

As we have seen, intentional strategies are overtaken by events and often lead to efforts to deal with change that are dysfunctional. There is a risk that they may leave companies in a constant state of flux. With emergent strategies, top management still sets the strategic direction and domain, but the specific (emergent) business strategies emanate from the collective decisions of those close to the action as they guide the company towards its objectives. This is analogous to an airline flight

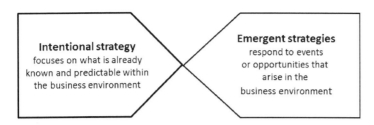

FIGURE 3.1   From intentional to emergent strategy

where planes are off the true course about 98 per cent of the time, but they still arrive at their destination because the pilot makes frequent small corrections.

This paradigm shifts the emphasis from formal strategic planning to building organizational capability featuring people-driven systems that enhance speed, flexibility and agility (Wright and Dyer, 1999). This also puts a different twist on the role of leaders because agile organizations are essentially self-organizing systems driven by individual initiative and self-control. Those in formal leadership positions may do very little formal planning; instead, their role is to facilitate, encourage and generally champion the new paradigm.

HRM plays a major role in crafting these new relationships, by fitting people to roles rather than specific jobs. Employees are selected on the basis of organization–person fit, rather than person–job fit. In consequence, the training and development experiences that follow allow staff to acquire the skills they need to function effectively in this changed environment. Essentially, HRM translates corporate strategy into human requirements that directly link corporate or business strategies with specific HR issues and programmes. This in turn allows for the more transparent measurement of the contribution of HRM to overall organization performance.

Consolidating around core processes and outsourcing

As mentioned above, companies have altered their formal strategic planning processes to increase their speed, flexibility and overall agility. A related trend is to consolidate the organization structure around core processes and to outsource the rest. The concepts of core competencies and outsourcing were preceded by the concepts of unrelated diversification and vertical integration in the 1960s. Noting the failure of numerous conglomerates in the 1960s and 1970s, many financial theorists, management academics and consultants began to support a more focused view of how widely a company should array itself, which usually translated to the phrase "stick to the knitting" (Quinn and Hilmer, 1994). In other words, stick to doing what you know how to do best. The advent of strategic business units that operate fairly autonomously, particularly in large multi-business enterprises, means that these days this problem has largely been overcome.

A firm's core competencies are generally not products, but knowledge, intellectual skills or unique systems that create a sustainable competitive advantage.

The notion is to leverage something that you do very well, and which is not easy to copy (Hamel and Prahalad, 1990). Thus, while an outstanding product design will usually be imitated fairly quickly, the intellectual skill that produced the design may be very difficult to copy.

Quinn and Hilmer (1994) state that intellectual input accounts for virtually all the value added in the service sector in the United States, which accounts for 79 per cent of all jobs and 76 per cent of all value added. Therefore, core competencies represent the bulk of a company's intellectual capital and profitability. Conventional wisdom extends this argument to suggest that if some aspect of a business is not a core competence then it should be outsourced to another firm that can do it cheaper, faster and better than you can. There are some good examples of this practice.

The Dell Computer Company does not manufacture anything. The company's core competencies are in direct marketing to the public, real-time assembly to customer specifications and outstanding after-sales service. Dell invests heavily in training and development to maintain this competitive advantage. Similarly, Nike Inc. outsources 100 per cent of its bulk shoe production and only manufactures key components of its 'Nike Air' system. They create maximum value by concentrating on the core competencies of product design, marketing, distribution and sales.

Quinn and Hilmer (1994) recommend that no more than three to five activities in the value chain should be targeted as core competencies because, as work becomes more complex, it is difficult to achieve excellence in a wide variety of activities. A recent study reported in the Business Exchange on how the world's leading companies manage supply chains (Benjabutr, 2012) supports this. The list below shows that these are very successful companies; however, their activities and the order of activity vary and depend on the industry, as can be seen from the list:

1.   Boeing and AirBus – aircraft manufacturing
2.   Benneton, Zara, Addidas – fashion
3.   Unilever, Coca Cola – consumer products
4.   BMW, Ford, Hyundai – automobile manufacturing
5.   Intel, HP, Dell, Samsung – technology
6.   Tesco, WalMart, Amazon – retail.

A summary of the main best practices in the value chain gives, in order of importance:

1.   strategic sourcing
2.   supply chain design
3.   demand management
4.   new product development.

The role of HRM is critical in identifying and maintaining core competencies. These are usually identified through benchmarking and HRM is either responsible for, or involved in this activity. Because core competencies represent a heavy investment in human capital and competitive advantage, the HRM systems that support those key staff must also be of a very high standard. It is hard to imagine that anything other than high-standard HRM practice could maintain high-standard core competencies and the people who represent them.

Outsourcing is the other side of the coin regarding the concentration on core competencies, and it involves benefits and risks. Until an activity has been benchmarked, a company may not know how well it performs. When Ford Motor Company carried out a massive benchmarking study on 400 sub-assemblies for the Taurus–Sable line they were surprised to discover that many internal suppliers were nowhere near the standard of external suppliers (Quinn and Hilmer, 1994). Where there are a relatively large number of suppliers and mature market standards, it makes sense to outsource.

Normally, if strategic control of an activity or unique process were important it would be kept in-house. Similarly, if its strategic importance were low, it would be a candidate for outsourcing. At the intermediate level it would probably be bound by a contractual arrangement.

Caution is needed when choosing to outsource, as will be discussed in more detail in a later section that discusses the flip side of downsizing. Nonetheless, one of the key concerns for HRM, and one that does not usually get enough attention, is the de-skilling that takes place when an activity is outsourced. The skill bases which a company has built up over a lengthy period of time can be lost very rapidly. Where the skill base needed for an activity is widely distributed in an industry, this is not a serious concern. Where the skill base is not widely distributed and there are few dominant suppliers, then a company may risk suppliers taking control. In some cases, by outsourcing a key component companies may lose the strategic flexibility to introduce new designs when they want them, rather than when the supplier permits (Quinn and Hilmer, 1994). Another issue is that once an activity is outsourced, the company loses control and may have reduced influence over the process, the quality or the timing.

Finally, outsourcing an activity extends the supply chain beyond a company's boundaries and thus beyond its internal control mechanisms. This can be problematic when supply chains cross national boundaries, particularly into developing countries. These and other considerations about supply chains are discussed in the next section.

Supply chain development

The assumption underpinning emergent strategy is that the business environment is too chaotic and unpredictable to be forecast accurately with conventional strategic planning methods. This means businesses need a more flexible structure to place managers closer to the action. Focusing on a few core processes with the rest being outsourced also suggests a more flexible structure.

The need for flexibility, the ability to respond quickly to changing circumstances and generally do everything faster, is clearly not compatible with the traditional bureaucratic structure. In order to develop an organizational architecture corresponding to these needs, many companies have redesigned their activities in relation to their supply chains. In a sense, the supply chain becomes an organizing mechanism for fitting elements together and removing barriers. It is, essentially, a move away from functions towards processes.

Modern supply chain theory rejects the traditional view of an organization being composed of distinct functional entities (Anderson et al., 1997; Kampstra et al., 2006). These 'functional silos', as they have been called, are seen as an impediment to the smooth flow of products, services and information across the internal supply chain of various management systems, as well as external components such as suppliers and customers. Figure 3.2 presents a simplified supply chain with its internal and external components.

The early view of supply chain management (SCM) is that of an integrated, process-oriented approach to procuring, producing and delivering products and services to customers. This includes sub-suppliers, suppliers, internal operations, trade customers, retail customers and end users (Anderson et al., 1997).

Contemporary SCM is a progression in logistics management, which has gone through several stages. Initially logistics was concerned with the relationships between warehousing and transportation. These two functions were integrated by physical distribution management which resulted in the need for less inventory through the use of faster, more frequent and reliable transportation (Metz, 1998). This was enabled by more advanced communications between the various components of the supply chain, integrating production plants, regional and local distribution centres (Metz, 1998).

A second stage in the development of SCM was the inclusion of logistics, which incorporated manufacturing, procurement and order management functions. This stage was made possible by advances in information technology, worldwide communications, computer-aided design (CAD), computer-aided manufacturing (CAM), along with the ability to store, access, analyse and exchange large amounts of data (Metz, 1998). In complex supply chains, such as those for the automotive industry, manufacturers rank their suppliers by a tier rating of 1–3, based on their strategic importance to the production process. (Kampstra et al., 2006).

External	**Internal**	**External**
→	→	
Suppliers	Management systems	Wholesalers
Contractors	Manufacturing, procurement, logistics, product design, etc.	Retailers
Sub-contractors		Customers

FIGURE 3.2   A simplified supply chain
Source: Entrekin (2000). Original version copyright © 2001 International Labour Organization. Revised and updated version copyright © 2013 Lanny Entrekin.

These days we refer to 'integrated supply chain management', where the supply chain is lengthened to include suppliers at one end and customers at the other. This represents a progression from a two-stage supply chain in the 1960s to a seven-stage or longer supply chain at present day (Entrekin, 2000). These developments have largely been made possible by dramatic advances in information technology (IT). IT provides more information, more accurately, more frequently and globally than at any time in history. This makes it possible to digest, analyse and model information in sophisticated decision-support systems in ways that allow organizations to cope with the increasing complexity of supply chains. Systems thinking, total quality management (TQM) and business process reengineering (BPR) have also contributed to the development of SCM by requiring managers to understand how various management processes interact in order to make them more efficient and productive.

Activity-based cost accounting (ABC) is another important advance supporting SCM. ABC gives process-based financial information that allows a much more specific allocation of costs than traditional function-based cost accounting. This technique provides an understanding of where the costs really lie and thus enables the improved design of integrated processes.

Disaggregated supply chains

Most manufacturers and service providers have traditionally outsourced some aspects of their production or service activities. Automobile manufacturers source components from hundreds of specialized suppliers while retaining the core processes of product development, manufacturing, assembly, marketing and sales. Similarly, banks have traditionally outsourced functions such as cheque clearing, some data processing and other 'back room' activities to specialist service providers.

However, the outsourcing of entire production or service functions is a more recent phenomenon, resulting in the disaggregation of supply chains. Call centres are an example where companies such as banks, utilities and other service providers have outsourced customer service to a specialist provider. In his popular book of 1998, Charles Handy described these as 'doughnut organizations', as they retain their strategic core functions and outsource the rest.

Most mass producers of apparel and footwear outsource production while retaining their strategic core functions of product design, marketing, procurement and logistics, together with internal management systems such as finance and HRM. As noted previously, external supply chain relationships can vary from a purely arm's-length contractual arrangement to high involvement of the purchaser and supplier. The literature suggests a number of possible relationships. Table 3.1 illustrates the potential complexity of modern supply chains, not only to do with the efficient production and distribution of goods and services, but also to do with corporate social responsibility in relations across the supply chain.

With the constant pressure to increase productivity and lower costs to remain competitive in the global market, MNCs have looked to their supply chains for the

TABLE 3.1 Range of possible relationships between companies and their suppliers

	1. Contractual arms length	3.	5.	7.	9. Fully integrated
Supply strategy	Many suppliers, contractors and sub-contractors	Many suppliers, contractors and sub-contractors	Several preferred suppliers and contractors who supply several companies	One or two suppliers who produce exclusively for one company. Company-owned operations centre located in region of production, e.g. Hong-Kong	Wholly owned production facilities
Factors of production emphasized	Emphasis on low cost/speed to market/low to medium quality	Emphasis on low cost/speed to market	Emphasis on low cost/acceptable quality	Emphasis on low cost, high quality/speed to market	Emphasis on cost and high quality
Location	Lowest cost developing country	Developing countries	Developing country	Transitional or recently developed country, e.g. Singapore/Brazil/India/Mexico	Europe/North America/Japan/Australia/New Zealand
CSR strategy	Meet local labour standards, e.g. minimum wage/hours/child labour	Meet local labour standards No code of conduct	Meet local labour standards/code of conduct	Exceed minimum labour standards/code of conduct/labelling scheme	Meet or exceed developed country labour standards/invest in training and retaining staff

Implementation and monitoring	Meet local minimum labour standards	Meet local minimum labour standards/minimal CSR emphasis	Minimal CSR function/third-party audit	Well developed CSR function/third-party audits	Part of strategic plan/HRM policies
Image and type of product	Low or no image apparel and footwear	Intermediate use products, e.g. rubber, products used in end production by others, bottles/cans etc. Little or no corporate or brand image	Medium to high quality image apparel/footwear/toys/houseware	High quality corporate and brand image sports apparel and footwear/personal products/food products	High quality corporate and brand image products, electronics/integrated circuits/computers/software/automobiles

Source: Entrekin, 2000. (CSR – Corporate Social Responsibility.) Original version copyright © 2001 International Labour Organization. Revised and updated version copyright © 2013 Lanny Entrekin.

answers. In addition to refining and improving processes in their internal supply chains, many companies have outsourced entire processes to lower-cost locations.

To achieve a comparative cost advantage over competitors, more and more MNCs have established production in developing countries that generally have much lower wage structures and mandated labour standards. As this phenomenon has dramatically increased in the past two decades, so has the concern of international agencies such as the ILO, non-governmental organizations (NGOs), national governments (particularly the United States), human rights groups and university students, among others. These concerns have crystallized around the ILO's concept of 'decent work', which embodies principles and standards relating to freedom of association, the right to collective bargaining, non-discrimination, and the elimination of child and forced labour. These concerns culminate in the rejection of 'sweatshops' where high-priced consumer goods, destined for developed country markets, are said to be produced in unacceptable working conditions that are unsafe, unhealthy and for wages that will not support a reasonable standard of living.

The development of SCM is part of a more general movement to streamline organizations so that they can deal with complexity and turbulence in increasingly shorter timeframes. The functional approach in the bureaucratic model is simply too slow and cumbersome to allow organizations to be proactive. Companies are therefore reconfiguring processes and relationships so that they can respond in real time to an ever-evolving landscape.

Reengineering and cycle time

Reengineering emerged in the 1990s as a favoured tool for achieving dramatic improvements in critical measures of employment such as cost, service or speed (Hammer and Champy, 1993), and is still prevalent today. The term is often misused as a euphemism for downsizing in announcements to employees and the financial markets (ILO, 1999). Reengineering, which often includes downsizing, basically refers to thinking about how things should be done now, as opposed to how they were done in the past. This almost always leads to organizing work around processes instead of functions, as mentioned previously. Reengineering advocates the radical redesign of processes and structures and it can be very painful and unsettling for both managers and employees.

Reengineering has a mixed track record, sometimes yielding spectacular results and sometimes failing to reach its objectives. For example, Ford Motor Company discovered that Mazda (a company that Ford holds a controlling interest in) handled accounts payable with five people as compared with Ford's 500. Through reengineering, Ford implemented a totally electronic system that reduced the number to 100 (Daft, 1998).

On the other hand, a large survey of 99 completed reengineering projects undertaken by Davenport (1995) showed that two-thirds were judged as producing mediocre or failed results. These findings are still relevant despite the passage of time and are supported in more recent European findings that indicate 50–70 per cent of large reengineering projects fail over a five-year period (Stefanescu and Stefanescu, 2008). The most important reasons cited for these poor outcomes related to lack of attention to the human dimension, poor communication, and the anxiety and stress that were created. Other reasons related to unrealistic expectations, a short-term perspective, inadequate resources, lack of ownership of the projects (Davenport, 1995) and lack of employee involvement or appropriate support from management (Stefanescu and Stefanescu, 2008). Because reengineering is expensive, time-consuming and almost always painful, Daft (2007) suggests that it is best suited to companies that are facing major dislocations in the nature of their competitive environment, such as in telecommunications. Hammer and Champy (1993) identified several recurring themes associated with successful reengineering projects that are equally relevant today, including:

- combining several jobs into one
- empowering workers to make decisions
- performing process steps in a natural order
- replacing functional teams with process teams
- shifting the focus on performance measures and compensation from activities to results
- making managers act as coaches, not supervisors
- making executives act as leaders.

There is a saying that "everything that goes around comes around again". Very little on the above list is new. Job redesign, worker participation, cross-functional teams, at-risk compensation, mentoring and transformational leadership have all been around since the early 1970s. The probable reasons why these recycled ideas occasionally work now, although they were generally unsuccessful then, have to do with stability, structure and implementation. The 1970s was a relatively stable environment in which bureaucracies still worked reasonably well. These experiments took place in structures that had not changed and were generally tried in isolation rather than in combination, as suggested by Hammer and Champy (1993).

Cycle time, as discussed previously, refers to the length of time it takes to create and produce a product or service; it is a relatively new term in the lexicon of globalization. If a company's cycle time is consistently longer than that of competitors it will never enjoy the 'first mover' advantage. Consider, for example, Dell Computer Company (mentioned previously). Computers are ordered online and built to requirement. This leads to fast cycle times, so the computers are delivered within 5–7 days (Dell.com, 2009) and the company has minimal inventory costs. Like cost reduction and productivity improvement, cycle time is a more aggregate measure of the combination of techniques used in the attempt to achieve a competitive advantage. These include rethinking the strategy–structure nexus, consolidating around core processes, outsourcing, supply chain management and reengineering.

The use of teams

The use of teams precedes globalization and is probably the most consistently used mechanism for organizing work. With the extensive restructuring and downsizing that has taken place in the last decade, organizations have become much flatter and managers' spans of control have widened dramatically. The rule of thumb in the 'personnel management' era was that a manager's span of control should not exceed 8 to 10 subordinates. This implied close supervision of subordinates in fairly highly structured jobs that allowed little discretion for individual initiative or decision-making.

This scenario is clearly inappropriate in today's globalized environment and companies have had little choice than to move towards team-based structures. The origins of teams can be traced back to the Tavistock studies of post-First World War (cited in Trist and Bamforth, 1951). This was followed by Swedish experiments with the team-based production of automobiles usually associated with Volvo (Pasmore, 1995). Interest in the United States was evident in the 1960s with the early use of teams at Procter & Gamble and the much publicized teamwork system at General Foods' pet food plant in Topeka, Kansas (Kraut and Korman, 1999). Today, companies such as Boeing, Healthways and Bayer use teams to enrich problem-solving and improve performance and quality (Jacobsen, 2008). Teams are finding new importance and are common practice in high-performance organizations (Messersmith and Guthrie, 2010), where social relations and interconnectivity are needed to achieve both performance and satisfaction outcomes (Lengnick-Hall et al., 2009).

Generally, teams are defined as groups of individuals working interdependently to solve problems or accomplish tasks. The emphasis here is on *interdependently*. This distinguishes teams from groups of people who happen to work in the same location on similar jobs. The main types of teams and their distinguishing features are listed below.

There are six types of teams; three are permanent work arrangements and three are temporary work arrangements. The three permanent teams are:

1. self-managing work teams which deal with daily work activities and have a high level of autonomy and task interdependence;
2. work teams which deal with day-to-day work with some level of supervision;
3. management teams consisting of senior-level managers dealing with strategic decisions with a high level of autonomy.

The three non-permanent teams retain functional responsibility while working on specific assignments:

1. Cross-functional teams combine expertise from functional areas that require these inputs for specific work assignments. These teams usually have moderate autonomy and task interdependence, and stay on the job until the task is completed.

2. Problem-solving project teams work on specific tasks to solve problems and improve work processes or design new products. They usually have moderate autonomy and task interdependence and remain until the task is completed.
3. Virtual teams are geographically dispersed and seldom meet in person. These teams work on common assignments and exchange information electronically, usually with complete autonomy and low to moderate task interdependence.

One of the important differences between the teams described above is their permanent or temporary nature. Self-managing work teams, work teams and management teams tend to be permanent arrangements, whereas cross-functional teams, problem-solving project teams and virtual teams tend to be temporary. Perhaps the most important types to date are permanent self-managing teams and temporary cross-functional teams.

Self-managing teams are important because they represent a realization by management that if people are properly selected, trained and resourced they can effectively manage themselves, take the initiative and make decisions. This has two important effects. First, people are empowered to use their own abilities and this enhances motivation and group cohesiveness. The second important effect is that these teams release managers from close supervision so that they can pay more attention to strategic issues. This, then, is one of the main mechanisms that allow companies to alter their structures from tall hierarchies of authority to self-organizing forms that are more flexible and agile. The manager's role involves less command and control and more resourcing, training and facilitating.

Cross-functional teams are equally important as, by definition, they function across boundaries. One of the major drawbacks to the traditional function-based bureaucracy is the difficulty in communicating across departmental boundaries to find joint solutions to common problems. Disputed issues would often need to refer several levels up the hierarchy to a common boss for resolution. Cross-functional teams are usually established with the necessary expertise from two or more functional areas to accomplish a specific task or solve a mutual problem. Cross-functional teams are used to design new products, services and processes, and are extensively used in reengineering. Members retain their functional responsibilities and disband when the project is complete. Assignment to cross-functional teams is also an excellent developmental experience for young talent.

Increasingly, teams are operating with members from diverse cultures and from diverse locations and remotely from each other as a virtual team. This poses some unique problems to be managed. Humes and Reilly (2008) argue that providing the opportunity for individuals to explore their own values, beliefs and behaviours, especially in relation to the way they see their own societal values and cultural background, are ways of breaking down the barriers to present misunderstandings. This exploration should include their time expectations, their cultural relationship structures, the use of hierarchy and power and sharing their ideas about these with other team members.

Team-based work arrangements are not a panacea, nor are they appropriate for all situations. Geographically dispersed sales representatives working on commission, or people stitching clothes on a piece-rate basis, will probably gain little from being called a team. Work teams are most effective when there is a high degree of interdependence requiring a high degree of collaboration and cooperation to accomplish tasks (Lengnick-Hall et al., 2009). Work teams are not created by simply calling a group of workers a team. They will be most effective where the tasks are complex and well designed (Patel and Conklin, 2010). If a group's work is routine and unchallenging, highly programmed with little opportunity for initiative and feedback, teams will probably have little impact on productivity (Hackman, 1987).

A recent review of 120 'top teams' by Hackman (2009) identifies some important considerations that help make a team successful. First, the team must be real in the sense that all members are able to effectively contribute and, for this to happen, it must be clear who is part of the team. Having dissension in the team is not a problem as this can actually raise the standards by promoting different points of view. This is quite different to having non-team players who undermine the team, which is not recommended! Second, the team needs a compelling purpose and direction regarding what members are supposed to be doing together and what they need to achieve. Third, there needs to be an appropriate mix of members, with clearly designed tasks. Fourth, the organization needs to support and recognize members with appropriate rewards, HR systems and information systems. Lastly, they should be coached as a team, so they understand the group processes. Focusing on individual performance undermines team performance.

The major challenge for HR practitioners in introducing team-based work is to review their assumptions relating to the new work environment, and then to adjust their approach from individual HR practices to those appropriate to teams. Many of the assumptions underpinning management and human resource management practices were formed in previous eras, particularly the 1960s and 1970s. This was a period of considerable stability where tall hierarchies of authority worked reasonably well, change happened more slowly, jobs were relatively long-lived and had discrete responsibilities. Clearly, assumptions of that era are not applicable to today's hyper-energized environment, with flatter, more agile organization structures and shorter cycle times.

Assumptions that need rethinking revolve around motivation, structure and accountability. With regard to motivation, earlier assumptions were primarily concerned with individual needs and rewards and had a short-term focus. The new assumptions have a longer-term focus and are concerned with group needs and rewards. Regarding structure, earlier assumptions were concerned with independent work, with tightly written job descriptions and strong work boundaries, whereas the new assumptions need to be concerned with interdependent work, collaborative work practices and a longer- term focus. Regarding accountability, earlier assumptions were concerned with individual responsibility, functional specialization and a command and control reporting structure. The new assumptions are concerned with shared responsibility, horizontal reporting and self-management (Kraut and Korman, 1999).

Study guide

Review questions

1. Explain the build, operate and transfer model.
2. Explain the difference between intentional and emergent strategy and the relationship of each to the organizational structure.
3. Discuss the advantages of consolidating the core processes around an organization.
4. Explain what is meant by outsourcing.
5. Explain some of the challenges model organizations confront in dealing with disaggregated supply chains.
6. What is meant by reengineering?
7. Why is cycle time important to organizations?
8. Explain some of the advantages organizations seek when using employee teams.

Discussion questions

1. Many argue that strategy should always precede an organization structure; however, others argue that structure can sometimes precede strategy. What is the basis of this argument?
2. Many organizations have outsourced non-core activities in the hope of streamlining their core functions and reducing costs. However, some organizations have found that outsourcing has failed to deliver the advantages that it promised. Discuss why this may be so, drawing on examples from your own experience.

Online activity

Conduct research into a company that operates in your region and consider how it balances the tension between planned and emergent strategy.

1. What competitive local forces and broader Delta forces influence the strategic choice?
2. What are the implications for recruiting, rewarding and retaining employees?

Case study: Desert Dining

David Williams was reflecting on a seminar he had recently attended about the use of teams to improve morale and productivity. David is a Sales Manager for a company that produces and distributes a line of dinnerware in the Southwest states of Arizona, New Mexico and Texas. The company, with the name 'Desert Dining', is headquartered in Phoenix, Arizona, and specializes in desert motifs on its line of dinner plates, cups and saucers, serving dishes, dessert dishes, soup bowls and a line of linen dinner napkins and table cloths.

There are 30 sales representatives spread across the three states that call on retail and wholesale homeware stores and general merchandise outlets. The product line is considered to be high quality and appeals to an up-market, formal dining market. The seminar had influenced David to think about whether he could use the team concepts to improve the performance of his sales force.

He acknowledged that some of his sales representatives were more productive than others and that if perhaps more ideas were shared by the more successful ones they could improve overall performance. The sales force presently meets as a group twice a year at headquarters to review sales targets, performance criteria, any new product additions, and to attend a sales seminar/workshop with a marketing guru from the local university. This takes place over three days, of which one day is for travel to and from their locations.

Each sales representative is assigned to an exclusive sales territory and is supplied with a company car that can be used for personal use. Remuneration is based on a base salary plus a 20 per cent commission on sales above an assigned quota. Although the base salary is a living wage, most sales representatives exceed the base quota and make commissions that represent a good salary. They are also recompensed for documented work-related expenses.

Questions

1. Are any of the concepts in Chapter 3 appropriate for David's sales force?
2. Which, if any, of the team concepts presented in Chapter 3 might be applicable to David's sales force?
3. Is the remuneration package in David's sales force appropriate for the use of teams?

Further reading

Benjabutr, B. (2012) How World's Leading Companies Manage Supply Chains? scm-operations.com. 2 December. http://bx.businessweek.com/china-manufacturing/view?url=http%3A%2F%2Fwww.scm-operations.com%2F2012%2F11%2Fsupply-chain-case-study-analysis.html.

Dierdorff, E.C. (2012) Members matter in team training: Multilevel and longitudinal relationships between goal-orientation, self regulation and team outcomes. *Personnel Psychology*, 65(3): 661–703.

Hewlett, S.A. (2009) Top Talent: Keeping Performance Up when Business is Down (Memo to the CEO). USA: Harvard Business Press Books.

Patel, P.C. and Conklin, B. (2010) Perceived labor productivity in small firms – the effects of high-performance work systems and group culture through employee retention. *Entrepreneurship Theory and Practice*, March: 1042–2587.

World Economic Forum (2012) The Global Gender Gap Report 2012. http://www. weforum.org/issues/global-gender-gap.

4

MANAGING THE CHANGE PROCESS

This chapter explores fundamental change frameworks and discusses how to manage and implement change. Previous chapters have discussed the influence of the external environment on organizations; here we focus on the internal processes and strategies organizations use to adapt and improve performance capacity. Our intent is not to be prescriptive, but to provide an overview of the basic principles that underlie the change process and the problems that can arise. A quick look on the internet will show that various consulting firms offer a variety of approaches; however, in essence these are variations on the fundamental strategies we present here. Implementing any change strategy is likely to require, to varying degrees, consideration of some or all of the following:

- Appropriate frameworks and processes to manage the change. These include strategies and ways of diagnosing, implementing and evaluating any change.
- The dimensions of change. These can include planned or reactive changes that range from slow or minor changes to incremental change over a longer period or large-scale rapid transformations.
- Understanding the internal forces that occur at different levels of the organization to assist or hinder change.
- Matching the change strategies to the management style and strategy.
- The importance of effective leadership in paving the way and supporting the organization during change.
- Recognizing and managing the impact of changes within and across the organizational system. Changes in one part of the system or organization usually have a flow-on effect to other parts of the system. Some of these can be easily identified beforehand, whereas others emerge during the process, but regardless of their origin they have to be managed.
- The reasons why people resist change and how to overcome this resistance.

Resistance often emerges as conflict before or during the change process. Positive conflicts can stimulate innovation and acceptance, whereas negative or dysfunctional conflict can cause the change process to fail. Implementing effective human resource management practices can help to change employee behaviours and assist with cultural change. How can an organization develop a strong pivotal or core culture that matches the organization's objectives? The human resource management strategies of recruitment, selection and placement, and performance management need to be aligned to the organization's goals and, when implemented effectively, foster change.

The relevant steps for planning any strategic decision include diagnosing the current situation, exploring the options, then developing and implementing a plan of action. This can be implemented in the following way:

- understanding the external environment and how changes in that environment will impact on the organization;
- identifying the core objectives and role of the organization;
- exploring and creating realistic previews of where the organization wants to be in the future and how well these match with the environment;
- comparing the current situation with the desired future and identifying any discrepancies;
- developing plans to solve the identified problems, or address the discrepancies, so as to move the organization toward realignment with the organization's goals.

Different levels of an organization have different objectives. Recall that in Chapter 1 we identified that organizations can be thought of as a system in which all components work in tandem with other parts of the system, from top to bottom and across the different organizational functions. These generally follow a configuration like that demonstrated in Table 4.1, but differences arise due to the firm size, type of industry and stage of development.

Most of the above is fairly straightforward and will be readily understood. One of the more important elements that is not so well understood is the impact of structure. In simple terms, structure is the way the organization divides tasks and establishes reporting lines to make up a chain of command, so that individuals are accountable at various stages of a process. *Structural* change refers to the rearrangement of the organization's design components. The structure is the framework used for coordinating different activities and resources to ensure each component works towards a sub-goal that contributes to the overall goal of the organization. Structure defines reporting lines, span of control and levels of accountability, as in whether authority is centralized or devolved.

Restructuring has been popular in recent times and one of the major approaches has been to flatten the hierarchical layers in the organization to have greater worker involvement. The advantage of this is that decisions can be made faster, because they are often made by the person on the front line. This in turn means that the

TABLE 4.1 The internal organizational components of an open system

	Inputs	Internal organization	Measures
Top level or organizational goals	Vision – Mission – Strategy. Choices depend on external opportunities and threats and organizational capability	Management systems, i.e. finance and administration, type of structure, choice of technology, controls for product or service quality, HRM and culture	Measure of success, i.e. market share, ROI, environmental impact, customer satisfaction, staff turnover and satisfaction
Group or operational levels	Work coordination	Structure of tasks – whether shared, professional groupings or task groupings. Interpersonal relationships within and across functions. Performance standards	Effectiveness, i.e. decision quality, cooperation and customer satisfaction
Individual	Cooperation with others; individual contributions	Individuals' knowledge, skills, ability and contribution to their job (i.e. engagement through the job characteristics model)	Individual effectiveness, i.e. quality and quantity of performance, absenteeism, satisfaction, and personal development

ROI: Return on investment.

organization can be faster in its response to the demands of clients and suppliers or other relevant factors in the external environment.

Restructuring offers a wide variety of choices. These can range from minor changes in the physical layout, to introducing or decreasing a layer of supervision, through to downsizing the workforce and rearranging departments or breaking the organization into smaller business units. Changes across an organization's infrastructure are more complex to introduce because they interfere with the interconnectedness. For this reason, Spector (2007) argues they should not be undertaken at the beginning of a change process, but be left to the later stages, where they can be used to improve and reinforce connections that appear to be working well in supporting strategic realignment.

More extreme and more difficult to manage is a restructuring that involves mergers and acquisitions where different systems, and particularly the cultural systems, are non-aligned. This can create some real problems, particularly if one company perceives it is the victim of a takeover and the relationship between the companies is strained. A recent example of this was Porsche wanting to take control of Volkswagen. Volkswagen and their other major shareholder, the State of Saxony, reacted angrily to what they saw as a lack of transparency when Porsche secretly bought derivatives to try to take over the company (Milne and Saigol, 2008). Resentment over this contributed to a difficult ongoing relationship with regard to their cooperation. The takeover bid also worsened Porsche's financial difficulties, and there are still some residual issues with lawsuits from shareholders over the purchase of the Volkswagen shares. Despite the difficulties in their relationship it was eventually announced in mid-2012 that Volkswagen would acquire Porsche (Bryant, 2012). It will be interesting to see if their strained past will have an effect on their relations in the future.

The physical layout is regarded as the easiest to change and it is certainly easier to change than the behavioural systems, yet even small changes might need to include behavioural, structural and technological changes. For example, altering the physical spaces of an office layout by adding a piece of equipment can lead to a change in the operational process, a need for training and a reorganization of reporting relationships within a subunit. Taking this perspective of the organization as a system open to its environment, when planning such a change, considers the flow-on effects and interactions that might occur within the unit and in other subunits, so that these can be adapted to maintain alignment or equilibrium. This recognizes that components of a subsystem are interrelated and interacting, therefore changes in one part of the system will cause changes in another and, as in ecological models, all components of the system need to be dealt with together (Espinosa and Porter, 2011).

Another type of change is techno-structural change, in which the organization redesigns technology and structure interdependently. This is usually done to accommodate changes brought on by the introduction of new technology and the resultant changes in working arrangements. Technological change has increased at an accelerating rate over the past 20 or 30 years, so that nowadays most organizations are heavily dependent on technology, but gaining the best of the technology often requires upgrading skill levels and instilling high levels of knowledge among employees. Increasing skills and technology have combined to change the way work groups operate; individual employees have gained a greater level of involvement and there is more focus on teamwork. This has occurred for three reasons.

First, those who do a job usually have a better understanding of how it can be improved; second, increased involvement promotes greater ownership and motivation; and third, increasing task complexity means that many roles have areas of interdependence, so are performed more effectively by a team rather than individuals. Importantly, clues to a more workable structure are often identified from situations where individuals informally bypass the current structure to improve an outcome (Spector, 2007). When the structure is a barrier to getting the job done, individuals find ways around this by bypassing the formal structure or using their informal network.

Technology is not just about computers on desks; it refers to the broader technological support and processes an organization uses to provide goods and services. These days, measurement systems are usually aligned with technology. Sophisticated computerized management information systems that provide internet access for employees to manage their own human resource records, access online training, order stock and track products and orders have become commonplace. Technological measurement systems can be used to gather, assess and disseminate information on group and individual activities. On the one hand, technological solutions can replace people in any number of tasks that humans find repetitive, boring or uninteresting; whereas, on the other hand, we have become so dependent on technology that a power failure in an office building can close work down to such an extent that workers may as well go home.

Apart from machinery, technology can also refer to the methods and job design. Car manufacturers like Nissan, Ford, Toyota and General Motors rely on integrated computerized systems to coordinate manufacturing processes. These systems incorporate robotics, logistics, production tools and processes. In most cases, up-to-date technology provides companies with a competitive advantage, although there are exceptions to the rule. One small family-owned woollen mill in the Scottish Lowlands has stuck to using old-fashioned looms because it is able to do short runs using high-quality yarns and sell these as exclusive products to fashion houses. The ability to produce short runs with the old-fashioned low-cost equipment gives this company a competitive advantage over the more mechanized modern mills.

Technology has opened up tremendous opportunities for new businesses. Five-Senses is a small Australian company that sells boutique roasted coffees. The company started by selling to retail outlets and cafes, and then expanded to selling over the internet. Internet sales grew rapidly, changing the nature of the business operations. Previously, small numbers of staff were selling large batches to a small number of retailers; now they are selling small batches to many consumers. Changes to the technology have changed the structure of warehousing, transport and packaging. This change in strategy has lifted the level of processing required to deal with small orders, and has led to increased employment of part-time and packaging workers, which provides different challenges for maintaining the company culture.

Just as technology impacts on structures, it also needs to match the needs of people. This is referred to as the socio-technical system. While the social and relationship needs of the people who perform tasks need to be taken care of, the mechanics and tools of technology have to be there so that performance outcomes are met. This means individual persons and the machine or technology need to be able to work in harmony together – as was alluded to in our opening tipping-point proposition.

A number of strategies related to the design of jobs are available to organize this balance. These include the way work groups are arranged; empowerment to be involved in decision-making about the job and how it is conducted can help by promoting job enrichment or enlargement. This can range from decisions about the job, to self-managed work teams, and participation in broader decision-making. For example, computer giant IBM attributes the success of its transformation to the ideas and suggestions of employees. Anthes (2006) quotes IBM's Chief Information Officer, Brian Truskowski's claims that over fifty thousand of the company's three hundred and thirty thousand employees contributed their ideas and suggestions to help distil the company's corporate values. Employees' ideas were used to close the gap between those values and the company's business practices.

There are many examples of organizations that have taken this approach: IBM, Southwest and Continental airlines, Toyota and, increasingly, government agencies worldwide have embraced greater employee involvement. Kochan (2006) argues that employee involvement also aids corporate governance because there is greater transparency and decisions are held more accountable. Again, the IBM story serves as a good example of how employee involvement can do this.

Behavioural change strategies address the people or human resources component of the organization, including all levels of management and staff. The aim is to change employees' values, attitudes and behaviour. Behavioural strategies are fundamental in any change process because no change can succeed without the adoption and engagement of the people involved. Changes that address the formal human policies and processes, such as recruitment and selection, performance measurement, and employee development, occupational health, safety and equity, recognition and rewards and attrition, actually influence the informal cultural system.

It can be quite frustrating for consultants when organizations think of culture simply as a soft system that can be changed alone. Changes that address fundamental processes for realignment are quite critical because these are what support cultural change. By this we mean that improved customer focus, for example, is not just a result of communicating the need for this, but it is about employing the right people, giving them the right skills, support and rewards and having the right systems in place to deliver this.

Behavioural change is generally regarded as a 'soft system change' as it is harder to measure and involves a lot more subjectivity about assessing what is really going on. Think of the organizational elements as a mutually dependent social system. The concept of mutual interdependence suggests that the success of the organization and its members are intertwined. Improvements in key performance indicators, whether quality, customer service or return on investment, will benefit the organization and allow it to pass on these benefits to the employee, thus promoting goodwill and maintaining that performance. From the employee's perspective, this is expectancy and equity theory working in tandem. Employees who contribute effort expect rewards, and it is only fair that these are given.

If employees perform well, they stand to gain more through recognition and rewards and the employer gains through improved productivity. In this type of environment, having different perspectives or understandings among employees and management adds richness and insights to the decision-making process to the benefit of all. An excellent example of this is the US-based company W.L. Gore & Associates. This company has operated a flat and flexible organic team-based structure for years (W.L. Gore & Associates, Inc., 2012). Leaders emerge within the teams as needed because of their ability. The company repeatedly makes it into the Fortune 500 listing, and is also consistently listed as one of America's best companies to work for and ranked at number 38 in 2012 (CNN Money, 2012).

Employee involvement and participation in decisions means power is shared and diffused throughout the organization. Of course, there are downsides. Shared decision-making can take longer and political coalitions and power plays have more room to surface. The soft system approach does not view conflict as bad; rather, conflict is a way to explore and expand new ideas and understanding, provided that it remains focused on the organization's problems and is not interpersonal conflict.

Our experience is that employees do not react negatively to calls to improve performance, quality of service or value to the customer, and in fact often have many good ideas on how to improve these. Regardless, they need to understand why changes are being made and accept that change will deliver a benefit. If employees do not see the sense in a change or do not believe it will work, more work is required to establish a shared understanding of the purpose and outcome of a change. Change strategies that focus on improving morale, motivation and employee commitment usually provide the best return to both employees and the organization, and may not be anywhere near as expensive as high-cost investments in technology or large structural change. As Whitaker (2010) points out, simple things like asking staff about what is important to them can be motivating and lead to performance improvements, or it can be as simple as thanking an employee for a job well done.

Nonetheless, many organizations find people and in particular the culture of an organization the hardest to change. Changes within the human resource system can be quite complex. If we take, for example, what at first glance might appear to be a simple change to a policy on promotions, we can see that this has flow-on effects to the infrastructure. This can be in terms of staff movement and choice of whether to promote internally or externally, which in turn can affect employee motivation and commitment, recruitment and selection choices, performance management, rewards and sanctions. It can also impact directly on teamwork, performance and the organization's culture through a variety of measurement systems, as shown in Table 4.2.

Is there a best way to implement change?

The short answer is no, it depends on each set of circumstances, but there are some useful principles to guide the process and help achieve a successful outcome.

TABLE 4.2 Measurement systems affected by human resources decisions

Behavioural	Policies and techniques	Technology
• Motivation/Commitment	• Performance management	• Work/job design
• Job satisfaction	• Recruitment and selection	• Methods and
• Leadership	• Training and development	equipment
• Teambuilding	• Work coordination	• Quality circles
• Employee engagement	• Career development	• TQM
• Turnover	• Succession planning	
• Culture	• Control systems	
	• Rewards	

Change can be influenced to varying degrees by the management style, philosophical choice, ability to adapt or react and the opportunities and threats present in the external environment; organizations need to take account of the variability that affects them and adopt a contingency approach. On the one hand, a collaborative or participative approach is more likely to garner staff engagement and increase the chance of success. However, when decisions need to be made and implemented in a short time frame, the organization is forced toward centralized decision-making, even when that is not the preferred philosophical option. Survival, in times of crisis, may well depend on a dictatorial approach!

Many companies that have tried large-scale changes have struggled because they are unable to measure, control or sustain the multiple changes that are required. Consider the challenges faced by United Airlines. The airline is the world's largest carrier and employs over 85,000 staff, operates 5.5 thousand flights daily across six continents; 142 million passengers were carried on over 2 million flights in 2011 (United Airlines, 2012). In December 2012, eligible employees received a bonus for their best performance in 2012. Eligible employees are paid a bonus of $50 if 80% of domestic or international flights arrive on time, and if both are on time this means $100 bonus. This strategy was implemented years ago at a time when customer dissatisfaction with some services and the harsh economic climate motivated the company to look at ways to improve customer satisfaction. Specific problems included departure delays, airplane cleanliness and complaints about customer service. This level of performance is being sustained because the airline's approach has embedded the importance of service within the organization's culture.

Small-scale changes can also founder if employees do not understand or accept them. It is worth keeping in mind that even large-scale change, which flows across the whole organization, starts with a first step. Informed decision-making based on industry knowledge and experience and a good diagnosis and planning can mitigate some of the risk. Have a clear understanding of what needs to be achieved and the milestones that can measure and track progress. Taking small steps allows for evaluating and fine-tuning before implementing further changes. The specific approaches each manager chooses usually hinges on the urgency of the change and the individual's own philosophical approach.

As well as the Delta forces, the internal situation and capability also influence the choices that are available to respond to change. The change choice isn't just a matter of having an effective strategy. Demands for increased shareholder wealth can limit access to funds to support redevelopment, retooling or investments in staff. An organization's size, asset base, technology base, skill base and culture as well as the dimensions and scale of the change can limit the available choices.

Another crucial element that influences the choice is the quality of leadership. Poor leadership was cited as one of the reasons General Motors struggled to adapt to a world of increasing fuel prices and falling sales. Problems with the company's internal governance and years of turmoil led to a massive divestment of assets and the company faced bankruptcy until a bailout by the Federal government bought up 26 per cent of the company. Despite this, in 2012 the future of the company is still uncertain as falling share prices and market share question how effective the new leadership and direction of the company are (Muller, 2012).

The nature of planned change

Change and development strategies can be broken into three stages. The first is to understand why change is needed, which includes diagnosing the internal and external conditions including the rate, pace and urgency for change. Two analogies about change are worth discussing here. The first is the calm waters analogy that suggests problems are diagnosed, change is implemented and the outcome achieved in a three-step process that leads to ongoing stability. This is comparatively rare, but is still applicable in some businesses that operate in stable markets. The second analogy is that change is much more erratic, constant and unpredictable and more akin to white water rapids. Companies need to be vigilant, proactive, responsive and sometimes reactive to deal with this type of change. Given the nature of globalization, change can come from anywhere in the world and virtually overnight for some businesses. A good example of this is the closure of Borders bookstores, discussed in Chapter 2. Recognizing and accepting that change is needed is the first step to dealing with both types.

The diagnosis needs to include any changed goals, problem issues and symptoms. It is important to separate the issues and symptoms, as responding to symptoms only will fail to deal with the source problem. The second stage is to design strategies to implement change. The third step is to evaluate the outcomes of the change. Assessing how effective change has been allows for adjustments as needed to ensure the change is sustainable over the medium to longer term. Keep in mind that effective implementation can and should be measured in a number of ways, such as the impact on staff and other resources, customers, cost effectiveness, growth and timeliness. Next, we explore some of the practical strategies and processes used to implement change. Different approaches for gathering information are the starting point.

Diagnosing the organization

A 'one size fits all' approach will not work, so any change strategy needs to suit the environment and situation. What suits one organization may not necessarily suit another. Understanding the current issues allows for an effective problem diagnosis and is always a good starting point. This is critical for two reasons. Firstly, understanding what one is changing ensures the right changes are made and change will be for the better; and secondly, having a good understanding of the current situation increases the likelihood that core issues, rather than symptoms, are addressed. For example, an organization may identify problems with internal communications and decision-making; yet a closer inspection might identify that these symptoms have arisen from an inappropriate or poorly aligned design and structure that isolates workers into silos, or from a lack of resources. An example that illustrates this point is Canadian manufacturing company Blount Canada Ltd, who initially responded to customer complaints by replacing equipment to produce better quality products. Problems were only solved when they embraced quality improvement and changed employees' attitudes to embrace a culture of quality (Piper et al., 2003).

A good starting place to identify problems or opportunities for improvement is to talk to the people who are either experiencing the problem or dealing with that aspect of the organization's operations. Customers can provide useful feedback on their expectations and experiences of products and services; suppliers might identify opportunities to manage the supply chain or value add. Employees often have a good understanding of how work processes can be simplified, improved and made more efficient or effective. Taking a proactive approach that takes this holistic view gives a much richer picture of how to solve problems and enhance development within the organization, and gives the organization greater opportunity to create and shape its future.

Change starts with an accurate understanding of the organization's external and internal environments. In planned change, the situation is diagnosed and plans are implemented in a staged response, although, in practice, this is not always possible. Sometimes change is opportunistic or a reaction to events outside an organization's control, as was discussed in Chapter 3 in relation to emergent and planned strategy. Even organizations that have relatively stable external environments, such as supermarkets or undertakers, have to compete, and sometimes quite fiercely, for their share of the market. The more rapid the pace of change or dynamic the external environment, the less opportunity there is to plan and incrementally implement a response, but there still needs to be a sense of purpose and focus. The steps involved in implementing change show this as an iterative process, as demonstrated in the cycle shown in Figure 4.1.

The first step is to diagnose what is actually happening in the organization. This might mean a problem or an opportunity, but it is something that triggers the awareness and identifies there is an opportunity for improvement and this leads to the second step. Before starting to make changes, identify what the goal or

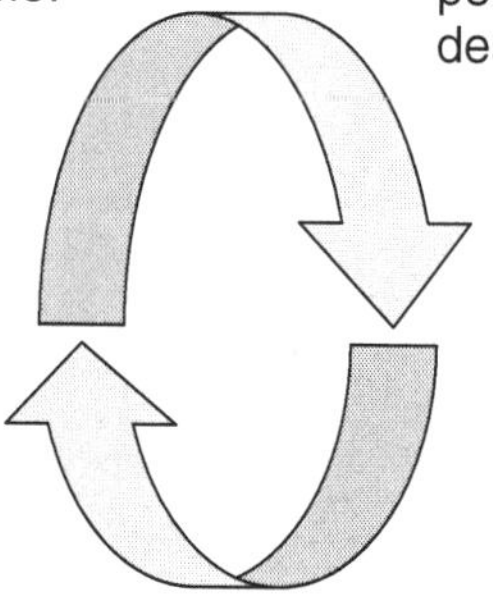

5. Evaluate against
the desired outcome.

1. Identify the gap in
performance from the
desired future goals.

4. Implement the
solution – and monitor
progress solution.

2. Diagnose the problems
associated with this gap
and accept need to change.

3. Explore alternative

FIGURE 4.1   The change cycle

objective is likely to be, so that the gap between the current and the desired performance can be identified. This leads in turn to a recognition or acknowledgement that change either does or does not need to occur. This sounds obvious, but key players failing to act or accept the need for change will undermine chances of success. If change is to be the outcome, collect and analyse relevant information that will allow a better understanding of the true nature of the problem or opportunity and what will be required to make the change. This provides the basis for developing alternative courses of action, from which the most appropriate choices are selected and implemented.

Consider, for example, the changes at United Airlines that we referred to earlier. Falling customer satisfaction and complaints about departure times, staff attitudes and airplane cleanliness contributed to falling standards; thus the organization had performance problems to address. The future the company wanted was to be a leader in customer satisfaction. For United Airlines, the diagnosis came from customer satisfaction surveys and flight records. Different organizations could choose different solutions, depending on their human and financial resources and market opportunities. Once a solution is implemented the impact needs to be tested. United's results suggest that this eventually led to often more than eight out of ten flights operating on time, customer satisfaction targets were exceeded and more than 80 per cent of customers said they would recommend the airline to others. Note that this example provides specific and thus measurable and quantifiable targets.

The aim is not to re-impose old solutions or seek a quick fix, but to understand the core problems, so these can be addressed. It may be that only symptoms can be treated in the short term, but the fundamental causes must be dealt with in the medium to long term. The real issue is to understand what is happening and why it is happening. Some commonly used diagnostic strategies include:

• An analysis of the Delta forces.

- An analysis of the competitive environment (Porter (1980) identified these as: competitors, threat of new entrants, threat of substitutes, labour supply, and other stakeholders).
- A stakeholder analysis. This helps to identify all direct and indirect stakeholders and their interests in the change agenda. The analysis should explore how each will be affected so that decisions can deal with both positive and negative responses. Change is not always welcome and the organization needs to acknowledge and decide how it will deal with any likely confrontations.
- SWOT analysis (the strengths and weaknesses of the current state of the organization and the opportunities and threats that exist in the future). *A limitation is that this may not identify hidden or less obvious issues.*
- A future search conference: this is where organizational members work together to develop a picture of what is likely to be the reality at some point in the future.
- Other investigative techniques, such as the Delphi approach, scenario planning and other forms of brainstorming, as will be discussed later.

What are the drivers for change? These usually relate to the Delta forces, with external drivers relating to competition or other changes in the external environment and internal drivers relating to improved capabilities in terms of skills, financial resources, behaviours and attitudes. Knowing what the desired goal or objective is helps identify the gap between the current situation and the future. Each organization needs to ask three questions:

1. where do we want to end up?
2. what do we need to do to achieve our objectives?
3. how will we know when we have achieved these?

Shared dissatisfaction about the current situation provides the impetus for change. Only when individuals and groups in the affected part of the organization are aware of the need to change will they buy in and commit their energies to making that change happen.

Diagnostic tools and processes

This section covers some of the diagnostic strategies and the frameworks for deciding how to intervene and implement changes. There is some overlap with some of these techniques, but broadly, this section describes the rationales for using various approaches, whereas practical applications will be covered later in the section on HRM practices.

The first step is to collect data on what is happening and why it is happening. The choice of how data is collected depends on the issue, but using multiple measures to combine qualitative and quantitative methods is preferable for a number of reasons. Using several different methods, or multiple measures, allows the information to be cross-checked and this will greatly enhance the validity and reliability of the information. Quantitative information relies on numbers and can be used to confirm opinions about what is happening in terms of revenue loss or growth, turnover, wastage, hours lost, number of accidents, and can also give a numerical value to a consensus of opinions, such as attitudinal job satisfaction. Qualitative information is more in depth and relies on discussing a range of issues around a topic with individuals so that a much richer consensus of opinions is produced. Of course, the collection of any data can be constrained by the time frame, urgency and demand on resources.

A starting point is to understand the factual or objective data already held within the organization. For example, given that many Western countries are experiencing ageing populations and labour shortages, the gender, age and seniority of the employees can be a source of information for longer-term planning. Similarly, knowing the qualifications and competencies of staff helps with workforce and succession planning and flexibility. Profit and loss statements, inventory, labour costs, staff turnover, sales turnover, production costs, wastage, lost time injuries and their costs, and turnaround times are just some of the objective data sources that provide useful information for tracking performance and identifying areas that need to change.

The next step is to collect data about the tacit knowledge held by individuals.

There are a variety of ways that data can be collected. One quantitative measure that is relatively easy to implement is the use of surveys or questionnaires. These can be either pen and paper exercises or online exercises where employees or other respondents, such as consumers, self-report. They are usually anonymous, relatively easy and cheap to administer, and can serve as a benchmark. The downside is that they only gather limited data and may not tap the source of problems and can also be subject to error, for reasons such as people completing them in haste, missing or misinterpreting questions or pursuing a personal agenda.

Interviews have the advantage of allowing two-way communication and thus provide richer data. Respondents have the opportunity to explain their point of view and the interviewer can ask for clarification. Questions usually start as broad open questions that encourage the interviewee to express their opinions of the problems, issues and solutions; an example of this type of question is "Tell me about the organizational/work barriers that prevent you achieving your work goals". In other situations an unstructured interview may be preferable, as this allows the interviewee to talk freely about issues that they see as important. While interviews are a rich source of information and promote employee involvement, they need to be kept focused and on track. In addition, care must be taken to ensure that interviewees are representative of the wider organization and can participate without fear or favour of repercussions.

Another approach often used by consultants, and equally applicable for managers, is *observation* of both behaviour and processes. Observing employees and their co-workers can give managers insights into what really happens in an organization in terms of work performance roles and relationships. Researchers caution that the person/s conducting observations need to be skilled in interpreting individual behaviour because of the risk of misreading body language and other cues; however, if these are merely used as a starting point and the information is clarified, observation can be an extremely useful tool for managers.

Behavioural observation can be time consuming and therefore expensive and runs the risk of distorting behaviour if employees know they are being watched. Similarly, observing processes can identify weaknesses where, for example, employees are performing tasks that are not necessary, there is overlap, or where there is an opportunity to question why a task is being performed in a certain way. Observing employee behaviour also provides clues about the culture and employee morale, but again, this needs to be interpreted accurately. An excellent way of validating your observations is to check your understanding with those being observed. This has the additional benefit of developing a shared understanding of that meaning.

Employees at different levels of an organization have different experiences of the reality of the organization. Whichever method is chosen, the purpose is to obtain feedback from employees or other stakeholders to get a better understanding of what needs to change, how it might change and what can be achieved. Managers should not just assume that employees will view the need for change in the same way they do! Because of the job knowledge employees hold and their position, they may have very different perspectives and ideas about what needs to change and can often make very constructive suggestions. Therefore, it is important to inform, educate and involve staff at all levels so they understand why change needs to occur, the urgency and importance of making the change work, how they can contribute and that their contribution is valued. Lack of information and understanding limits their ability to contribute and commit. Employees often have constructive suggestions, ranging from operational to strategic initiatives, and can be a powerful force for implementing change effectively.

Appreciative enquiry

Appreciative enquiry engages all levels across the organization! Simply put, the need is to focus on what is done well and build on strengths, rather than focus on the negatives and what is not going so well. Focusing on problems can lead to the organization seeking someone to blame, which casts a negative slant on the change process and can undermine individuals' confidence. It can also imply that the organization's problems exist because of problem employees. This does not mean that poor performance should be ignored, but it should be confronted and dealt with appropriately through an effective performance management system.

If an employee is not suited to his or her role, the organization needs to confront and deal with this. It has the responsibility of ensuring it has the right people, in the right place, at the right time and that individuals are accountable. The outcome or the consequences of actions may precede change, but *focusing on the problem means the change process starts with a backward-looking orientation*. A more positive and forward-looking outlook is to focus on elements that have worked well in the past, or are currently working well, and build on these. This sends out a more positive message that energizes people. By using positive reinforcement, the intent is to focus on the positives so that these are increased and the negative behaviours and processes will fall away to be replaced by something more positive. A useful process that can assist organizations with this is force field analysis, proposed by social scientist Kurt Lewin.

Lewin's force field analysis

Lewin's (1952) three-step model explains how to build on the strengths of the organization and remove barriers that prevent change occurring. Despite criticism from some practitioners that this is a static model (we do not believe it is), rather than an adaptive model, it is still very useful. Think of it like this: the starting point is the 'current state', which literally means identifying where the organization is currently and what the issues are. The next step is to look at the 'desired state' which is, in essence, the goal or outcome the organization wants or seeks. The current state provides the baseline that helps the organizational members identify what needs to change when it is measured against the desired future state. Identifying what is working well or, conversely, not working, and assessing these against the vision the organization is working toward, allows strategies to be put in place to address any shortfalls.

Recall our earlier mention of the white water and calm waters analogies. The reality is that the organization may be facing a number of issues concurrently and these can be at varying rates of urgency, in terms of both implementation and outcomes. At face value, it is easy to view Lewin's model as a holistic process, which would limit its ability to deal with the multiple implications of change. However, its strength lies in that it can be a useful stepped process for dealing specifically with each issue.

Evaluating the issues facing an organization at a particular point in time allows the forces pushing for or driving change, and those hindering or causing resistance to change, to be identified. While these are in balance and the forces are of equal pressure, change is not likely to occur. Movement towards the desired state occurs when there is disequilibrium or dissatisfaction with the *status quo*. Without dissatisfaction, there is no motivation to change. The most satisfactory outcome is achieved when the restraining forces are removed or weakened, which allows driving forces to move the organization towards change. The model has three stages:

Step 1: Unfreeze. Unfreezing is about removing barriers or causes of resistance to change. Lewin argued that the forces that held the organization to its current pattern of behaviour needed destabilizing before change could take place. The force could be a range of issues such as personal motivations, patterns of behaviour, desire for power, lack of vision and rewards or sanctions. Once these are identified, 'unfreezing' serves to alert the organizational members to the need for change and provides the motivation for the change to occur. For example, transparency about stock prices and increased market risk serves to let employees know that change is needed. Awareness of the problems at United Airlines and a strategy that benefited employees allowed the company to make a positive turnaround.

This is quite different to the approach taken by the Australian company Pacific Brands, where the sudden announcement that Australian factories would close down and work would move offshore caught employees and unions by surprise, particularly as this occurred just after the CEO was given a considerable salary increase (Robinson, 2009). If unfreezing means preparing the ground to make the change, then the announcement of the CEO's pay increase was counter-productive. Better information about the true state of affairs and working with the unions and staff to resolve the problems could perhaps have helped create an environment of support to seek solutions to the company's problems.

The past generous benefits at Pacific Brands were an unsustainable drain on profits. Although this sounds simple to remedy, it can be quite a difficult process. Often people are identified as the first restraining force for change; however, the reality is that employees often face the dichotomy of wanting the organization to be effective, but at the same time are fearful of what the change might mean to them as individuals. Individual staff and work groups have a lot invested in keeping things the same, and threats of change can bring about an increase in conflict, power plays, the formation of coalitions and political lobbying in the workplace. The possibility of such behaviour often correlates to the individuals' perceived risk. So it is a wiser strategy to identify the possibility of these types of behaviour and put strategies in place at the group level to minimize any symptoms of resistance.

Once the driving forces and the obstacles to change are identified, strategies to remove obstacles can be implemented. Obstacles that impede the ability to change might include such things as lack of resources, training or skills, management competence and technology, to name a few. It may not be possible to remove all restraining forces; however, they need to be sufficiently reduced to allow the change to occur. In most cases, increasing the driving forces escalates resistance, so weakening the restraining forces is always the preferred option. For example, if the barrier is lack of knowledge, skills and ability, then an investment needs to be made to improve these. Increasing the driving forces can work if focused on survival issues.

Step 2. Movement or a transition occurs once the organization recognizes that there is a need for change and starts removing the barriers to change. The ideal is to achieve change or movement towards the objective the organization wants, rather than escalate unproductive or blocking behaviours. During this phase the organization needs a clear roadmap or plan of what has to be achieved. The organization decides who the appropriate people are to drive the change. What levels of power and support are needed to gain acceptance and motivate employees to embrace and accept change? Do they need external assistance from a consultant? Sometimes an outsider can have a clearer view of what is happening than an insider. Taking account of all contingencies that pose opportunities or threats is critical during this phase.

Step 3: Refreeze. This stage seeks to re-establish equilibrium so the organization's members are inculcated with the new way of doing things and do not regress to earlier behaviours. Refreezing aims to re-stabilize the organization by cementing the new pattern of behaviours, relationships and culture. Some argue that stability is unlikely in today's environment, but think of points of stability regarding an issue, rather than a stable organizational environment. Once adjustments are made to the structure and practices, the policies and procedures need to be updated and aligned with the new culture.

A comparison between the United Airlines case and Pacific Brands is not about the strategic choice of the organization, but about how each company handled this. For example, using Lewin's model to identify the driving and restraining forces in relation to the Pacific Brands case might have helped the company to handle the changes with much less damage. In 2009, the company announced it would close seven factories, cutting 1850 jobs, following a mid-year loss of A\$234.5 million, despite profits of A\$116.6 the previous year (ABC, 2009). A further 6,000 jobs would be kept in Australia (Gluyas, 2009). Pacific Brands manufactures clothing under some iconic brand names, including clothing brands Bonds, Berlei, King Gee and Holeproof, as well as footwear company Clarks. The company had been receiving subsidies from the government of approximately \$10 million annually for the previous two years, to upgrade its infrastructure. Thus the 2009 loss was a shock to shareholders and employees about what was really going on. Certainly, the increased value of the Australian dollar and substantial increase of cheap Asian products into the Australian market were factors; however, a second sticking point was that apart from the government subsidies, the CEO had nearly trebled her own salary after taking on the position earlier in the year (Gluyas, 2009).

The Textile Clothing and Footwear Union, employees and the Australian government all spoke out quite vocally against the company; the government claimed the money was given to provide opportunities to grow and develop the business locally, the employees complained they were given no warning, and other unions became involved to try and stop the company moving equipment offshore (SBS World News, 2009). Until this time the company had marketed its products as *Australian made* and enjoyed strong branding because of this. The past three years have been fairly turbulent for the company and it continues to struggle, suffering further losses in 2012. A new CEO took over the reins in August 2012, but it is still too early to assess whether Pacific Brands can recapture its place in the market. Figure 4.2 is an example of how Lewin's model could have identified the risk factors involved in the driving and restraining forces for this case. Adequate unfreezing of the organization might have increased focus on the jobs that were to be retained, better protection of the brand and timing of the decisions made. The company could have also worked in tandem with the union to try and manage the process much more effectively.

As previously mentioned, some researchers criticize Lewin's (1952) model as being too inflexible and linear, claiming it is only suited to an environment with a slow pace of change. However, it was never Lewin's intention that the model be

Forces driving change	Forces blocking change
• Financial loss A$234.5 • Increased competition from cheaper imports • Higher labour costs than competitors maintenance costs • Poor recent safety record • Need to expand for survival	• Staff expectations • Unionisation • Branding as Australian made • Financial Support From Government • CEO Pay rise of 170% • Closure of 7 factories • 1,850 Job losses (6,000 jobs retained)
Unfreeze means to prepare the organisation for Change by considering how to overcome restraining forces.	*Needs new strategy, structure and processes and culture to maintain the changed organisation* processes

FIGURE 4.2   Sample of restraining and driving forces for Pacific Brands

interpreted in a linear way. Indeed, his view was that change is a constant and that life and group interactions are never static. In fact, Burnes (2004) argues that Lewin's model has much more in common with complexity theory and the contingency argument that we have already proposed as part of the open systems theory approach.

R egardless, Lewin's model is a simple and practical model for understanding the impact of change on employees. It allows choices to be made depending on the urgency and importance of particular events. Individuals, workgroups and managers can all use the process to identify what needs to change and the barriers likely to impede progress. It can help employees understand why a particular change is required and so helps prepare them. The danger in using this model, as with any tool, is in how it is applied. Like any analytical tool, the model should be used as a dynamic process. It can provide an overarching framework for analysing what needs to occur and the steps needed to plan for change. It is not simply a case of analysing the current situation, unfreezing, moving, then refreezing. Other contingencies need to be taken into account during implementation, so adjustments to accommodate these are made. Organizations need to continually scan their internal and external environment and adjust their progress, or realign some goals if this is necessary.

Diagnostic matrix

We have already identified that organizations need a range of systems, as was seen in Table 4.2. This table shows horizontal connections down the organization from senior managers to the lowest-level employees, and includes the structure, technology and systems for decision-making and coordinating the activities of employees as well as human resource management practices. The vertical systems operate at the different layers of the organization, such as the individual, group and organizational levels. Spector (2007) suggests that diagnosis should seek to identify any non-alignment within and across the vertical and horizontal elements, starting at the organizational level. For example, does the business model match to and align with the vision and industry analysis? Questioning all the links helps to draw out core issues and provide a way of dealing with information in a structured and manageable way.

We recommend using more than one model or approach to making a diagnosis because looking at a problem from another perspective helps uncover gaps in knowledge and provides a checking mechanism when making decisions. It is quite clear to see that if Pacific Brands had mapped the impact of the proposed changes on all of their various systems, such as the human resources, structure and financial systems, a discrepancy would have been found between what was happening at the strategic and individual and group levels. This is not to suggest that the financial decision was the wrong one, but, as in Lewin's model, understanding the ramifications of the company's decisions on the various players and components means the organization could have handled them differently. Because change usually needs to happen at all levels of an organization, the diagnosis also needs to occur at each level so that flow-on effects can be identified. Simply looking at the pay structure at each level could have alerted the organization to the fact that there was considerable incongruity between what was happening at the top and the bottom. Diagnosis needs to include all affected systems and take account of the flow-on effects from one system to another, as discussed in the open systems model.

Driving the change process

Apart from an accurate diagnosis, strong leadership is also important to drive the change process and help it gain acceptance. This is discussed in more detail later in this chapter. The leader of the organization may not be the primary change agent but still has an important role. The leader must be seen to be visible and actively support the change process if employees are to get the message that it is important and worthwhile. The change agent who implements the strategies can be drawn from various positions internal or external to the organization. Regardless of whether they are internal practitioners, such as training and development staff, or functional managers or a cross-functional team, or whether they are an external party sourced to assist with the change, they require good people skills, business knowledge and an understanding of change processes. The implementers of change need to have highly developed:

- project management skills;
- communication skills;
- problem-solving skills;
- good interpersonal skills; and
- integrity to follow through with any actions committed to. They need integrity to explain why something does not occur if follow-through cannot occur. In essence they need to 'walk the talk';

- knowledge of their limitations and the ability to work within them;
- ability to establish a clear structure, or rules to work by, so people know where they stand.

This means they need a good understanding of the organization and its objectives, excellent interpersonal skills, a high level of emotional intelligence and knowledge of their own limitations. Workers are often fearful about what the change will mean for them, and the change agent needs to gain acceptance of the change by those affected if it is to be successful. This demands sensitivity when dealing with people, especially when they feel there is a lot at stake.

Having good consultancy skills and the ability to listen to what people have to say can often provide insights that can improve the change process. Goleman (1998) describes emotionally intelligent people as those who are able to display empathy for others; they have the ability to monitor their own responses and react appropriately, while at the same time they use their intelligence to uncover what is really going on. These individuals are able to work across functional boundaries and with people at all levels of the organization. They are also mature enough to set aside their own personal agendas and focus on what is best for the organization. This requires a high level of mutual trust. A recent interview with Paul Polman, CEO of Unilever, highlights this thinking:

> It's true that you cannot talk yourself out of things you've behaved yourself into. Trust is easily destroyed and takes a long time to rebuild
>
> (Bird, 2009).

Overcoming resistance to change

Understanding the organization's ability to change is part of the diagnostic process. The benefits of implementing change need to be weighed against the costs imposed and the ability of the organization to adapt. There are cases where the strain on internal resources, workers and economic resources outweigh the benefits of the change and these can be identified through a force field analysis. This helps identify the strength or urgency of the blocking or restraining forces and the strength or urgency of the forces driving change. Some common causes of resistance to change at the organizational level include:

- Inability to respond; this can occur when the organization is too large or bureaucratic to respond quickly and capitalize on the opportunity presented, or lacks the foresight to innovate and respond.
- A structure that prevents rapid adaptation and decision-making.
- Lack of resources; these can range from finances, management skills, to low morale and/or lack of commitment.
- Escalation of commitment to failed decisions or threats to established power relationships.

- Analysis paralysis; for example; the reduced cycle times can mean the organization has limited ability to predict the likely outcome and so it hesitates over making a decision and the opportunity is lost.
- Decision-making structures which can help or hinder the change, depending on the circumstances. Centralized decision-making allows for a quick response, but may not get support from others across the organization. Decentralized decision-making can help engage employers and gain acceptance, but has a slower response time.
- Previous failed attempts at change, which make it harder to gain commitment and undermine trust in decision-making.

How individuals react to change relates to their personal wants and needs as well as their relationships with both the organization and its members. Again, it is worthwhile to think of the two previous examples of United Airlines and Pacific Brands. Individual choices are influenced by trust and commitment, task design, skill development, advancement opportunities, rewards and recognition. In high trust organizations, employees are more likely to go along with an urgent decision that excludes them, but they still need to be kept informed of how the change effects them, and included in how the change will occur. Some of the reasons individuals resist change include:

- Fear of the unknown. Individuals are unable to assess how to adapt to the change if they do not know what changes are likely to occur. Uncertainty increases anxiety and fear about the outcome, which is more likely if trust is low, the individual feels the alternatives are limited or has had previous negative experiences. Fear increases the tendency to exaggerate or selectively focus on negative impacts of the change.
- Self-interest, where individuals are content to remain in their comfort zone. Some people dislike changes to their routines or habits, but are likely to be more accepting if they can see the benefits for themselves or the organization.
- Threats to established relationships, such as the breakup of friendships or a work team.
- Changes to job roles, or increased task challenge.
- Misunderstandings about what is likely to happen and how it will affect individuals.
- Threats to job security, whether real or perceived.
- Economic implications of job loss or reduced advancement opportunity.

Understanding employee concerns about change provides an opportunity to deal with the cause of resistance. On the basis of her work in assisting individuals to cope with death, Elizabeth Kubler-Ross (1993) proposed that individuals who suffer an emotional loss go through discrete stages of emotional responses, and these stages can also apply to other life events. Individuals move through a range of emotional responses, though this does not always happen sequentially and their emotional state may oscillate between anger, denial, exploring options, depression and acceptance. Scott and Jaffe (1989), who recognized that individuals going through organizational change could suffer the same sense of sense of loss and equally devastating emotional responses, later adapted this work. These authors argue that change is also associated with letting go of the past, which engenders a sense of loss, and this is more severe when individuals feel they have little control over the outcome.

The initial responses to change are either to deny that the change will occur or that they will be affected, or to become angry or depressed about what will be lost, which keeps the individual bound to the past (Scott and Jaffe, 1989). In contrast, the journey for some individuals may be one of exploring what change means for them; this allows them to explore and consider options and then move towards these, which has a future orientation. Understanding how people react to change is important, for several reasons:

- It allows the organization to acknowledge that anger and denial are normal human responses as they are ways of protecting and holding onto the past.
- It proposes a way forward whereby individuals can be encouraged to look to the future by exploring their options and committing to a choice of action.
- It identifies that individuals might need to move through the various stages, albeit at different rates, before they are able to make a decision about the future.

The uncertainty that often surrounds organizational change can leave individuals in 'no man's land' as they do not have sufficient information to be able to choose one course of action over another and this can prevent them moving on to exploring their options and making a decision. Instead, they become stuck in the denial and anger phase. People cannot make a choice if they do not know the likely gain or loss! Depending on the circumstances, being clear on the implications of change allows employees to make decisions about their future.

As the Pacific Brands case shows, past success made it very difficult for employees to accept that the company had moved into such a dramatic level of unprofitability. In addition, it was even more difficult to accept for many of the factory workers who were long-term employees and had no job alternatives.

A way to manage this is to find ways to acknowledge the positives and negatives of the past and then encourage people to focus on the future. Not knowing what the outcomes of the change will mean for the individual exacerbates fear. Wherever possible, give individuals back some control and as much information as is available to help them make choices about their future. This is one very good reason for committing to no job losses early in a change process, if this is possible, because it takes away some of the pressure caused by uncertainty. Kotter and Schlesinger (2008) have long argued that the best strategies for overcoming resistance to change, which is also the means to unfreeze an organization, include:

- Education, which promotes employees' understanding of why change needs to happen and provides the knowledge, skills and abilities needed to make the change.

- Communication, which allows sharing of information about what is happening and why it is happening. Face-to-face communications are the most effective as they provide the opportunity for interactive dialogue. Employees can ask questions and have their concerns dealt with, which helps minimize misunderstandings and rumours. It also provides the opportunity to solve problems and jointly develop innovations as employees can often contribute ideas or information about opportunities and threats that management may not be aware of.
- Involvement and participation to give employees a say in the changes that are taking place, so they have a greater sense of ownership over the changes. Involvement might mean that employees have the opportunity to influence management decisions, whereas participation means they contribute to or make some decisions. The reality is that the people who do a job are usually better placed to understand what needs to change and can provide solutions that are realistic and doable. If the solutions do not make sense to employees, they will certainly not be committed to them and they are unlikely to be effectively implemented.

Lewin also recommended two other strategies, but these are less preferred than the four above. These may be necessary if time is of the essence or some key players are resistant and need to be involved; however, these strategies can escalate resistance to the change.

- *Cooption.* In some cases, it can be appropriate to engage those who do not support the change into the process, particularly if they have influential roles. Becoming more engaged helps them become more accepting!
- *Coercion.* This is the least preferred option as it may cause resistance and lead to negative repercussions, but again the hope is that by engaging groups or individuals they will come to be more accepting.

Organizations do have the power to require employees to accept the change if they want to remain with the organization and this can work if there's not a lot of emotional engagement in the impact of the change, but it is the least preferred option. The organization can discipline workers for noncompliance, but the downside is that forcing change on reluctant workers escalates resistance, which leads to increased turnover, absenteeism and noncompliance. Turnover of talented workers is especially a problem because they are the ones the organization most needs to keep, but they also find it easier to find alternative employment. On the other hand, workers might appear to accept the change and only work to rule and perform to the barest minimum, which falls short of what is needed for change to be successful.

Successful change efforts focus on specific goals and are based on a careful analysis of the current situation, including the external financial, social, technological and political competitive environments. Evaluating the available technologies, resources and raw materials helps establish whether achieving the desired future state is realistic. Fundamental questions managers need to ask include:

- Why do I need to make changes?
- What is the goal to be achieved?
- What choices do I have?
- What are the options to manage what happens?
- Who will be affected?
- How will the organization and individuals be affected?
- How will I deal with the consequences?
- When and where are changes needed?
- How can they be best implemented?
- How will I know when the objective has been achieved?

In reality, it is often not this simple. As previously pointed out, changes in one part of an organization have repercussions in other parts of the organization. Scenario planning that helps predict and plan to either manage or avoid such events in advance is the ideal, but this is a quick alternative to formal planning. This does not always allow you to predict some outcomes, but it does help to simplify the various alternatives. Flow-on effects can emerge in the least expected areas!

Study guide

Review questions

1. Explain the difference between planned and reactive change and the implications this has for organizational strategy.
2. Discuss reasons why the members of an organization might resist change. How might Lewin's model be used to assist in overcoming resistance to change?
3. What steps can an organization use to develop a core culture?
4. Explain the relationship between job design and structural change.
5. Using an example of either an organization you have worked for or the school where you are studying, explore the interactions between the different types of technology used by that organization.
6. Explain why leadership is important during a change programme.
7. Explain three strategies an organization can use to diagnose the need for change. How practical are these diagnostic strategies for an organization that you are currently working in, or have worked with in the past?
8. Critically evaluate four reasons why individuals resist change. Explain whether you think these reasons will always lead to change resistance.
9. Explain the different emotional responses individuals can have to change and explain why it is useful to understand these responses.
10. List some appropriate responses that can be made to help both individuals and organizations cope with change.

Online activity

1. Conduct an online search and investigation into the changes facing the airline industry worldwide over the next 10 years. What factors are driving this change? What are the likely impacts and challenges for airline companies?
2. Investigate the legal implications of terminating employees within your country.

Case study: Downsizing the maintenance section

Mike Evans left the meeting room feeling very uneasy. He was the only one of the five managers present at the meeting who had opposed the decision to outsource all maintenance activities to a local firm of contractors. It was common knowledge that Des Conway, the general manager, was a good friend of the owner of the contract firm and that they regularly played golf together. Des had proposed this company, claiming they were the only large company that was situated locally and therefore the only ones who would be able to take on additional work at short notice. This was particularly important given the high likelihood of a new contract with one of their major distributors that was likely to lead to a 20 per cent increase in production. As the production manager, and therefore manager of the maintenance section, Mike was the one who would be charged with telling three employees they no longer had a job. He had argued in the meeting that he could not see the justification for outsourcing the maintenance section as it was always busy, had good camaraderie and the workers were very responsive to the needs of the manufacturing section, there was plenty of work and no down time. Des claimed the outsourcing initiative was a cost-saving strategy that could save the company 'considerable' money and provide improved flexibility, but had not produced any hard figures of what the savings would be. Unlike the workers they currently employed, the contract workers were not unionized and were being paid at the minimum wage.

Mike Evans was highly regarded in the company and felt that he had enough credibility to ask for some time to properly analyse the alternatives of outsourcing maintenance and some in-house alternatives. When asked by Des what he wanted to achieve, Mike listed the following points:

1. Compare costs of increasing internal capacity with the costs of outsourcing.
2. Estimate the costs of using overtime to meet increased demand.
3. Evaluate whether there is a direct correlation between an increase in production and an increase in maintenance.

4. Estimate the cost of adding an internal maintenance worker on a one-year contract to cover the increased maintenance demand on a trial basis.
5. Avoid an almost certain confrontation with the union over unfair dismissal, given the good performance of the maintenance crew.

Discussion questions

1. Identify the ethical and management issues raised by this case.
2. Would you classify the change to outsourcing as a reactive or planned change? Explain your reason.
3. Are there other steps that Mike could take?
4. What alternative strategies would you suggest to Des?

Practical exercise

1. Working in pairs or small groups of three to four people, draw on one member of the group's work experiences in an organization where change has occurred, to:

    a) Explore and identify the interactions between different internal organizational components that were affected by the change. Refer to Tables 4.1 and 4.2 to help identify the different levels that are impacted by the change. (Examples of the changes that could be discussed include a change in strategic direction to develop and market a new product, a restructure of the organization, or changes to improve the focus on customer service.)

    b) Use Lewin's force field analysis to identify the driving and restraining forces and discuss strategies that could be used to overcome the restraining forces.

    c) Explore how the Delta forces influenced the various changes described above.

    d) Discuss some of the appropriate diagnostic strategies that could have been used and the benefits and disadvantages of these in a practical setting.

2. The concept of appreciative enquiry and engaging employees across the organization sounds all very well in theory, but what advantages or problems might you see in implementing this in practice?

Further reading

Battilana, J., Gilmartin, M., Sengul, M., Pache, A.-C. and Alexander, J.A. (2010) Leadership competencies for implementing planned organizational change. *The Leadership Quarterly*, 21(3): 422–438.

Fiedler, S. (2010) Managing resistance in an organizational transformation: A case study from a mobile operator company. *International Journal of Project Management*, 28(4): 370–383.

Furst, S.A. and Cable, D.M. (2008) Employee resistance to organizational change. *Journal of Applied Psychology*, 93(2): 453–462.

Hutzschenreuter, T., Kleindienst, I. and Greger, C. (2012) How new leaders affect strategic change following a succession event: A critical review of the literature. *The Leadership Quarterly*, 23(5): 729–755.

5

IMPLEMENTING CHANGE

This chapter presents some frameworks for implementing change. These are not prescriptive, but are a starting point to frame questions and answers to guide the change process. The reality is there is no 'one size fits all', and although we can learn from other organizations, and in some cases replicate their successes, managers should choose the strategy that best fits their organization. Solutions need to be relevant and appropriate to the particular circumstances of the individual organization and its members.

Change is not just about making decisions regarding positioning in the marketplace and taking account of external factors, such as the industry structure, customers, competitors, suppliers, possible substitutes or new entrants, the rate and pace of change, as well as opportunities for growth and expansion; both the formal and informal internal systems affect the organization's ability to respond. The human resource processes of selecting, developing, appraising and rewarding employees and the measurement, control and structural systems form part of the formal processes of the organization that were discussed earlier. The most important informal aspect is the culture that develops. The culture is the basic assumptions, values and patterns of behaviour shared by members of the organization, and these can aid or hinder change. Changes that go against the organization's culture are not only harder to implement, they are also much more likely to founder.

The choice very much depends on the time-frame, the risks of both implementing the change and not implementing the change, the costs, urgency and scale of the change. Where time permits, an incremental approach is easier for the organization to manage because it allows an idea to be tested in one part of the organization. Incremental changes can be reviewed and refined before being implemented across the wider organization. When the change is tested as a pilot project, it should be tested in an environment that gives it the maximum chance of success, rather than in an area where it is less likely to succeed. This helps establish whether the change is workable and likely to be successful and also allows for any adaptations that might make it more workable. It also helps to identify if the change is not likely to be successful so that a costly full-scale programme can be avoided.

On the other hand, some argue that incremental change only makes adjustments to the status quo and therefore is not truly innovative. Innovation differs from change in that it encompasses either a new approach or a new way of doing things, rather than just an adjustment of the status quo. The reality, of course, is that this usually involves change. Implementing change in an incremental way is easier to manage for the organization and is therefore more likely to be successful for most. However, another reality is that innovation in the form of a new product, idea or technology is often needed to sustain competitive advantage and integrating this will result in adaptation within the organization. Radical change may be needed, but is usually only successful in dire or extreme circumstances.

Often, the best people to go to for solutions or innovations are those inside the organization who understand the unique context of the organization, and its processes. There are also occasions when the fresh perspective of an outsider can provide insights not obvious to those closely involved with the problem or issue. Each organization needs to weigh up the advantages and disadvantages of the various approaches and select what is most appropriate for itself. Partnering with an external consultant and a knowledgeable insider can provide unique insights. Sometimes it is difficult for an insider to 'see the woods for the trees', so to speak, and the consultant can bring a fresh perspective and uncover issues that are not immediately obvious – an approach that is effectively similar to benchmarking.

Understanding what is currently in place, and measuring this against the vision of the future, helps identify which strategic approaches or processes can best help make the change successful. There is considerable information available in the literature and from the International Labour Organization on the various modalities, and how these processes can be implemented. The key issue here is that there are similarities among these models, and in the main they are adjustments to a basic approach that fits specific circumstances. Some of the major systemic approaches to change are:

- customer focus
- best practice
- management by objectives
- quality management (Total Quality Managment, ISO (International Organization for Standardization) and the Baldridge Prize – which is an American National Quality Award)
- strategic management
- six sigma
- core values
- employee involvement

- organizational learning
- lean management
- benchmarking.

Regardless of which approach is chosen, the choice should be based on best-fit criteria. It is always better to tackle what is doable, rather than attempt the ideal and not be able to see it through because of lack of management or employee support, lack of resources or time.

Kotter and Schlesinger (2008) provide the following long-established and proven advice for implementing change:

1. Create an awareness of the pressure for change.
2. Establish and publicize a clear vision.
3. Ensure the organization has the capacity for change, in terms of its physical and emotional resources.
4. Start by identifying and implementing some first steps.
5. Managers and leaders need to model the way.
6. Reinforce the change through recognition and rewards and realigning policies, procedures and the organization's culture.
7. Evaluate the impact of the change and work toward continual improvement.

A good starting point is the future search mentioned in Chapter 4, to develop a picture of the future and help establish a vision for that future. Understanding what the future holds helps us shape the organization to fit into that future. Rather than making plans for the present day, this approach focuses on considering what the environment will be like in five, ten, twenty, or even fifty years or more. This does not mean this future will come to pass; these longer planning periods simply represent a planning horizon that needs to be continually updated to align with the here and now and shorter term. This helps the organization understand where it might position itself for the future and what it needs to do to remain viable and grow.

Many large corporations worldwide do this. For example, Toyota has been a forerunner in developing hybrid electric vehicles. The Toyota Prius is still dominating the hybrid car market with its third-generation offering. Incorporating the technology into the company's other vehicles means Toyota has been able to capitalize on its first mover advantage and now holds approximately 60 per cent of the hybrid market and is well ahead of its competitors.

Choice of strategy depends very much on the desired outcomes and the available resources within the organization. For example, if morale needs to be improved, then strategies to improve interpersonal dynamics and relationships and to build trust are required. One time-honoured tradition in implementing effective change is to build on what works well. When change is needed quickly, often because of survival needs, the efficiency versus effectiveness argument arises. Sometimes short-run changes need to be made to survive an immediate situation, but may not fit with the longer-term outcomes. It would be naïve to say that short-term gains are unimportant – failure to achieve these can undermine longer-term prospects. An example of this might be downsizing or rightsizing, as some call it, to reduce overheads and improve short-term profits. The longer-term loss of knowledge and experience may end in a net loss rather than a net gain. Outcomes that balance efficiency, effectiveness and satisfaction are a better strategy. This leaves the organization with long-term advantages and builds, rather than depletes, the organization's capability. Neither does it ignore the financial imperative to be productive.

Changing the organizational structure

An organizational structure needs to perform two fundamental roles. The first is to divide the activities of labour into workable components. The second is to coordinate activities within and across the various components to achieve the organization's goals. Choices depend on the strategy, size, technology, age and type of employees, and the environment. Organizations generally operate at some stage along a continuum that at one extreme is mechanistic or bureaucratic and at the other is flat, flexible and adaptive. Generally, tall and centralized organizations are referred to as mechanistic organizations, because they resemble large machines that once in motion are hard to stop. This type of organization has a tall hierarchy with systems and rules to maintain command and control and relies on bureaucratic processes. This is practical and sensible. Policies and procedures are merely a means to an end and are developed to help ensure coordination and control. The disadvantage is that they can impede an organization's ability to respond by slowing down decision-making, as communications have to pass through various management layers. Compare the complexity of coordinating the different layers of a worldwide organization such as Exxon to that of a small local accountant's office where everyone is located in the same office.

The bureaucratic processes in large organizations can take on a life of their own. In an environment of rapid change, they can quickly become out of date and/or irrelevant as circumstances change. Nonetheless, having rules and regulations in place is critical because they provide boundaries to let people know what is expected of them. The downside is that if they are rigidly applied, or adhered to at all costs, they constrain employees' behaviour and ability to make choices when exceptional circumstances arise. This is particularly a problem when organizations need to respond to emerging issues. In such circumstances, employees may work to what is written, rather than to what is needed for the benefit the organization or its customers. Therefore, rules, procedures and policies should never be treated as an end in themselves. At the other end of the continuum, an organic organization is much flatter, with a very limited hierarchy. This means decision-making is devolved so that the organization is more flexible and responsive and can more easily adapt as the environment changes. Twenty-first century organizations tend to be flatter and more organic so they can respond quickly to events that are occurring beyond their control.

While some organizations are purely mechanistic (for example, the classic mass production factory of Henry Ford) and others are organic (for example, small innovative high-technology firms), depending on their size and industry, many are not truly one or the other but have various combinations of mechanistic and organic features. This is obvious when comparing an assembly process in a mass or large-batch manufacturing plant that is focused on cost control, against research and development or marketing activities that need innovation and responsiveness within the same organization. The determinants of an organization's structure can be seen in Exhibit 5.1.

Exhibit 5.1   Determinants of organizational structure

The following five factors help to determine the structure of an organization:

The environment: A stable environment makes change predictable, so organizations are better able to function with a mechanistic structure and centralized control. A rapidly changing environment means organizations have to change quickly to be responsive and so a flatter or flexible structure is required. Similarly, organizations that operate in a complex environment or have many stakeholders or products need to decentralize power so that decisions are made at the point of activity to improve both timeliness and decision quality.

Strategy: The structure needs to align with the strategy. If customer service is a key strategy, employees need sufficient decision-making ability to respond to customers' needs on the spot. A cost containment strategy might require devolution of budget management to workgroups who are held accountable, or, in other circumstances, might be controlled through centralization and increased bureaucracy. The choice depends on a combination of imperatives.

Size: The size determines the level of devolution and centralization needed. In a small organization, a manager or owner is able to meet with and discuss matters with all staff; whereas knowing all employees is unmanageable in a large organization. As organizations grow larger, bureaucratic processes are used to ensure conformity and consistency, and so these types of organization tend to have greater levels of centralization. The ideal is to find a way to balance the need for responsiveness and employee involvement, but still retain sufficient control to ensure objectives are met.

Power and control: The choice of how much to decentralize is influenced by the environment, size and how much power managers are prepared to share with others. This choice is influenced by the strategic goals, plus their individual perceptions, values and individual preferences. Trust is a key factor. Where there is mutual trust between managers and subordinates and a culture of acting within agreed boundaries, devolution of some decision choices is both possible and desirable.

Technology: Most people use the term technology for the activities surrounding machines that deliver technological outputs, such as computers, the internet, telephones and manufacturing systems. However, technology can have a much broader meaning, as to how knowledge is applied or used to help humans adapt to or improve their environment. In this sense, it is broader than just the tools that are used.

The role of technology deserves greater explanation as there are three meanings for technology (Winner, 1997). The first refers to the tools or equipment, the second refers to the skill-based activities, routines and procedures that surround how the equipment is used, and the third refers to the organization or social arrangements that allow us to gain the productive benefits from the first two. These distinctions in how we use the term technology are important because they identify the different perspectives that need to be addressed when implementing new technology or adapting technology into the structure of an organization.

From a management perspective, technology can be organized in such a way that it integrates with the social systems. Employees are more likely to accept technology if they have the skill base to gain full use of the technology. The technological system also needs to be maintained. Therefore, technology pervades all aspects of an organization's work; it affects the design of jobs and workgroup relations and how well these are coordinated and controlled. For example, it can increase task specialization and reduce the breadth of an individual's skills so they are doing highly repetitive work, which in turn increases management control, but at the same time it can severely degrade an individual's job satisfaction. An example of this might be in a call centre where individuals are given carefully controlled scripts to respond to customers.

On the other hand, the same technology may also give individuals greater freedom by increasing the range of skills they require and by removing repetitive tasks and allowing more time for thinking, decision-making and innovating, provided that the technology does not produce so much information that people are overwhelmed with it. In this way technology influences recruitment and selection, performance management, training and development, promotional prospects and occupational health and safety, so it affects employee values and attitudes, morale and work–life satisfaction. Nonetheless, each of these outcomes, including how technology is used and integrated, remains an organizational choice.

Four internal issues to consider when designing an organization:

1. How will tasks be divided, or broken up among the sources of labour? This often relates to how specialized or skilled a task is. Highly specialized and simple tasks can be very repetitive to capture economies of scale; however, complex tasks that require a high level of skill and specialization are less suited to being broken up, so individual or team approaches may be more suited.

2. How much decision-making authority will be retained by the organization or allocated to employees? This relates to the type of task as well as the knowledge and skill levels of employees.

3. How many direct reports can be managed by each manager or supervisor? This directly relates to the chain of command that flows through the organization. Regardless of where control and authority are held, how wide should any individual's span of control be? As pointed out earlier in this book, the span of control is much larger now than previously.

4. How appropriate is it to departmentalize different functions and decide whether activities are grouped around specific tasks, locations or products or processes? For example, a manufacturing process might be grouped around specific components of a product, with highly repetitive tasks and centralized control, or it may be devolved to work teams, where individuals with different tasks and skills contribute to an end-product.

Notwithstanding the importance of the above factors, the most fundamental choice that affects the structure is the decision to centralize or decentralize control. The desire for accountability, the width of an individual manager's span of control and the amount of time it will take to implement a response are tied to the organization's ability to adapt. Once this choice is made, the next decision is with regard to the advantages and disadvantages, or the costs and benefits, of centralizing control and decision-making or devolving these, in whole or in part, to other parts of the organization.

Another consideration is the level of task complexity and work specialization required of individual jobs or group tasks. Complex tasks in particular are difficult to standardize and break up into components; they also demand greater autonomy so workers can respond to individual contingencies or problems as they arise. Generally, and although managers need to make the choice that best suits their needs, the answer to the dilemma of deciding how much authority and autonomy should be devolved is to err on the side of giving greater ownership to employees, particularly if job satisfaction and commitment are valued.

On the one hand, tasks need to be divided to capture synergies that give economies of scale; on the other hand, further additions lead to a point of diminishing returns, and diseconomies of scale emerge. For example, this tension surfaces in overly bureaucratized systems as delays in decision-making and processing, or in under-controlled systems as nepotism and/or a lack of accountability. The tendency these days is to have flatter, more flexible structures, such as network or process-based structures, because these are much more responsive to customer needs. Giving employees access to customers, suppliers and other stakeholders helps organizations to be more responsive in turbulent modern environments and is the basis of the high-performance work system approach and employee empowerment (Camps and Luna-Arocas, 2012; Razi and More, 2012). The greater the level of contact, the more connected are employees to the organization's imperatives!

The key to designing a structure is to combine elements in a way that best helps achieve the organization's strategy. The 'strategy drives structure' view implies that the organizational units are aligned to most cost-effectively and efficiently achieve pre-defined strategic outcomes, as set out in a strategic plan. The alternative view is that structure adapts to emergent strategy where the timing, specific focus and goals arise out of opportunities that present. The ideal is to design a structure that captures the advantages of both the strategic and emergent strategies, which is why flatter, flexible structures with less rigid boundaries are becoming more common.

One final aspect worth considering when designing jobs is to think of the impact on individuals and workgroups. In the 1980s, Hackman and Oldham developed a model which is equally relevant in today's environment. Hackman and Oldham (1980) identified that, to be job satisfied, individuals needed five core characteristics designed into their work. These core job characteristics are:

1. skill variety – so that individuals use a range of skills at work;
2. task significance – so that the job is valued as one that is important to the organization or society;
3. task identity – so that the individual has a sense their contribution is identifiable;
4. feedback – from the job, or others such as supervisors or customers; this lets the individual know how well they are doing;
5. autonomy – so the individual has some sense of self-determination or choice over what they do.

Hackman and Oldham argued that having these attributes in a job helps to foster three important psychological states: firstly, that work has meaning; secondly, the worker knows how well they contribute; and so, thirdly, the worker develops a sense of responsibility for what they do. The model recognizes that perceptions of a job are influenced by the complexity and level of challenge within the task and an individual desire for challenge and growth. Taken together, these help explain how well individuals perform, and how job-satisfied they feel, or conversely, their disengagement and dissatisfaction. The concept behind the job characteristics model is that meeting psychological needs through the job design influences an employee's relationship with his or her work and encourages motivation and work involvement (Hackman and Oldham, 1980).

The job characteristics model is still widely used in research and for assessing how to restructure jobs, because it provides a framework for enlarging and enriching individual jobs (Albrecht, 2012; Truchon et al., 2012; Christian et al., 2011). Changes to work processes can integrate individuals' social needs with the technical and task components, then work becomes a more enjoyable and satisfying place. The aim is to ensure that individuals are exposed to as full a range of the psychological attributes proposed in the model as possible. Armed with this knowledge, jobs can be enriched by increasing the range and scope of characteristics within individual jobs.

This should not be more of the same if the work is boring or repetitive, but it should introduce changes to the task that provide some stretch or challenge and increase the attributes that are lacking. Autonomy and feedback address all three of the psychological states and therefore are deemed the most important attributes. Having the sense that a job provides autonomy, or is important or significant, and knowing the outcomes helps to promote job involvement (Albrecht, 2012). Such results are consistent across developed countries, and are also emerging in studies in developing countries. A recent study in India identified that job components that matched individual values promoted both intrinsic and overall job satisfaction (Kumar, 2012). Similar results in Pakistan identified that empowerment through the job and employee participation also positively correlated to job satisfaction (Syed and Yan, 2012). Of course, it is also important to recognize that individual perceptions about what is valued and important can vary, depending on the employees' experiences, hopes and expectations. This fits well with the SAS example cited in our opening chapter.

To identify what works well, look to relationships where components fit together or integrate. Signs include positive feedback from customers, evidence of good productivity, good working relations and cooperation among staff, or innovation. Relationships and patterns can emerge because individuals have found they work well, even if these are outside the formal structure of the organization. Conversely, dysfunctional work patterns and relationships signify the need for change. Unsatisfactory results mean the job or task might be better if taken apart and reorganized differently. Again, look at the organizational, work group and job levels. A good starting place is through the HR strategies of job analysis and performance management, but synergies can also be identified through other diagnostic processes. Use diagnostic processes to map the flow of work to help identify arrangements that work well so these can be capitalized on and integrated into an aligned structure.

Measurement and control

Managers use the measurement and control systems to track productivity, performance and change and the need for resources. Measurement systems, such as financial, quality, inventory or information technology systems, provide hard data that helps to identify what needs to change and how successful change has been. Measurement systems and controls help identify what needs to be done on a day-to-day basis and how daily activities feed into short-term goals, such as monthly targets, and medium-term or strategic objectives.

Controls and measures come from one of three sources. First, they can come from the market or external environment in the form of government rules and regulations or customer expectations. Second, they may be rules or policies and procedures imposed by the organization to measure and track its progress. Third, controls can be imposed informally by the espoused values, beliefs and attitudes that make up the culture. Balance is needed across these three sources.

These three control systems act as a counterbalance. Rules and regulations provide boundaries that let people know what they are allowed, or not allowed, to do, whereas the culture can provide the same boundaries where there is ambiguity as it shapes the way we think about how we do things. Therefore, the culture lets people know what is acceptable and what is not acceptable. Underpinning these is market control because obviously companies want to stay in existence, either to make a profit or to provide a service. Shifting the emphasis in the control and measurement systems helps disrupt current activities and signal change. How well it is accepted is moderated by the operating environment, organizational leadership and the history of change within the organization.

Measurement systems allow the organization to control what is happening and reduce uncertainty. Control systems not only measure outcomes, they also provide parameters that protect both the individual and the organization. There are many situations where the risks and the decision choices remain constant, so the controls can be standardized, as occurs with standard procedures or policies, and these are referred to as bureaucratic controls. At another level, the external environment may force controls on an organization, as occurs with occupational health and safety, insurance and equal opportunity requirements. Nonetheless, there are many complex situations where it is difficult to define parameters to guide decision choices beforehand, so organizational culture can act as a control to guide behaviour in times of uncertainty. This is not to suggest that one form of control is better than others, but to acknowledge that all have a role to play in maintaining and shaping the desired behaviour of employees.

The culture is manifest in the shared values that let people know what is or is not acceptable. If the culture has drifted so that undesired behaviours are occurring, or the culture needs to be strengthened, adjusting the rules, regulations and/or policies can provide a transparent and enforceable way to reshape desirable behaviours and gain a correction. The challenge is to get the balance right so the rules and policies do not actually become a barrier to individuals making choices that reflect the needs of the organization. The ideal from the organization's perspective is to get the balance right so that if policies and procedures are either too restrictive or too free, there is another mechanism that protects the interests of the organization and individuals but still provides scope for them to exercise choices they have the knowledge, skills and ability to use.

Communication

Some researchers and practitioners suggest you can never communicate too much during a change process; however, the quality of the communication is what really matters. Communication needs to use an appropriate mix of media that targets the interest and engagement levels of the employees and provides usable information in a way that they can identify with (Linke and Zerfass, 2011). Thus communication needs to be consistent, timely and clear in intent, so sufficient information is given to maximize understanding without overloading the recipients.

Communication during times of change usually serves one of three purposes. The first is simply to get information out so that people understand what is happening. Next, employees need to be motivated to 'buy in' to the change process, and third, to gain their input and involvement. Different types or phases of the change process can require different communication strategies. Fundamental to any change strategy is the need to engage employees in two-way conversations about how changes can be implemented and what impact this will have on them.

The value of two-way communication cannot be overstated. Armenakis and Harris (2002) argue that failure to communicate or ineffective communications are a primary reason that change efforts fail. Managers need to think about who will be affected, what the likely impacts are and how individuals, work groups, subsections and departments are likely to respond. Everybody needs to know what is happening, especially those who are likely to be affected. Those in influential positions, whether they are in formal positions such as managers, supervisors and union representatives, or informal opinion leaders, should be harnessed to spread the word in a positive way and gather feedback on the mood and concerns of organizational members.

Acknowledging that sometimes there are limits on what can be publicized, particularly if third parties are involved, letting employees know about the what, why and how will encourage participation and shared ownership. Participation through suggesting remedies or opportunities for improvement can be a motivator for employees. However, as we discuss in the leadership section, sometimes action needs to be implemented urgently, and the risk of delays because of participation can make this strategy inappropriate.

Communication needs to be face-to-face whenever and wherever possible. The two-way nature of face-to-face communication allows for a two-way dialogue. It not only minimizes the risk of harmful erroneous rumours spreading, but can allay fears by giving employees the opportunity to ask questions, clarify concerns, raise solutions or engender innovations managers are not aware of. To be effective, communications with staff need to address the following five keys identified by Armenakis et al. (1993):

1.   why change is needed;
2.   the confidence or belief that the change is achievable;
3.   the change truly is in the best interest of the organization;

4. the organization will provide the resources and support needed to make it happen;

5. in what way will employees benefit from the effort involved in making the change?

Armenakis and Harris (2002) argue effective communication addresses three overlapping phases of change: readying the organization for the change; gaining acceptance to execute the change; and embedding or institutionalizing the change. Various strategies are available, but Armenakis et al. (1993) recommend going further than just telling employees about what will happen and why it will happen. Shared opinions from internal and external sources provide the opportunity to learn about what is happening and prevent isolation. Discussion and involvement allow employees to work through the implications and achieve a better understanding of them. Extending participation to joint decision-making gives greater ownership and understanding of the outcomes and subsequently gains commitment to them.

Dealing with conflict

Conflict can be both a positive and a negative force. Positive conflict can stimulate innovation and acceptance and provide an opportunity to explore the likely impacts of the change. Alternatively, negative or dysfunctional conflict because of anxiety or interpersonal confrontations can sabotage or hinder the change process and, too often, can cause the change process to fail.

Conflicts should not be brushed aside, but are better viewed as opportunities to re-evaluate the validity of a decision. Inability to confront and explore issues of conflict has contributed to group think and poor decisions in a number of famous cases, such as the Challenger Space Shuttle disaster or the crisis of confidence that led to the run on the Northern Rock Building Society in England in 2008. Group think occurs when differing opinions are suppressed so that conflict is not allowed to surface. A more constructive approach is to put in place strategies to examine why the conflict is occurring. Viewing conflict as an opportunity makes it more likely to be a source of innovation. When people do not feel free to disagree, nothing is likely to change!

Conflict is not always obvious. It is often easier to deal with conflict that is out in the open, whereas conflict that is not discussed or exposed can undermine employees' performance. This can be a particular problem in countries with rigid structures or processes, where employees are treated as commodities. Disgruntled employees will choose to work to rule or take sick leave at a critical time when the organization needs their allegiance.

Leadership

A combination of leadership and good management is best when implementing change. Leadership strongly influences what actually happens in an organization on a day-to-day basis and there is no doubt that leader behaviour and style have a strong influence on an organization's culture (Tombaugh, 2005). Much is made of the leader as an important figure for setting the company's vision, and there is no doubt that leaders can inspire, transform, support, enable and motivate an organization. Effective leaders also need to be good managers, or, if management is not a strong part of their skill set, they need to make sure they are supported by good managers.

Leaders and managers have to be aware of the risk of self-deception. In a recent business programme interview Matthew Quinn (Hooper, 2008), one of Australia's leading CEOs and managing director of the property development company Stockland, identified that it is critical for leaders to surround themselves with people who are prepared to give an honest opinion and question the organization's actions when they feel this is necessary. Quinn says such actions should be applauded and valued, rather than punished.

An individual's ability to make rational decisions is bounded by their level of knowledge, experience and intellect and their interpretation or 'sense making' of past and present situations as well as the available information. Depending on education, culture, personality and past experiences, individuals interpret the same information in different ways. Years of experience in dealing with organizational change has identified that managers and employees often have very different understandings of reality within the same organization, because they view events from different perspectives. The essence of collaborative and flexible approaches to change is to capture and work with these perspectives. A number of approaches to do this are discussed further on.

Although we argue for employee participation in change in general, there are situations when participation is not called for, or when participation can actually limit the organization's ability to respond to change. Leaders need to be both responsible and accountable for the organization's decision choices. Sometimes there is not time to explore the options; sometimes leaders need to make urgent decisions! In other cases, greater employee involvement can generate conflicting views and ideas that are time consuming to resolve, or escalate tension within the organization, and therefore decisive action on the part of a leader is in the best interests of all.

Other examples occur when the leader has to make decisions based on having a macro perspective, or confidential information, such as might be the case prior to a merger or acquisition. Releasing information prematurely can damage negotiations. Similarly, if the external environment limits the ability to choose among strategic responses, there is little point in involving people in decisions where ultimately they have no ability to affect the outcome. Similarly, the scale and extent of the change can influence the choices. There is a vast difference between a minor change that can be undertaken over a period to a full-scale transformation of the organization that may be required if an organization faces bankruptcy.

Personality, experience and the environment all influence leadership styles. Collaborative leaders involve employees, so they have considerable say in what happens; others can take a more limited consultative approach that takes employee opinions into account. The leader can set the whole tone of the organization. An autocrat who does not communicate with people encourages others to act in the same way! This reduces transparency in communication throughout the whole organization. In turn, the leader who is accountable and open to question and new ideas encourages others to be the same.

Cultural change

Culture refers to the values and common meaning a particular group of people share. Much as a country's culture is distinguished by the common attributes and values shared by its citizens, organizations develop a culture of shared meanings. Culture is displayed through the normal patterns of behaviour; these demonstrate what is valued and what is considered acceptable (Schein, 1986). These shared values and attitudes affect how people work together; the patterns of behaviour that develop can either support or be a barrier to the change process. The cultural attributes can include many facets, ranging from tangible artifacts like the office layout to jargon used and the rewards and sanctions handed out. Other less tangible attributes such as ethics, commitment, concern for others, also help to define the culture and what is, or is not, acceptable.

Culture serves a valuable purpose because it defines the acceptable standards of normal behaviour, or 'norms', within work groups and provides informal rules to get on with others in that environment. Cultures develop because groups find ways of adapting and integrating behaviours that work well for them and then want to pass on this knowledge so that others will behave in the same way (Schein, 1986). The values associated with a given culture show up in a number of ways, such as being friendly and inclusive of others, the standard of professionalism or sharing a common language of acronyms or abbreviations.

The artifacts, symbols and stories of the organization let people know what is important and help identify the culture (Schein, 1986). For example, dress code is an artifact that can help to identify who belongs in a group, whether it is a company uniform, professional suit or casual dress (for instance, a policeman or air steward is instantly recognizable). Symbols can be the company logo, a quality assurance stamp or exemplary customer service. Stories about the organization's survival, triumphs or ability to overcome adversity also help socialize individuals to the cultural norms and build a cohesive culture. For example, the stories about the beginnings of Virgin, Ebay, Google and Nokia bring images to mind that signify important aspects of these companies. Taken together, these provide boundaries around the shared meaning of how members think and behave.

What attributions do you make?

How does dress signify something of the individual values and what assumptions do we make when we see a person in uniform? Consider a nurse, a policeman, a member of the Salvation Army or the pinstripe suit of a barrister.

Building on Schein's (1986) work, Johnson and Scholes (1997) referred to the intertwined components of culture as a cultural web and, along with the rites, rituals, stories and artifacts, included the influence of the organization's structure, power and control systems in this web. Understanding what happens with each of the individual components allows managers to map and integrate the current culture to identify components that need to change. Breaking apart the cultural components helps identify which parts need to change and how this can be achieved. The hub of the web is the organization's culture, which is influenced to a greater or lesser degree by each of the individual components that go to make up the culture. The elements that make up the web are briefly described below:

- Stories are the past events that are talked about. Ready examples are seen in the heroic myths of the beginnings of Dell, Microsoft and Apple Computers. Retelling these stories lets the listener know that tenacity and innovation are valued. Similarly, negative stories can serve as a warning and a lesson for all in the organization. What are the current stories about your organization? Who are the heroes of these stories? What message do they convey to staff and customers?
- Symbols and visual or tangible artifacts signify what is valued by the company and send out a message about the organization. These include the company logo, dress codes and state of the premises. For example, the Qantas emblem of the flying kangaroo signifies it is uniquely Australian. Aboriginal motifs on staff uniforms, the emblem on the aircraft and the company's advertising campaigns focus on Australian symbols.
- Rituals and routines are the way things are done. These make up rites of passage that let people know what to expect and help to define the way things are done; for example, having regular morning teas to meet and greet each other sends a very different message to newcomers compared with an organization where individuals remain behind closed doors. Similarly, organizing regular training meetings, or involving employees in decision-making, demonstrates how management values staff. Think of the difference between a university and a hospital. There are many similarities in that both are bureaucracies that engage in teaching, research and community service. However, for most employees the hospital setting is much more rigid in the routines of shift handovers, work rosters, crosschecking of medications, triage and other treatment procedures.
- Organizational structure encompasses the defined formal structure and reporting lines that appear in an organizational chart and the informal structure, where power relationships have developed because they work, to benefit individuals or the organization. Does the structure encourage involvement or does it just treat employees as numbers? The informal or unwritten structure that is supported by relationships is often overlooked, yet it can be a powerful force for resistance to change when power bases and coalitions are threatened.
- Control systems – do they align and support the desired culture? Control mechanisms include both the measurement systems and the policies and

procedures that support these. For example, consider the human resource management systems governing recognition, rewards and sanctions, financial measurement and quality control systems. How well are they enforced, or are they too rigid? Are they adapted to the current practices, technologies and customer needs?

- Power relationships – who holds power to influence decisions? Senior management holds real power; however, power is not shared equally. How do people use their power bases, and do individuals or coalitions work for their individual benefit, rather than the organization's? How is power wielded? Are rules rigidly enforced, or is there sufficient flexibility to allow for rapid responses to extraordinary circumstances? Is power abused? Keep in mind that those who act as gatekeepers, or control communication and technology, can also wield significant power and influence.

Organizations can have different cultures, although it is usual to expect all members to share a dominant set of values. The dominant values are core or central for all organizational members and should be congruent with organizational objectives. Human resources (HR) strategies of recruitment, selection, placement and performance management should support these values by making sure the right people for the organization are selected and appropriately socialized to the patterns of acceptable behaviour. If the core values are consistent, sub-cultures among subgroups, where attributes, values or patterns of behaviour of their own arise around different professions, work roles or locations, can be useful to bond members to a particular group. Having subcultures is not of itself a problem, provided peripheral norms support the core values. They become a problem if subcultures interfere with the core values and allow groups to focus on their own agenda rather than the organization's. For this reason, the core values are best inculcated when socializing new members.

New entrants are socialized into the organization both formally, through the HR process of orientation, and informally, by how they are accepted and treated by others. Both the formal processes and the behaviours manifest in the informal values help shape the culture of an organization. Employees quickly learn who has informal power, who engages in political behaviour and who has the ability to sanction or promote their acceptance. In this way, culture helps individuals make sense of their environment so they can shape their behaviour to fit in and be accepted by others. Where individuals deviate from the expected behaviour other organizational members can shun or ostracize them and so bring pressure to bear to get them to comply with the group norms. Group pressure that seeks or enforces compliance in return for acceptance is how culture also acts as a control mechanism.

In some ways, having a strong culture can be a double-edged sword. Aligning the culture and values is likely to assist change. We say likely to assist here, because there are situations where the culture can also create a situation where employees stand together to block the change. On the one hand, a strong culture fosters a sense of identity and can promote feelings of belonging, trust and commitment based on the perception that individuals' values fit with the organizations. This is more likely to promote employee involvement in, and commitment to, the change process as employees feel that they are in this together. This sense of unity fosters integration between the individuals and the organization's goals and promotes quality of work-life; the downside is conflict and political behaviours if employees want to block the change.

Assumptions influence the choices people make; for example, seeing another employee penalized or lose their position can lead others to assume the organization is harsh and rigid in its application of performance management policies. This may be far from the truth and a completely false assumption! A useful analogy of organizational culture is the iceberg metaphor. Like an iceberg, much of what defines the culture is hidden. The deeper you go below the surface, the more difficult it is to pin down the beliefs and assumptions individuals make about the world around them, as Figure 5.1 shows. To check employees' assumptions, ask why the individual or group thinks as they do. This allows misunderstandings to be clarified. Sometimes actions cannot be explained, but the manager can make an informed choice about how to deal with the situation. The reality is that there are many situations where the organization does not, indeed should not, pass on information about employees or events that occur.

The level above the surface contains the tangible artefacts that are visible cultural components. This is at an objective, conscious level where judgments are made based on what we observe, experience and think. Attributes are visible things like the logo, documented policies and procedures, quality of customer service, the physical layout of the offices and quality of fittings, the plant and equipment. These can demonstrate what is valued in the organization. The iceberg analogy suggests that as we move below the water line, we also move to a deeper level that is more subjective than objective. At this level feelings about trust, commitment and

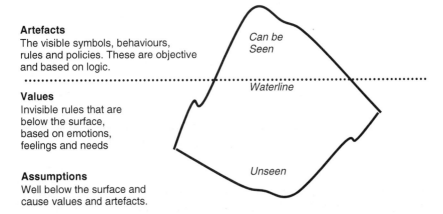

Artefacts
The visible symbols, behaviours, rules and policies. These are objective and based on logic.

Can be Seen

Waterline

Values
Invisible rules that are below the surface, based on emotions, feelings and needs

Assumptions
Well below the surface and cause values and artefacts.

Unseen

FIGURE 5.1   The organizational iceberg

loyalty emerge and are observed, for example, in common behaviours, shared ethics and language used.

At the deepest level, individuals make assumptions about what they expect from the organization and usually they are not even conscious of the choices they make. Assumptions are based on how they perceive their experiences within the organization and are also influenced by their past experiences and expectations; for example, employees who have been retrenched or suffered disadvantage through organizational change in the past are more likely to assume they will suffer negative consequences this time round. Conversely, the same applies if their past experiences have been positive. Good examples of these relationships are to be found in the failures of companies such as Enron Corporation, Arthur Anderson and Worldcom in America, the HIH Insurance Company in Australia and the Italian company Parmalat in Europe. Dysfunctional behaviours led to a pervasive culture where the systems inside the company become so eroded that no-one in the organization was prepared to speak out.

Many change management strategists recommend involving employees in the change process, yet Hofstedes' work on individual differences in societies suggests that Western societies tend to be more individualistic than Asian societies and therefore workers in the West are more likely to want involvement than workers in other countries. This appears to be a simplistic interpretation. We would argue, for example, that Asian workers would want to be involved, but in a way that is congruent with their own individual and group values.

The reality is that choosing to work with the preferred choice of people within a system, even if this is not perceived as optimal, usually is a better choice in terms of workability. Where employees oppose change, they are more likely to be obstructive and can block what might otherwise have been a successful strategy, in many varied and subtle or not-so-subtle ways.

How do you set about changing the culture? Just having a new vision of the future is insufficient! Consider the United Airlines example we referred to earlier. The change worked for United because the company addressed each issue it identified as contributing to its problems. Cultural change requires considerable time, effort and consistency, and most organizations underestimate, rather than overestimate, the amount of each of these. On the basis of historical evidence, a number of authors have some very similar thoughts to offer on how cultural change can be achieved.

Firstly, expect the change to take a long period, maybe up to five years or more. On the other hand, if the urgency for the change is apparent to everyone, the culture may change more rapidly. There are always some people who will accept the change readily and others who, for whatever reason, be it personal or organizational, are likely to resist. Not everyone will come on board, but it is critical that management gets the engagement of opinion leaders and a sufficient critical mass of support. Increase the speed of a cultural change by recruiting new staff who already have the values that are needed. A second critical step is to understand the prevailing culture and build on and reinforce existing positive attributes.

Reinforcing and building on what already works and paying less attention to the values that no longer fit reduces the risk of increasing resistance to change, caused by attacking the culture head-on. Challenging cultural values is usually perceived as an attack on personal values. This sends the message that the employee's *values* are undesirable or unacceptable. A better way is to focus on the positive, rather than the negative. There may be cases where negative values have to be addressed, but, as with all forms of negative feedback and criticism, this should happen privately on a case-by-case basis and should not form part of the public message to the organization as a whole.

There are several approaches to identifying values. The first of these is to examine common behaviours to understand what they mean. Ask questions like: "What happens, and why does it happen?" "How do we relate to others – inside or outside the organization?" "Why do we behave in this way?". Another way is to understand the values by exploring the assumptions that underpin them. The questions to ask here are "Why do we believe that?". The third approach is to examine the tangible elements of the culture such as the artifacts, symbols and rituals, and question the values that underpin these.

The best way to rebuild or form a new culture is to promote and publicize the best elements of the existing subcultures. This has the added benefit of recognizing those individuals or groups who are 'in sync' with the organization. Another strategy is to encourage innovation and development. O'Toole and Bennis (2009) point out that encouraging honesty and transparency is critical, even when management hears what it does not want to hear; if senior managers admit their mistakes, this makes the same possible for their subordinates. Encouraging employees to find new ways of doing things promotes involvement. It also provides an opportunity for implementing new frameworks in which the desired values can be inculcated. Finally, a good way to develop a new culture is to actually live that culture.

Living the culture means that at all levels, and particularly all management levels, the desired values are upheld in all interactions and activities on a day-to-day basis. If management lives the values that it espouses, this demonstrates to the organization as a whole the importance placed upon these values. If management does not abide by the values, or uses a 'do as I say, not as I do' approach, it undermines the values and in fact reinforces undesirable behaviour and demonstrates that the values underpinning policies and procedures are not valued by the organization itself. It is also important not to get distracted from the endpoint or goal. A final comment! – Choose a range of strategies from those listed above that you believe will work best in your environment.

Empowerment and involvement

There is no doubt that modern organizations with educated workforces find that a consultative and participative approach is more successful; however, involvement is also culturally bound and may need to be adapted to fit with what the workforce expects or can deal with. There are many benefits to involving employees. The main rationale is that the people who do a job often have a better understanding of what the problems are, and how they can best be solved. As workforces become more educated and technology becomes more complex, tasks often require multiple skills or team involvement, so that in some cases the specialized skills or knowledge required among a work group are beyond the scope of an individual manager. Employee participation in the workplace increases motivation and is thus self-perpetuating, as it leads to increased involvement and commitment to the organization (Kumar, 2012; Latham et al., 1994; Razi and More, 2012). It also provides better access to information, which reduces political by-plays and improves decision-making and job satisfaction (Witt et al., 2000).

How to implement employee participation and involvement has received considerable attention from both researchers and practitioners. Unfortunately, it is not just a matter of stating that employees can be more involved or participate in decisions. An appropriate framework needs to be set up to ensure that both staff and management know what is expected; this helps set in motion a clear process of transition. It is often taken for granted that participation is a pretty straightforward and easy process to set up – just tell people they can participate or be involved!

The reality, however, is that unless the roles and processes are defined, the ambiguity surrounding these just creates conflict and stress. In some cases, managers are perceived to manipulate employees to gain the outcomes they desire; for example, managers can outwardly seek open participation, but circumvent this by selecting the employees that participate to ensure they get the outcome they want.

An extremely useful framework proposed by Black and Gregerson (1997) provides a five-dimensional framework for considering how to implement participation in decision-making. Firstly, consider why participation is to be implemented, whether participation will be informal or formal, whether employees will have a direct say, or be indirect as in having voting rights, being mindful that some people will have a stronger desire for participation than others; however, all should have the opportunity. Be quite clear on what issues employees can participate in; is it just to be about job design and working conditions or strategic issues? Employees also need to be clear on what level of involvement they can expect; is participation the opportunity to express an opinion or to make a decision? The final criterion they recommend is to make the process of decision-making clear, so employees know what to expect; will decisions be made in meetings by a show of hands, or in a confidential ballot?

Kotter and Cohen (2002) suggest ways of bolstering empowerment during times of change, including: hearing about the experiences and success of others, which can help bolster confidence for being successful; having recognition and reward systems that demonstrate confidence in the employees, which further promotes self-confidence and expectations that they can achieve; and providing feedback to help align decisions with the organization's vision. Disempowering subordinates does not work (Kotter and Cohen, 2002) and this is embedded within the concept of high-performance work systems (Aryee et al., 2012). Managers who fear letting go of their power and try to control everything undermine any sense of empowerment.

Teamwork – Inter-group development and goal setting

Organizations increasingly rely on teamwork. Unfortunately, just putting a group of individuals together and expecting them to work as a team does not work. Because individuals bring different attributes in terms of their personality, work experience, and skills and knowledge, teamwork can be undermined by conflict, power struggles and some members taking advantage of the effort of others and being 'free riders'. In a study of 496 employees from 10 different industries and across 15 organizations, Casimir et al. (2012) found that building relationships and social capital are ways to overcome negative behaviour that emerges among groups. Waddell et al. (2007) identify some strategies groups can use to deal with problems, and also stress the importance of strengthening and nurturing relations. These strategies include:

- sensitivity training, which aims to help members have a better understanding of their own behaviour and interactions within groups;
- process consulting, which aims to help group members solve problems and leaves them with the skills to do this for themselves in future;
- interventions by a third party, which can be used to resolve interpersonal issues within a group through problem solving, mediation or adjudication;
- team building, where deliberate strategies are put into place to build and enhance the group's relationships so they can work together more effectively.

Managing people through the change

Harvard professor John Kotter (1995) stresses the importance of incorporating the following steps when implementing change. Despite the passage of time, these are equally as relevant in today's workforce:

- create a sense of urgency so people know the change just has to happen;
- guide the change with people who are committed to it;
- be clear on what you are aiming for;
- communicate, so everyone is informed and understands what's happening;
- make internal changes (i.e. structure, technology) to remove obstacles to the vision;
- be systematic and go for short-term wins to build on gains;
- keep up the momentum by using small gains to help overcome greater challenges;
- embed the changes within the culture – so that it all fits.

Considering the economic turmoil that we are experiencing, some argue that a long-term vision is probably unrealistic, given that it is impossible to predict what might happen in the next 12 months, let alone the next five years. However, the purpose of a vision is to provide a guiding framework of where you want to end up and it's important not to confuse the vision with the goal. Having a vision gives a sense of purpose and keeps the change effort focused. Perhaps most important of all, the vision serves as a reference point for the choices and progress that are made. This way the endpoint can be realigned, adapted or even changed as circumstances warrant. Also, achievements can be identified and celebrated so that everyone is aware of what has been achieved.

The reality of change in organizations is that change can affect macro outcomes; however, the individual's job may not change, so the individual does not recognize the impact of the change. Quite often people at the coalface do not actually see the impact of the change. Macro measures of improvement such as letters of thanks, improved turnaround times, reduced costs for raw materials and reduced production error rates may not be visible to individual employees. Therefore, people need to be made aware of the outcomes on a day-to-day basis.

The other issue that warrants some brief discussion is the need to ensure that employees have adequate resources, not only physical resources but also time and information. The reality is that when organizations move into a change process it often follows a period of uncertainty or stress. This means employees can be tired and stressed when going into a change process. Employees are often stressed and worried about their own future and have an added workload burden. Organizations that are financially struggling often adopt what is termed a fortress mentality; they look inwards and focus on applying internal constraints to exercise greater control, which is often the opposite of what they need to do! Not investing in new technology or skills poses a dichotomy between what they would like to do and what they realistically can do. This calls to mind the saying "*you can't downsize yourself to prosperity*"!

Organizational learning

One strategy that has received a lot of interest in the literature and from practitioners is the concept of organizational learning, or the learning organization. Peter Senge (1992) argues that a learning organization is one that continuously expands its ability to create its own future to improve performance, profitability and innovation. Knowledge and information are critical to the success and survival of organizations that want to produce the best quality goods and services. Of course, it is not the organization *per se* that learns, but the people in the organization who are able to learn, and their collective knowledge contributes to the organization's success. In that sense, a learning organization is one that is peopled by individuals who create and share their learning. In this way, others can add to gaps in the incomplete knowledge of individuals. The aim is to create an environment, or culture of learning, in which members strive to improve and use their knowledge to effect improvements through change. Although Senge (1992) provides a framework that defines a learning organization, it is important to recognize that the concept is essentially a philosophical view or approach that uses a range of tools to seek continuous improvement.

The value of learning from experience was first raised in the late 1970s, when Argyris and Schön (1978) identified the need for organizations to harness the knowledge gained when they solve problems so this could be stored for future reference. Throughout the past 40 years many different explanations for organizational learning have emerged in the literature, which has created some level of confusion for practitioners. However, Chan and Scott-Ladd (2004) suggest these differences arise from philosophical differences about what learning means, how it can be implemented and what its goals are. Both the how and what are important!

There are five key attributes that help define a learning organization:

1. Systems thinking, so that members recognize and respond to the interconnectedness of each of the components. This is inherent in the open systems model that was discussed earlier in this book. The external environment, resources and stakeholders can influence the choices an organization has, and it must therefore react with adjustments in its strategy, technology, structure and task design and its measurement and staffing systems.
2. The need for individuals to gain and improve their skills through continuous learning so that they achieve 'personal mastery' (Senge, 1992) over the tasks that they need to perform; in consequence, they can contribute to improved capacity within the organization.
3. Having a shared vision of what the organization stands for and what it is striving towards.
4. Having a shared mental model or perception of what is important to the organization. This means the assumptions and generalizations about the organization are shared among its members (Easterby-Smith and Araujo, 1999). This is particularly important since individuals make sense of their environment on the basis of their individual experiences and assumptions, and their perceptions can be distorted.
5. Lastly, the concept of shared learning encourages individuals to contribute to their own and others' learning, so they can learn from each other and share their own knowledge.

Levitt and March (1988) identified some pitfalls organizations need to be wary of when they implement a learning strategy. One is the risk of claiming a cause-and-effect association from learning, when in effect there is really no association. For example, if employees were given training on customer service and consequently customer satisfaction improved, there may still be no association between the two. This can be overcome by setting specific measurable training objectives that address specific outcomes. For example, if dealing with difficult customers, timeliness and courtesy were issues, the measures might be to observe how employees deal with conflict or critical incidents, letters acknowledging exemplary service, and the time taken to approach customers.

The second problem occurs when organizations or individuals assume that a solution that worked in the past is the best one for the future. Pharmaceutical giant Procter & Gamble found this out to their cost when successive growth strategies saw the company get into financial difficulty. The turnaround came when A.G. Lafley was appointed CEO and the company refocused on core business and restructured, shedding over 138,000 workers from across 80 countries (Markels, 2006).

The third problem is a belief in the organization's ability that blinds the members to the need to change or improve their technology. This could well relate to Avon, which has finally made moves to replace its CEO after ongoing problems and a further fall in stock value of 45 per cent in 2011 (Lublin and Karp, 2011).

Fundamental to implementing a learning strategy is having well-designed programmes and processes that deal with a range of strategic outcomes. For example, in a study of organizational learning in the hotel industry in Malaysia, Arshad and Scott-Ladd (2008) identified that some of the strategic targets included customer service, high-quality facilities, products and accommodation that were provided at competitive price rates. Organizational learning strategies were developed to focus on how all staff, from management right down to the kitchen and housekeeping staff, could best meet their respective targets.

Implementing organizational learning requires building on the strengths of the organization. Many companies, from Shell to General Electric, Samsung and Honda, have successfully used this strategy, but that does not mean that they use the same strategy. Each organization has to choose what best fits its environment and capacity so that it deals with its own unique issues. The aim should be to continuously improve at the organizational, group and individual levels. Popper and Lipshitz (2000) recommend looking for evidence of information processing at each of these levels through a demonstrated capacity to collect, analyse and use information, not only in relation to the presenting problem, but to be able to abstract the learning into other settings. There also needs to be evidence of how knowledge is retained and accessed.

Some of the strategies that organizations can use include learning from your own and others' experiences, to refine and improve a process or activity. Levitt and March (1988) suggest this includes components of problem solving, experimentation, internal benchmarking, conducting research and development, encouraging suggestions and using other information-gathering ideas such as brainstorming.

Other strategies include training and development programmes, external benchmarking with competitors or those who are known to set industry standards, as well as seeking feedback and information from consultants, suppliers and customers, or other stakeholders such as newspapers, government agencies and trade shows. The internet or World Wide Web is also a great source of information. A final area for organizations to gain new knowledge is through mergers or acquisitions, which give access to the practices, standards and the knowledge of another company.

This is not to say that just increasing the level of information is sufficient. Information that cannot be acted upon or does not add value is worth little if it does not add to the organization's learning. One risk is that the internet can overload people with a lot of useless information, so that with so much information it is very difficult to sort out what is of value. The knowledge needs to be linked to practices within the organization that actually add value and should add to practices, processes and procedures. What makes the difference is the nature and quality of the learning experience, the sharing and diffusion of information, the commitment and valuing of learning services embedded in the organizational culture and the recognition that learning is aimed at strategic performance outcomes and the good of the organization. Providing opportunities like this helps to bind the employees to the company and this is what adds value to both employees and organizations (Ready, 2009).

Benchmarking is one strategy drawn from the organizational literature that warrants further discussion. Benchmarking allows an organization to learn the specific steps that lead to product or process improvement by learning from others who are leaders in a particular field. This has become a popular method because it is relatively inexpensive to copy what others do. The downside is that what comprises best practice in one situation may not be suited to another situation or environment.

A differing environment, other contingency factors or differences in resources and internal capability may make the transfer of knowledge less useful, or it might even be useful for generating alternative solutions. Pfeffer and Sutton (2006) rightly point out that copying others can speed up the learning and can be cost-effective, but this is not the same as being an innovator or leader – being as good as a competitor is not the same as being better. Some further suggestions adapted from Pfeffer and Sutton (2006) include:

1. Don't treat old ideas as if they were new
2. Be suspicious of 'breakthrough' ideas and studies – investigate and check how genuine or reliable they are. Simple formulaic solutions seldom work for complex problems
3. Celebrate and develop collective good ideas
4. Emphasize the drawbacks as well as the benefits
5. Use success (and failure) stories to get the message across, but not at the expense of reliable research to aid accurate diagnosis and informed choice
6. Demand evidence – robustly challenge and analyse ideas.

Don't just accept ideas because they are what everybody else is doing, or they are the flavour of the month. Be suspicious of the ten easy or simple steps that are supposed to solve a complex problem. Think through the implications of what it means for the particular organization and work systematically through an adequate diagnostic and implementation process. Sometimes time is short and decisions need to be made quickly, but the reality is that you can only work with the information you have. It is hard to let what appears to be a good opportunity go past, but there are situations where long-term interests are best served by not grabbing an opportunity that is not fully understood. Complex systems usually have many interacting elements and subsystems and these benefit from the breadth of knowledge that is shared through collective decision-making (Espinosa and Porter, 2011).

Summary

This chapter has examined the processes of change and introduced strategies any organization can take up or adapt to their situation. Fundamental to these is recognizing that change has a systemic impact and requires a systemic response. Change events can be episodic or continuous, or vary from large to small scale, and change strategies that have the support and involvement of staff are more likely to be executed effectively. We cannot stress sufficiently the importance of understanding what needs to change before making any change and the advantages of taking an incremental approach. Perhaps one of the most talked about systemic approaches in both the current literature and practice is that of viewing the organization as a learning organization.

Technology has allowed many organizations to become flatter and this is likely to increase along with the pace of change. The increasing pace and extent of change means it can be difficult, or in some cases impossible, to predict all changes and manage these in a linear way (Styhre, 2002). This means managers need to deal with the tension of keeping control of the internal processes and structures, while at the same time devolving responsibility, decision-making and accountability to employees or operatives at lower levels. To make this transition, the organizational culture needs to be adaptive or change readily as it is increasingly difficult to predict the future and the adaptations to change that organizations will have to make.

In summary, the first step is to understand what is and what can be, why it should be and how to make it happen. Deal with core issues, rather than symptoms. Encourage participation and shared ownership with all members of the organization. Some basic guidelines that can help with the implementation of change are outlined below:

- Make sure top management is involved and there are people appointed to champion the change.
- Have the strategy mapped out before you start. Have a plan, a vision, establish milestones, measures and outcomes.
- Conduct a pilot test to check the efficacy of a project and fine tune it before it is taken to a wider implementation.

- Use an incremental approach to change and start with issues or areas where change is more likely to be successful. This lets people know that the change can be successful and helps build support for change.
- Take the opportunity to learn from mistakes.
- Ensure employees have access to sufficient resources.
- Build in opportunities for employee involvement and teamwork to engage the hearts and minds of employees in the change process. Through involvement, create a shared responsibility in the redesign of roles, responsibilities and relationships. Change can be more successful if planned and implemented by teams.
- Consider the boundaries where change has a flow-on effect or is not likely to impact other components of the organization, and make sure you sequence the change logically and appropriately.
- Recognize that you need to minimize the risk for both the organization and individuals. If individuals feel they are at risk, they are less likely to commit to and support the change.
- Understand the push–pull factors affecting the organization. Ensure that everyone is aware of the driving forces; look for and address areas of dissatisfaction or restraining forces.
- Use the diagnosis as an opportunity to create shared understanding.
- Identify the behaviours that you want and use behavioural shaping strategies such as positive reinforcement, through such strategies as praise and recognition to promote these. Alternatively, non-recognition or sanctions can extinguish behaviours.
- Measure success with a balanced scorecard – this approach recognizes that all stakeholders have needs to be met. Although these needs may differ from time to time, overall each should be treated equitably in recognition of their importance to the organization's long-term sustainability.
- Keep a balance between the 'hard' and 'soft' sides of the organization. Innovation can only occur if innovative people are encouraged and innovation is valued as much as analysis (Rigby et al., 2009).

Study guide

Review questions

1. Explain the difference between change and innovation.
2. What are the seven necessary steps for implementing change?
3. What are the four key issues that need to be considered when designing an organization structure?
4. Explain the key differences between a tall mechanistic structure and a flat organic structure.
5. Explain the job characteristics model. Do you agree that this is a practical and useful model for modern organizations? Explain why.

6. Explain the three sources of controls and measures used by organizations and provide an example of each.
7. Explain the importance of communication and three purposes of communication during a change programme.
8. Explain why leadership is so important during a change programme.
9. Explain the features that make up the cultural web.
10. Discuss the iceberg metaphor and explain how it can be used by organizations to understand the impact of and manage change.
11. Explain the five key elements that define organizational learning.

Activity

Consider an organization you have worked in or currently work at and map out a cultural web for that organization.

Discussion question

Many organizations are moving towards the flat organic structure. However, this is not without risks in terms of coordination and control. Why do you think this is so?

Case study: Jack n'Wills' latest acquisiton

Getting a promotion is an exciting opportunity for anyone, so Steve Lim was excited when he was asked to manage Jack n'Wills newest acquisition, a micro-brewery and its attached small restaurant on the outskirts of a west coast city. Steve had been assistant manager for three years at one of the company's eastern states plants and had been frustrated by what he considered were outdated management practices. Jack n'Wills was named after the company founders, who, due to a shared interest in brewing, had started their first micro-brewery eleven years ago. The company now owns fifteen breweries that are located on the outskirts of major regional centres across the country. Jack and Will have always followed the strategy of brewing and manufacturing locally and sourcing employees from the local area as much as possible. Only key management staff and senior brewers are moved between sites.

Jack and Will negotiated this latest acquisition and agreed to retain all existing staff, even though they realized the micro-brewery was overstaffed. This could be dealt with over the medium term. Steve is not particularly happy about this as his bonus and share options as a manager are tied to the performance of the site. His preliminary analysis of the brewery/restaurant's performance is that even though it is making a small profit, there are opportunities to reduce staffing. There is evidence of continuing customer complaints, and although these relate to minor issues that staff dismiss as complaints from 'difficult people', Steve believes this is evidence that more extensive staff training and management and control systems are warranted. He wants to target a 20 per cent improvement in profits in the next twelve months and this would require a 15 per cent reduction in staff.

When Steve first arrived to take on his new role, employees often referred to how Terry Knowles, the former owner and manager, ran the brewery. Terry had a reputation as a father figure in the company; he viewed the employees as his family and knew them all by name. Family members and friends of current employees were given preference when recruiting and this extended to offering holiday jobs to employees' student children. Terry believed this helped build close relationships and loyalty and worked as a quality control mechanism; staff would not recommend anyone who would not fit into the organization.

Steve is concerned at the recruitment practices. While Terry's approach allowed for speedy recruitment, from Steve's perspective the outcome is poor human resource management practices with negative employee attitudes, 'nepotism', and the growth of subcultures detrimental to the organisation's 'bottom line'. In spite of being in a niche market, under Terry the company was operating under a fortress mentality. Steve can see there are many opportunities for improving performance, and this is where he could set himself apart to demonstrate how effective his management approach can be. He can develop the plant to serve as a model for Jack n'Wills' sites in the future. He wants to extend the small restaurant outlet that is attached to the brewery, which in turn will further boost profits.

The existing workforce is 150 staff, of whom 30 per cent are employed in part time or casual positions. Steve Lim wants to replace any staff who do not live up to his expectations or fail to meet the new performance targets he has decided to implement. At a meeting Steve called with the managers and supervisors to lay out his plans for the future, the discussion became heated. Both the restaurant and production managers argued that Steve's approach was too harsh and went against the commitment given by Will and Jack. Chen, the production manager, exclaimed angrily: "*These people are good people and are worth investing in!*" Fatima the restaurant manager agreed, saying "*What Terry wanted suited Terry! He wasn't concerned about such things. We can change, but we need to bring the staff with us.*"

Three months later there have been some small improvements. Four of the poorest performers have resigned and a customer service training programme initiated by Fatima has just been completed. On the other hand, unionism is strengthening and the workforce is becoming more militant and aggressive. Last week Steve circulated a memo to staff setting out his performance expectations. At this morning's meeting, the union threatened to instigate rolling stoppages and have presented the following log of complaints:

- Lack of consultation over recruitment (Steve has advised the personnel department that all recruitment is to be based on merit).
- The company's poor safety record. Since Steve's arrival three workers have been injured; one fell from an elevated walkway and suffered a fractured pelvis, the second suffered lacerations and other minor cuts when he tried to jump over a spill from a dropped crate of beer bottles, and a third suffered chemical burns when cleaning vats. It turned out that Stores had sent the chemical to the maintenance department, undiluted and misla-belled. These incidents have aggravated a culture of conflict between staff and management.
- Lack of occupational health and safety training.
- Salaries for the workers are 4 per cent below the industry average and there has not been an increase in the past three years.

Questions

1. What change management issues emerge in this case?
2. Do you agree with Steve's focus on productivity, or do you think there are other ways he could deal with the problems facing this site?
3. What advice would you give Steve?

Online activity

List some of the major systemic approaches to change. Compare and contrast at least two of these models; for example, six sigma, management by objectives, customer focus, lean management.

Further reading

Espinosa, A. and Porter, T. (2011) Sustainability, complexity and learning: Insights from complex systems approaches. *The Learning Organization*, 18(1): 54–72.

Kim, T.G., Hornung, S. and Rousseau, D.M. (2011) Change-supportive employee behavior: Antecedents and the moderating role of time. *Journal of Management*, 37(6): 1664–1693.

Oreg, S. and Sverdlik, N. (2011) Ambivalence toward imposed change. *Journal of Applied Psychology*, 96(2): 337–349.

Pfeffer, J. (2010) Power play: acquiring real clout – the kind that helps you get stuff done – requires bare-knuckle strategies (Spotlight on the Effective Organization). *Harvard Business Review*, July–August, 88(7–8): 84–92.

6

HUMAN RESOURCE STRATEGY ARCHITECTURE

Turning to the subject of building and harnessing the human and social capital, we will consider such strategies as employee involvement, participation in decision-making. This includes when and how these strategies can be implemented.

This chapter will cover the issue of human capital as a strategic resource and a tool for bringing about change. Topics covered will include creating the enabling structures and space, building trust, the use of teams and knowledge management. The impact of labour force diversity, in terms of ageism, gender, generational differences and transmigration, will be discussed.

HRM practices in a changed environment

This chapter describes the major HR practices that should be operative in companies, and suggests how they may need to change in a globalized environment. It is important to put this into perspective, as there is a danger that the 'hype' surrounding globalization may overtake the reality for most companies in both developed and developing countries. Although virtual companies and virtual teams do exist, they do not represent common practice as yet. For many companies, the changes to HR practices will be incremental and evolutionary rather than radical. This perspective is consistent with the 'emergent' approach to strategy discussed previously, which is more about building capability and continuously realigning the company and its practices in relation to changes in the business and global environment.

The following topics are discussed in this chapter: the employment relationship; motivation and commitment; job security; the make-or-buy decision in HRM. In addition, it covers HR planning and forecasting; recruitment and selection; work analysis versus job analysis; competency profiling; performance management and remuneration.

The employment relationship: Motivation, commitment and job security

In the era preceding globalization, the employment relationship was characterized by stability, the prospect of long tenure and a reasonable degree of job security in return for adequate performance, conformance to company norms, and loyalty and commitment to the company. During that era, which lasted from the late 1950s to the early 1980s, the dominant personnel/HRM philosophy was what Kraut and Korman (1999) refer to as *self-enhancing motivation*. This motivational philosophy, as reflected in recommended HRM practices of that time, focused on an individual's need for personal growth and development, achievement and self-enhancement. These motivational theories were accompanied by the notion of goal alignment, which suggested that if employees could align their personal goals with those of the organization, they could move together to accomplish mutual objectives. Such ideas were advocated by many of the important management writers of that period, including: Argyris (1957); Herzberg et al. (1959); McGregor (1960); Vroom (1964); and Hackman and Oldham (1980).

The second theory, perceived as less important, is based on the idea of *self-protective motivation* (Kraut and Korman, 1999). This is essentially concerned with protecting oneself from forces in the environment that threaten one's sense of identity. This suggests that self-protection motivation is the force that underpins the need for personal and job security.

In an era of relative stability and prosperity, this was not an issue that created a lot of anxiety and it was generally perceived to be of greater concern to unions at a time when their membership and influence were declining. In this environment, HR policies and practices placed more emphasis on the self-enhancing approach to motivation and, although self-protection was seen as important, it received less attention from practitioners and theorists. Thus, there was an assumption that HR practices with this focus could serve the needs of both the company and the individual (Kraut and Korman, 1999). In effect, this corresponds to the above-mentioned notion of goal alignment.

The belief in continued relative stability ended in the mid-1980s with the start of an endless round of restructuring, reengineering and downsizing, particularly among large corporate bureaucracies. Many corporations underwent massive downsizing in the 1990s, some of them several times. For example, IBM went from 410,000 to approximately 225,000 in 1999 (Kraut and Korman, 1999). Computer World Canada reported in 2009 that IBM was to lay off 16,000 worldwide. In 2012, Wikipedia reported that IBM had 433,000 employees worldwide, compared to 225,000 in 1999. However, IBM Employee News and Links noted in December 2012 that of the 433,000, only 92,000 worked in the United States and that India has 120,000 IBM employees. In another example, the US Postal Service announced in February 2012 that it was cutting 35,000 jobs and had plans to eliminate 150,000 overall (Keane, 2012).

We believe that this chopping and changing, growing and downsizing suggests a lack of an overall strategy to cope with an unpredictable environment and preserve valuable human capital and organizational and tacit knowledge. In an effort to boost employment, US President Obama has been keen to bring more manufacturing jobs back to the US (Traub et al., 2012). Although jobs in this sector have been growing over the last three years, there are still close to 1.8 million fewer jobs in manufacturing than there were five years ago (Foxnews, 2013).

As companies transformed themselves from tall hierarchies of authority to flatter, more flexible structures, a certain degree of downsizing was inevitable. However, downsizing per se has never been a viable strategy for repositioning a company, although many corporations acted as if it were. Downsizing does serve the purpose of rebalancing the employment mix (sometimes referred to as 'rightsizing') and it does reduce costs. However, this should be part of a larger revitalization plan to reposition a company rather than a stand-alone measure. Because downsizing has such an impact on defining the new employment relationship, and because HRM has to work with what is left after downsizing, it is worth exploring in detail some of the hidden costs and effects involved. These should be understood before this course of action is implemented.

The global economic woes of 2008/9 led to sudden and substantial job losses by early 2009, with 129,000 losing their jobs in Canada in January alone (Smith, 2009). Job losses for the same month in the USA included 207,000 from manufacturing, 111,000 from construction, 76,000 from the temporary help industry, 44,000 from transport and warehousing and 45,000 from the retail sector (Bureau of Labor Statistics, 2009). In one day alone nearly 80,000 jobs were lost across the UK, Europe and the USA (Wray, 2009) as companies such as Caterpillar, Philips, General Motors, Corus, Pfizer and Caterpillar and numerous smaller organizations cut staff.

Nonetheless, as American academic and HR researcher Wayne Cascio (2009) points out, simply cutting numbers to reduce costs is a short-term solution, but can be more expensive in the long run. A diminished workforce is also likely to be demoralized and this will increase turnover, both of which can impede the organization's capacity to recover and grow again. Once the financial dust settles, people will have to be rehired and the cost of recruitment and placement may out-weigh the costs savings. Cascio (2009) does not argue against lay-offs, but says this should be the absolute last resort. Recently, employees at one of Alcoa's Australian sites agreed not to take promised wage increases to reduce overall job losses (Taylor, 2009). Wage restraint, or in some cases wage reductions or reduced hours, has been a successful strategy used by some companies to ensure the capacity and strategic viability of the company and protect workers' jobs.

The hidden costs of downsizing

Downsizing is usually undertaken to improve productivity and reduce costs. Yet surveys continue to show that the expected benefits are not realized in over half the cases studied. In the short term, costs are reduced because there is a lower wages bill, but reductions in staffing can also negatively affect productivity. The source of hidden costs is the poor morale of survivors, caused by increased stress, and its effect on work behaviour and attitudes. Many companies are aware of the negative aspects but still use downsizing to adjust their workforce capacity, and the practice of stealth layoffs (where small numbers are laid off over a period of time) is used to hide the full extent of downsizing to avoid any backlash (Gandolfi and Craig, 2012). The resulting job insecurity, increased resistance to change, misplaced energy and erosion of trust can have a staggering effect on overall profitability. Some of the hidden costs which have emerged from studies on this issue are presented briefly below:

- *Reduced productivity.* A review of the literature into studies investigating the impact of downsizing concluded that over the longer term, downsizing has not significantly improved financial performance but has significantly undermined employee attitudes and increased customer dissatisfaction and defection (Williams et al., 2011). A poll conducted by Ernst and Young (2010) found that 74 per cent of senior managers at recently downsized companies said their workers had lower morale, feared future cutbacks and distrusted management.
- *Higher turnover, absenteeism and more sick leave.* These are all direct consequences of a drop in morale, lower commitment, and lack of trust and loyalty. Such costs are very high. One study estimated the cost of turnover at 1½ and 2½ times the annual salary and benefits cost for each employee leaving. Several studies have affirmed that employee loyalty engenders customer loyalty and that loyal customers are the most profitable.
- *Decline in quality.* When layoffs take place without work redesign, quality often suffers. As 'survivors' try to learn the jobs of the displaced employees while continuing to do their own work, they become stressed and overworked. Quality and service inevitably suffer.
- *Decreased creativity, entrepreneurship and risk-taking.* Increased workloads for those who are left, uncertainty about the future, loss of experience and confidence in the organization erode risk-taking and innovation (Elmuti et al., 2010). This study of two large manufacturing organizations tracked outsourcing programmes and identified that reducing the workforce in this way negatively affected employees' attitudinal responses and increased the likelihood of turnover. Fear, resentment and loss are all likely to impact negatively on creativity.
- *Loss of key talent.* Companies often find that key employees and top performers leave during downsizing, stripping the firm of valuable human capital, critical skills and institutional memory. For example, an automobile company worker in charge of ordering steel accepted a generous early retirement package, but after he left, an order was placed for the wrong kind of steel. This produced a $2 million loss for the company in downtime, rework and repair. Organizational memory and expertise were lost when the purchasing agent left because no one was trained to replace him.
- *Poor external image.* Many companies show little concern for the impact of downsizing on consumers and potential recruits. Experience has shown that it

takes a lot of time and money to rebuild a tainted public reputation and brand image. Badly planned downsizing can hit minority groups, reducing the diversity that companies may have built up over time.

- *Increased legal and administrative costs.* Not infrequently, workers who have been made redundant sue their former employers and commit sabotage to express their discontent.
- *High social costs.* Society at large must bear significant costs when a company moves into or out of a community. Costs may include lost tax revenue, welfare payments due to job loss, retraining, drug abuse or alcoholism and outplacement services. The question is: "Who pays these social costs?" The answer depends on the company's social concern and community resources. Mass layoffs may also lead to social unrest, especially in countries with no safety net for displaced workers.

Having recognized the risks and hidden costs of downsizing, companies are discovering that better results can be achieved through more responsible approaches. A number of countries, including most member states of the European Union, have legislation on employee dismissals. Moreover, an increasing number of multinational companies with a social corporate culture have responsible global policies on laying off employees, even in countries without such legislation (ILO and European Baha'i Business Forum, 1999, Table 1, Chapter 3). International labour standards also exist which provide guidelines for socially responsible enterprise restructuring, mainly pertaining to procedural fairness. The most relevant instruments are the Termination of Employment Convention, 1982 (No. 158) and Recommendation (No. 166) (ILO, 1982).

Given the potential and actual costs associated with downsizing and other forms of restructuring, the evolving model for the employment relationship may take one of several forms. Kraut and Korman (1999) state that the assumptions underpinning the self-enhancement model of HR practice are no longer valid and need to be changed. They believe that the individual and the organization should be viewed as separate entities that can integrate their interests and cooperate under certain conditions, but not under others. This is essentially a contractual model where monetary rewards are generally more important than organizational rewards such as promotion opportunities and enriched jobs. However, it is worth bearing in mind Pfeffer and Sutton's (2006) argument that competition for rewards can actually get in the way of information sharing and cooperation that is critical to performance.

Another view, expressed by Lepak and Snell (1999), is that of 'organizational architecture', which places employees in different quadrants according to the value and uniqueness of their skills. Value refers to whether an employee's skills can add value by lowering costs or providing increased benefits to customers. Uniqueness is the degree to which skills are specific to a company and may be based on tacit knowledge. Lepak and Snell (1999) suggest that HR can use this four-quadrant model to decide whether to internalize or externalize employment and development decisions.

Essentially this model recognizes that employees possess knowledge and skills that are not of equal strategic importance to an organization. Distinguishing between different types of employee makes it possible to focus on the strategic allocation of resources for training and development. It also provides a framework for 'make or buy' decisions in HR. This refers to the management decision whether to develop skills and knowledge internally through training and development or to buy them on the market. To a considerable extent, this depends on the strategic importance of those skills and knowledge and their availability in the open market. Generally, the types of competence that are related to core processes will be developed internally and may involve 'tacit knowledge' that has built up over time. This knowledge resides in individuals and is usually not codified or publicly available. It may or may not reside in the collective memory of an organization.

Therefore, Quadrant 1 represents core employees. A company invests in these workers, providing training and development, remuneration and benefits and other self-enhancement programmes that will protect the company's investment.

Quadrant 2 represents, to a considerable extent, autonomous professionals such as accountants, lawyers, academics, software engineers and so on. These people have valuable skills that are usually not unique to a specific organization and are fairly widely distributed. Therefore, these skills can be obtained from the labour market and do not require investment in further professional development. These employees are generally committed to their career and profession rather than to a specific company and have a conditional loyalty at best.

Quadrant 3 represents employees whose skills are low in value and uniqueness. They represent labour as a commodity which is widely available and can be purchased and disposed of as required. This is a contractual arrangement, which is becoming increasingly common as companies, particularly MNCs, outsource many lower skilled jobs. These are not necessarily unskilled jobs, but rather lower skilled jobs that do not directly help create a competitive advantage. Temporary relief staff in offices, call centres, cleaning and maintenance are occupations that fall into this category. Although these people may not be considered core process staff in a strategic sense, they may well be core process staff to a service provider. In other words, it is not a question of whether these staff have value, but rather to whom they have value. The organization architecture model does not make this point sufficiently clear.

Quadrant 4 represents low value, high uniqueness staff that a company need not employ directly. They are low value in the sense that they do not directly add value to core processes or contribute to a competitive advantage. Their skills are unique in that a company does not need them often enough to justify their full-time employment. An example might be an alliance between a company and a university to carry out certain types of research on a continuing basis. In such a case, the synergistic value of the relationship exceeds the value each institution could generate on its own.

The HR architecture model clearly advocates a differential investment strategy for various categories of staff, depending on their capacity to contribute to strategic core processes and/or create value for customers. Lepak and Snell (1999) state that HRM researchers have tended to present a holistic view of HR practice, which suggests that high performance management practices should apply across the board to all employees. They have not differentiated sufficiently between the various types of employee. Similarly, Jeffrey Pfeffer (1998a) argued very convincingly for a more inclusive approach, although he did not comment directly on the use of segmenting architecture. A study of 702 companies, cited by Pfeffer (1998b), found that a one standard deviation improvement in HRM practices was associated with an increase in shareholder wealth of $41,000 per employee or about a 14 per cent market value premium. His book *The Human Equation* (1998a) and articles (Pfeffer and Sutton, 2006) present empirical evidence that strongly supports a direct relationship between a company's financial success and its commitment to management practices that treat employees as assets.

More recently, Combs et al. (2006) conducted a meta-analysis on 92 previous studies and found significant and practical evidence that implementing high-performance work practices (HPWP) improved financial performance, which is the reason they are designated as such, to the extent of 0.2 of a standardized unit for each increase in HPWP. These practices encourage employee empowerment and facilitate improved employee motivation through training and skill development, incentivized rewards and recognition and flexible working arrangements. Their findings also indicated that there was little difference depending on the suite of strategies used, suggesting that it is not just one particular HR strategy that makes the difference, but it's more about aligning the practices with the environment, the organization's context and its strategy.

A similar meta-analysis by de Waal (2007) examined 91 studies to help define the important features of a high-performance organization, as are summarized below:

- a simple flat organizational design that encourages teamwork;
- a shared vision and strategy that focuses on customers' needs and builds relationships with external stakeholders;
- operates as a learning organization focused on best practice and aligns employees' values to this to encourage innovation and allow risk-taking, and at the same time provides measurable stretch goals;
- provides job security in a safe working environment that protects the psychological contract; this includes incentives and rewards that are fair and support performance;
- nurtures talent;
- has strong leadership with high trust;
- seeks to optimize the value chain through continuous improvement;
- communicates goals and values and empowers employees through devolved decision-making;
- is externally focused on both the short and long term;
- makes effective use of technological systems.

If there is so much evidence of the success of high-performance work practices, why isn't every one using them? Pfeffer (2007) argues convincingly that the answer lies in the types of employment relationship that very prominent companies are developing. Pfeffer describes it as a disturbing disconnection that managers and companies ignore significant amounts of evidence that point in one direction and continue to move in another direction.

High-quality employment relationships require an investment on the part of both employers and employees. This mutual commitment leads to a form of psychological contract that satisfies the needs of both parties. The psychological contract refers to the perceived agreement made between the individual and the organization and is an unwritten and unstated contract that leads individuals to commit to a course of action in the belief that there is reciprocity (Rousseau, 1995; Pesqueux, 2012). The investment on the part of the employer would include a reasonable degree of employment security, relatively high compensation, and opportunities for training, development and personal growth. These are self-enhancement motivators because the investment on the part of the employee involves commitment to the company and its values, a certain level of loyalty, and willingness to be a team player and to deliver a high level of job performance.

These mutual commitments, accompanied by other high-quality HR practices, go a considerable way towards establishing high-performance work systems. Job security is particularly important because it stabilizes the relationship and people generally want stability in their lives. Take away job security and the relationship becomes destabilized and the psychological contract is nullified. Without a certain level of job security, commitment and loyalty are unlikely and the relationship becomes, essentially, contractual in nature. Self-interest on both sides has replaced mutual interest. The generally accepted proposition is that innovations in work practices neither occur nor are sustained over time if workers feel insecure (Auer et al., 2005).

The flexibility that is gained by reducing the workforce (downsizing) carries potentially high costs. As Pfeffer (1998a) has noted, companies that have invested in recruiting, selecting, training and developing their employees not only risk losing that investment, but also put important strategic assets on the market for competitors to employ. Pfeffer cites a number of examples, which are fairly common practice, of companies that tell new employees they are not offering job security but good training and external assistance to prepare for the next job. Pfeffer wonders why they are surprised when good people take up the offer and leave.

Summary

This chapter has considered the employment relationship and important related variables. These included the make-or-buy decision in HRM, motivation, commitment and job security. Four somewhat different approaches were considered about what the employment relationship might look like, although these are not mutually exclusive. Kraut and Korman (1999) take the view that individual and organizational interests are no longer totally compatible and should be viewed as separate entities. They do not view this as a hopeless situation, but rather as a reality of organizational life in a global environment. Their views seem to equate to contractual relationship being the norm in the future.

Lepak and Snell (1999) presented a theoretical model of HR architecture that segments employees into four quadrants according to the value and uniqueness of their skills in relation to the 'core processes' of the organization. This suggests different levels of investment in different categories of employees and in some cases there may be no investment in some employees. In this scenario core, employees are viewed as assets to be invested in and protected, while the others are largely of a contractual or alliance nature.

A number of authors (Pfeffer, 2007; Pfeffer and Sutton, 2006; Kling, 1995) present a more inclusive view that employees generally should be considered as assets, while not commenting directly on segmentation architecture. Interestingly, Kling referred even then to the need for high-performance work systems. These authors present a great deal of high-quality empirical evidence that show strong relationships between high-performance work practices and superior organizational and financial performance.

Sutton (2009) claims it is easy for managers to think of themselves and their own problems during difficult times such as we are currently experiencing. What they need to do also is to recognize the influence they have over their employees and the problems they face. He claims that when there is uncertainty and ambiguity workers tend to place greater emphasis on words and gestures (that in fact may have little or no meaning) in an attempt to predict what is likely to happen. His solution is for managers to be aware of their influence and be circumspect in the messages they give out. Being clear and unambiguous about the expectations and direction of the company helps to provide clear direction and lets workers know where they stand. This also gives them some certainty so they can make decisions. Sutton says compassion, understanding, control and predictability should be the watchwords for helping employees cope with difficult and uncertain times.

The final view presented in this chapter is that of a psychological contract between employers and employees whereby a mutuality of interests can be achieved. It is our view that this psychological contract must be underpinned by a certain level of job security to be sustainable, as this stabilizes the relationship and people want a certain amount of stability in this aspect of their lives. When job security is removed, as is common now, the relationship becomes destabilized and the mutuality of interests becomes separated. Under these conditions, the relationship becomes contractual in nature and self-interest on both sides becomes dominant. It is then difficult to see how a collective set of high-performance work practices can achieve the dual objectives of high performance and the protection of a considerable investment in human resources. The final section addresses more specific HR practices that HR specialists and managers may need to adapt or rethink in terms of their applicability in the global environment.

The relationship between strategy and human resources management can be seen in Figure 6.1. This model shows that organizational strategy is adapted to the changing environment and this in turn affects the various human resource activities. To be effective, these processes need to align horizontally across the organization, and vertically with the strategy.

External Environment

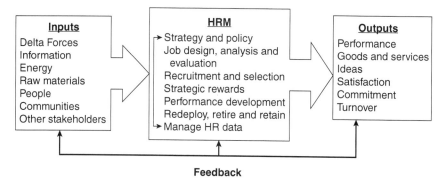

FIGURE 6.1   A strategic human resource management model

Study guide

Review questions

1. Explain how the employment relationship has changed in recent times in terms of motivation, commitment and job security.
2. What are some of the potential disadvantages of the effect of downsizing on a workforce?
3. Explain the meaning of the psychological contract.
4. Explain the meaning of high-performance work systems and work practices.
5. Discuss why employee loyalty is important.
6. Explain the relationship between organizational strategy and human resource management.

Discussion questions

1. Consider the component parts of organizational architecture as discussed by Lepak and Snell (1999) and explain the underlying rationale for this configuration when comparing an airline or large retail store.
2. Many claim that work is performed solely in exchange for monetary rewards. If so, what is the role of the psychological contract in a flexible, modern workforce?
3. Is a high-performance work system approach suitable for all organizations? Discuss the advantages and disadvantages of this approach in different business settings or sectors.
4. Given the mobility of the labour force and the different working arrangements that individuals have; contracts or short term employment, do you think loyalty to organizations is important?
5. Human resource practitioners advise that effective HR strategies help to manage the risk for both the employee and employer, but what does this mean in terms of delivering the organization's strategy?

Case study: Timber Design Pty Ltd

Timber Design is a company located in Fredericton, New Brunswick, on Canada's East Coast. The company specializes in designing and fabricating kit homes made with local timber which is primarily high-quality cedar. Cedar is readily available and is known for its excellent weathering quality. The designs vary in shape and size but most feature steep pitched roofs which are good for heavy snowfall locations, an open downstairs plan which includes living, dining, cooking and bathroom areas, and loft bedrooms.

The company consists of six sections comprising: logging, equipment maintenance, design, fabrication, logistics and administration, totalling 400 permanent employees. Markets include Canada, the United States, several Scandinavian countries as well as Australia and New Zealand. The kit homes are packaged in containers with detailed instructions for erection and shipped by the least-cost method, which is by rail and truck in North America and by sea to overseas locations. Prices range from $50,000. for smaller homes to $150,000. for more elaborate or custom designs, plus shipping costs.

As Timber Design has grown from a small operation serving local markets to its current larger operation, the Board of Directors has asked the senior management team to consider whether parts of its operations could be outsourced to other providers to achieve cost savings and to simplify the organization structure to better focus on core activities.

The executive team consists of the CEO, the finance and administration manager, the operations manager and the manager of human resources. The question facing the team was how to decide what was expendable. The HR manager said that he had recently read an article in an HR publication that suggested a human resource architecture model could be established to evaluate different parts of the organization based on employees' uniqueness and their ability to add value to the organization. What was not considered to be core activity could be outsourced.

Questions

1. List and discuss the components of Timber Design that meet the uniqueness and value criteria.
2. Use the architecture model discussed in this chapter to redesign Timber Design.
3. Is the notion of 'high-performance work practices' an alternative to downsizing?

Consider your current workplace

Strategic planning operates at three levels

Philosophy and vision	Policy development	Process and implementation
new products	A range of policies may	human resource system
low costs	be created: production	job redesign
service to customers	distribution	team development
efficiency	customer service	quality circles
quality	training	evaluative processes
increased morale	safety	
world leader	selection	
innovation	technology	

Identify one policy area which is of current importance to you and draft a policy statement. Remember that your policy should:

- Focus on the specific topic only
- Indicate the principles that should be followed
- Describe any guidelines that should be reflected
- Clearly identify who the policy covers
- Be written in a brief and concise manner

Further reading

Waiganjo, E.W. and Ng'ethe, J.M. (2012) Effect of human resource management practices on psychological contract in organizations. *International Journal of Business and Social Science,* 3(19). Retrieved from http://search.proquest.com/docview/1115580776?accountid=10382.

Williams, P., Khan, M.S. and Naumann, E. (2011) Customer dissatisfaction and defection: The hidden costs of downsizing. *Industrial Marketing Management,* 40(3) (April): 405–413.

Wood, S., Marc, V.V., Croon, M. and Lilian, M.d.M. (2012) Enriched job design, high involvement management and organizational performance: The mediating roles of job satisfaction and well-being. *Human Relations,* 65(4): 419.

7

JOB DESIGN AND FORECASTING

Job analysis versus work analysis

Job analysis is one of HRM's oldest tools, dating back to the 1930s. The role of job analysis has been to underpin other HRM activities and systems by providing a description of the jobs in an organization as a starting point for other HR functions. A job analysis yields a *job description*, which describes the duties and responsibilities of the jobholder, and a *job specification*, which describes the knowledge, skills and abilities that are necessary to perform the job. The job design is the basis by which employee capabilities and skills are assessed, and thus it is an important factor with regard to performance management, increases in rewards or compensation, training and development or taking corrective actions (Katou, 2012). The level of analysis is for a particular job or family of jobs that share similar performance characteristics. Job analysis is an input for the following HR systems:

- human resource planning – where jobs are the basis for predicting future human resource needs;
- recruitment – where job descriptions and specifications are the basis of the recruitment message;
- selection – where job analysis provides the selection criteria;
- performance appraisal – where job analysis provides the criteria for evaluating performance;
- job evaluation – where job analysis provides the basis for ranking and classifying jobs for remuneration purposes.

Because of the multiple purposes they serve, job analyses have been called the building blocks of HRM systems. Basically, job analysis is a procedure for collecting information about jobs. It generally uses one or more of the following methods to collect the data:

- *Observation* – is a method that dates back to the earlier part of the twentieth century, when it was used in time and motion studies and industrial engineering. It is useful for occupations where physical movement is involved, but not for studying knowledge-based occupations.
- *Individual interviews* – are used to collect information from a sample of workers holding the same or similar jobs; usually five or six interviews will yield consensus. The interview schedule probes various aspects of the job and ensures consistency from one interview to the next.
- *Group interviews* – are used for lower-level jobs involving large numbers of jobholders who might be reticent in an individual interview.
- *Structured interviews* – use questionnaires to collect data from a large number of jobholders. They are usually self-administered so that they do not require a skilled job analyst and can be machine scored. The disadvantage is that workers simply respond to what is on the questionnaire and cannot offer opinions or insights about the work.
- *Technical conference* – uses a panel of experts to describe the job and its requirements. These are usually supervisors who may or may not be former jobholders. The perceived weakness is that the conference does not involve the actual jobholders.
- *Diary* – refers to a jobholder keeping a written record of work activities. This has been used to study executive jobs, but has a number of drawbacks, notably the question of accurate recall.

Criticisms of traditional job analysis

Criticisms of job analysis are not new. Some managers and writers on management have criticized job analysis for "putting people in little boxes" and fostering a that's not my job" attitude. Strict adherence to tightly written job descriptions has often been the cause of demarcation disputes in heavily unionized areas. Some of the more serious criticisms are that job analysis:

- has a static focus on existing single jobs
- establishes rigid boundaries
- tends to be task oriented and ignores behavioural considerations
- limits innovation and creativity
- focuses on a person–job fit.

Are these criticisms warranted? The answer is a qualified "it depends on how you do it". There are, in fact, some serious concerns from the above list. As noted previously, job analysis is an old HR tool that came into wide use in an era of big, bureaucratically structured organizations (1940s–1970s). This era was characterized by stability, long tenure in jobs that did not change rapidly, and jobs that were primarily individually based in functional departments.

This contrasts with the environment of the 1980s, 1990s and the 21st century. The environment has increasingly been characterized by continuous, unrelenting change and massive downsizing which has created much flatter organizational structures, a much increased use of teams as a primary method of work organization and a process – versus a functional – orientation. We believe it would be precipitous to abandon the analysis of jobs and work altogether. Clearly, data are still needed for planning and forecasting, and to help workers understand what is required of them. Here again, we need to be cautious about the effects of globalization on 'old economy' companies and the pace at which they will need to change.

Not all companies are going to use teams as the basis for structuring work, particularly in developing countries. Piece-rates are still common in many industries and in some of the most successful companies, such as Lincoln Electric Company, the world's leading manufacturer of arc-welding equipment. Firms whose products require sewing and stitching, such as apparel and footwear, still pay their workers on individual, piece-rate systems. The argument here is not that companies will not have to change, most will, but that traditional methods may need modification rather than elimination.

Work analysis

Some writers argue that job analysis should progress to work analysis. Traditional forms of job analysis concentrated on describing the 'within-job tasks' that a worker would perform, thus establishing the boundaries between jobs and identifying the duties and responsibilities of a single job. This approach tends to ignore the 'between-job' relationships and skills that are critical in team-based work structures characterized by continuously evolving activities and conditions of employment, such as the increasing use of temporary workers.

The factors of change in today's business environment, noted above, suggest a need to consider alternatives to traditional job analysis. The following discussion contrasts traditional factors with emergent ones. Traditional job analysis made a clear-cut distinction between labour and management which focused on job boundaries and job compensation, whereas emergent factors are more concerned with teams, cross-functional responsibilities and collaboration. Job boundaries are less rigid and compensation is more team based in relation to the achievement of performance targets.

In traditional structures jobs were quite static and job requirements were fairly long lived with minimal interaction with co-workers. The focus was on within-job factors in jobs that didn't change much over time. In contrast, emergent factors featured jobs that are dynamic, interactive and encourage and value multi-skilling.

In traditional jobs accountability was to a supervisor and adherence to a prescribed set of job responsibilities. In contrast, emergent factors focus on accountability to the work group, customers and upholding group norms. Supervisors are more concerned with facilitating group work practices, training staff and resolving barriers to group progress. Traditional jobs of the past tended to feature long-term employment and stable conditions sometimes lasting a whole career.

Today's jobs, in part because of a decline in job security, tend towards shorter tenure with workers perhaps holding many jobs in a work lifetime. Does it have to be that way? The example of SAS Institute in Chapter 1 suggests it doesn't. Traditional jobs tended to feature cultural homogeneity with an emphasis on technical aspects of work, whereas today's jobs tend to feature cultural diversity that emphasizes the value of interpersonal skills. This is particularly true of international companies that operate in multiple cultures.

The major contrasts that stand out in the above discussion are the static versus dynamic nature of jobs and the work environment, the disappearance of rigid boundaries within and between work groups and the cross-functional nature of relationships. Therefore, work analysis will need to encompass a broader base of work relationships and configurations than traditional job analysis, that focused on individual jobs in a fairly static environment.

Sanchez (1994) suggests a number of changes to work analysis as follows:

- sources of data
- methods of data collection
- types of data
- level of analysis.

A later study by Lievens et al. (2004) identified that blending information related to the task and competency model improved rater reliability for predicting performance.

Sources of data

The traditional source of data has been the jobholder, referred to as the 'subject matter expert' or SME. The views of individual jobholders or team members should be included in any work analysis as they have a unique perspective from which to view the job or team environment. However, instead of a narrow focus on the individual and tasks, and the increased cross-functional nature of responsibilities and accountability to people other than a direct supervisor, this should be expanded to include other groups or individuals as legitimate sources of information.

These could include internal and external customers, focus groups and mystery shoppers in the case of retail operations. Expert groups of managers or supervisors, whose functions and processes need to interact, are another legitimate source of information for work analysis. This is not a huge adaptation from traditional job analysis, the major difference being the focus on roles rather than tasks, and on types of behaviour needed to facilitate cross-functional relationships.

Methods of data collection

Methods of data collection may not need to vary radically from the methods used for traditional job analysis. Interviews are still a valuable way of collecting work-related data, the biggest drawbacks being the time and expertise required to conduct them properly. The first author of this book has developed a method that helps to overcome the cost and time issues. This method has been used successfully with universities, a national telephone company, a state agriculture department, libraries, various government departments and businesses.

The method involves breaking the organization down into job families, which are groups of jobs with similar performance characteristics. Within a job family structured interviews are conducted with a small sample of jobholders or work teams to collect data. The data are then summarized and given to other jobholders or work teams, who were not interviewed, to validate the findings. This may include groups of supervisors or managers of the jobholders or teams, all of whom can suggest changes or additions. Experience with over 500 such interviews, in dozens of organizations, has shown that as few as five or six interviews can capture the essence of job and team roles in job families that may contain hundreds of jobs, as, for example, in customer service operations. The main difference between this method and traditional job analysis is the focus on teams rather than individuals and on roles and behaviours rather than tasks. The actual methodology is quite similar.

Advanced forms of information and communication technology may also facilitate work analysis. Teleconferencing and online surveys could make it possible to cut down on some of the more expensive and time-consuming face-to-face meetings with SMEs. It is also possible to monitor workers' telephone conversations with customers or record the number of keystrokes made in a data entry job. Although this type of performance monitoring is possible, the ethics are questionable from a privacy standpoint and such detailed monitoring may undermine trusting relationships.

Types of data

In traditional job analysis, the focus has typically been on tasks and the human attributes necessary to perform those tasks. To prevent the rapid obsolescence of job descriptions that result from what Sanchez (1994) refers to as "excessively detailed, molecular job analyses", he suggests the use of broader descriptors of both work behaviours and human attributes.

Cascio (2006) suggests using sets of broadly defined tasks or processes that are more characteristic of today's work assignments. Detailed 'laundry lists' of tasks tend to detract from the broader picture of what needs to be accomplished. Similarly, Klimoski and Jones (1995) recommend broader sets of worker attributes that incorporate strategic and team-oriented aspects of work. This fits fairly well with what Jackson and Schuler (1990) suggest as describing roles rather than simply jobs. A well-publicized example of this is the use made by Disney Corporation of behaviour modelling with its theme park employees to describe their role as actors and their customers as 'guests' to convey the desired message (Cope et al., 2011).

A new term that has entered the management lexicon is 'competency modelling' (Sanchez, 1994). The terms competency and competence are sometimes used to mean the same thing, whereas in fact competence refers to mastery of a skill and competency refers to a personal attribute or human capability (Lievens et al., 2004; Sanchez, 1994). Using this definition, competence refers to the assessment of worker performance in relation to specific tasks whereas competency refers to human capability.

It is this latter, broader definition of competency that is useful for work analysis. We will use the term 'competency profiling' to refer to the skill requirements and capabilities that an organization will require at a future point in time. This is a more strategic, future-oriented use of work analysis that is consistent with the notion of 'emergent strategy' and building organizational capability. For example, if a company outsources a major activity that used to be carried out in house, it may need to acquire capabilities in managing external relations and monitoring suppliers that it did not previously require.

Traditional job analysis most often focused on tasks at the expense of the relationships between groups and individuals and on the static processes, rather than the dynamic activities within a single job (Levine and Baker, 1991). Contemporary work analysis will need to concentrate on data that reflect a broader context, paying special attention to the qualities that fit people to an organization rather than to a specific job.

Level of analysis

Traditional job analysis has focused on tasks and the knowledge, skills and abilities (KSAs) necessary to perform them. Because a great many small (sometimes called molecular) tasks are likely to be required in today's work assignments, it becomes increasingly difficult to keep up with every minor change. It is not certain that this level of detail is useful anyway, given the change in focus from individual jobs to teams and processes. The study of behaviour tends to get lost in an analysis of detailed tasks. However, a behavioural focus is critical in work analysis because it provides information about what is done, how it is done and when it is done. In other words, it focuses on the larger domain of work.

Ideally, work analysis should consider a blend of both behavioural and job-focused criteria when describing work roles. Below are some suggestions for each type.

Person-focused criteria:

- adaptability
- decisiveness
- dependability
- initiative analytical skills
- communication skills
- interpersonal skills
- job knowledge.

Job/performance-focused criteria:

- work planning
- cooperation

- controlling
- organizing
- motivating and developing
- quality of work
- objectives.

Neither type is sufficient in itself. One focuses on the personal attributes that are important in fitting people into roles in the work environment, while the other focuses on the activities that constitute the roles. Any item on either list must be defined within the role context, as these criteria are the basis of performance appraisal at a later stage. The above lists are simply illustrative and may or may not be appropriate for a particular work setting.

This section has argued that job analysis needs to evolve to the broader concept of work analysis to be able to capture the essence of work and work relationships in today's work environment. To do this, HR must challenge traditional assumptions and practices relating to sources of data, methods of data collection, types of data and the level of analysis. We have also challenged the notion that job analysis is dead. Where traditional work arrangements continue to exist, as in individually based work systems, traditional job analysis may still be appropriate. In other cases, job analytic techniques may need to be adapted rather than discarded. Overall, we believe that the term 'work analysis' is more appropriate for today's work environment.

Human resource planning and forecasting

Human resource planning is a process comprising a series of activities. Planning is designed to help an organization evaluate its current stock of human resources and anticipate and prepare for future requirements. Human resource planning (HRP) is responsible for and encompasses many of the topics discussed previously. These include monitoring the forces of change (the Delta forces) to see how changes may affect an organization. For example, an age profile of the workforce may reveal gaps that correspond to predicted shortages in national and international labour markets.

Similarly, HRP has to fit with the corporate strategic planning model being used in an organization. We have discussed the nexus of strategy and structure and the tendency of companies to move towards an emergent model of strategic planning, based on the assumption that the environment is chaotic and unpredictable. In this scenario, planning leans towards building organizational capability to respond to change rather than trying to predict the future. Therefore, if HRP is based on a traditional model, with a long cycle time, it could be seriously out of sync with the requirements of an emergent model approach.

Human resource planning includes job analysis, work analysis, role analysis and competency profiling as tools that provide the starting point for HRP and many other HR practices. If a company has downsized and reorganized around core competencies, teams and processes, it may be inappropriate to use job analysis instead of role or work analysis. These examples illustrate the need for HRP to be integrated into the framework of corporate planning activities and to adapt older methods and acquire new ones as necessary.

HRP is usually portrayed as a five- or six-step process that is broadly defined "as an effort to anticipate future business and environmental demands on an organization, and to provide qualified people to fulfill that business and satisfy those demands" (Cascio, 2006: 177). Figure 7.1 illustrates the interrelated activities that comprise the HRP process.

The HRP process starts with organizational goals and plans, as well as with pertinent environmental factors and the analyses discussed previously as the forces of change. This feeds into an analysis of current human resources, which typically includes a talent inventory and various sub-analyses that complete the picture of current human resources. This is followed by various methods of forecasting human resource needs for the planning period. The gap between current and forecast needs becomes the target for the action plans that follow in the implementation phase. These plans relate to recruitment and selection, training and development to groom replacements, and the transfer, promotion and termination of internal staff. The final step is to evaluate the effectiveness of the process, with a feedback loop to the first step. If necessary, the process is redesigned.

Strategic planning typically takes place at three levels: long range, middle range and short range. Long-range strategic planning is undertaken by top management; it sets the strategic direction of a company and reflects the philosophy, goals and objectives of that company. Middle-range planning involves developing programmes and business plans that operationalize strategic plans for business units and departments.

INPUTS into human resource planning process	ANALYSIS of current human resources	FORECAST of future human resource needs	IMPLEMENT-ATION of the human resource plan	EVALUATION/ REDESIGN of the human resource plan
Organizational goals and objectives; Short- and long-range plans; Labour supply and composition; Economic conditions; Political and legal environment; Social and cultural values and norms	Skill inventories; Current performance levels; Ages; Potential; Salaries; Productivity; The number of workers at various levels, departments, and locations	Objectives for the programme; Budgets for implementing plans; The number of workers required at various levels, departments and locations; Characteristics of required workers; Policies governing selection of future workers	Research to gather necessary data; Identification of replacements; Training and development for 'grooming' replacements; Recruit, select and place from external sources; Transfer, demote, promote, terminate present employees	Cost/benefit analyses; Assessing degree to which objectives are met; Redesign based on changes in inputs, analysis, and forecast with implementation

FIGURE 7.1 A sequential model of the human resource planning process

Short-range planning is concerned with budgeting, programme scheduling, monitoring and controlling the results. The relationship of strategic planning to HRP is discussed as follows:

For each of the types of business planning there is a corresponding type of human resource planning:

- For strategic planning the corresponding activity for HRP is issues analysis. This focuses on plans for the future as well as internal and external labour availability.
- For middle-range business planning the corresponding HRP activity is to do with forecasting demand based on internal staffing, the level of turnover expected and the available projected resources likely to be available.
- Short-range HRP planning is largely to do with recruitment and selection, promotions and transfers, training and development, compensation and the estimated budgets to finance these activities.

It is important for the cycle time of the HRP process to match the cycle time of the strategic planning process. In a globalized environment, cycle times have been reduced dramatically to increase the speed to market for new products and innovations. Product development cycles have primarily driven this process and have become a key competitive strategy for many, if not most, companies. For example, Dell Computer Company reports that it has no product older than 11 months. It follows that the strategic planning cycle has to work within this timeframe. The discussion above shows that HRP also has to fit within the same timeframe. In short, HRP has to operate in the same 'real-time' planning framework as other planning systems.

HRM forecasting

HRM forecasting starts with a consideration of the goals and objectives an organization wants to achieve by a specific point in time. Typically, top management sets goals in terms of profitability, growth, production and service levels. The following points are examples of these:

- to increase profitability by 15 per cent in the following year (profitability);
- to open 20 new retail outlets in the next two years (growth);
- to bottle 20 per cent more cola in the next year (production level);
- to guarantee one-day delivery of all first-class mail within the state by 2015 (service level).

Note that the goals shown in the above examples are expressed in such a way as to provide planners with targets. For example, will there be enough qualified managers to staff 20 new retail outlets in the next two years? This question has implications for training and internal development and recruitment programmes.

How many people will be required to bottle 20 per cent more cola in the following year? How many people will be required to guarantee one-day delivery of all first-class mail by the year 2015? By relating goals to HR requirements, planners can indicate whether such goals are achievable within a given timeframe and whether they are cost efficient. Basically, all plans with human components have to be translated into HR requirements.

Methods of forecasting

There are numerous methods of forecasting, varying from fairly static approaches to quite sophisticated computer modelling. This section will consider several broad approaches, and then look at the internal process of replacement and succession planning. Broadly, the demand for labour derives from the demand for a company's goods and services. If other factors are constant (and they seldom are) increased demand for goods and services leads to increased demand for labour. The inverse of this relationship holds as well; that is, if the demand for goods and services declines, the demand for labour also declines.

Historically, HR forecasts were frequently made for short-, medium- and long-range periods. Short-range forecasts were usually for a period of 6 months to 1 year and covered fairly immediate needs. Medium-term forecasts were of the order of 1 to 5 years, with long-range forecasts being of the order of 6 to 10 years. These timeframes may have been feasible in a stable environment, but they are clearly inappropriate for a globalized environment where an entire industry can change quite dramatically in the space of one or two years. An example is in the world of finance, where banking, stockbroking and insurance have come together in a full-service industry, instead of being distinct and separate activities as previously. Short and intermediate forecasts are more likely to be the norm in future, with continuous updates replacing discrete, fixed periods.

1. Status quo forecasting is a simple approach, which assumes that the current supply and mix of employees is adequate for the forecast period. Planning simply involves replacing employees who are promoted or leave. This approach would only be appropriate in a stable technological environment in the short term, for example, a retail business in an area with little population growth.
2. Rule-of-thumb forecasting methods are based on extrapolating from previous experience. For example, a ten per cent growth trend over several years would be used to estimate the number of employees required for the next year. A similar rule of thumb might indicate that if a company maintains a ratio of one supervisor to 12 production workers, a forecast need for 144 additional production workers would require an additional 12 supervisors. Again, although this approach is fairly common, it is unlikely to be reliable and accurate in a volatile, unstable environment.
3. Unit forecasting is a 'bottom-up' approach to estimating the demand for labour. In its simplest form, it only requires managers to estimate their expected HR requirements for the forecast period. The estimates are totalled and become the overall forecast. This method, which is quite common, has some

obvious weaknesses, but it can be adapted to be quite a useful tool. Line managers should be involved in forecasting, as they are closest to the production environment. However, simply asking people to provide an estimate invites 'padding', the tendency to overestimate requirements to build in a safety factor, e.g. "I know I need two people, but I'll ask for three just to be safe".

A more formal version of this method is to use a structured questionnaire, which is required of each manager participating in the forecast. The advantage of the questionnaire is that it is standardized and asks managers to answer the questions that HRM wants answered, rather than what managers choose to tell. The structured questionnaire also makes it possible to compare results from year to year to reveal how accurate forecasts were and why they may have varied on such items as, say, the use of overtime. Exhibit 7.1 is an example of a unit forecasting questionnaire.

Exhibit 7.1   Unit forecasting questionnaire

1. List any jobs that have changed since the last forecasting period, and any that will change in the next forecasting period.
2. List any jobs that have been added or eliminated in the last forecasting period, and any that will be added or eliminated in the next forecasting period.
3. List the job requirements (skills, knowledge, abilities) for each job listed in 1 and 2 above.
4. List expected vacancies for each job category for the next forecasting period.
5. For each job vacancy, note whether the vacancy can be filled with present employees or whether additional employees will have to be recruited.
6. If the vacancy can be filled with present employees, note whether training will be required. Specify the nature of training needs.
7. What percentages of employees are performing their jobs up to standard?
8. How many employees in the next forecasting period will require training to perform their job satisfactorily?
9. How many employees in the next forecasting period will be absent due to military, disability, educational or other leaves?
10. How much overtime was needed in the last forecasting period and how much will be needed in the next forecasting period?
11. Any other organizational or work environment questions that are pertinent to forecasting demand.

The above example is not too detailed but could easily be expanded to include additional questions that might be pertinent. For example, information might be needed in connection with a change in production methods. Note also the implications for training and overtime.

The unit forecasting method is not itself a complete forecasting approach. Line managers' views should be included because they are closest to the actual work environment, but the internal environment is not the whole picture. It is also necessary to consider the external environment in which a company is operating. Here we need a broader overview of how the forces of change may affect a company, and line managers, by way of experience, education and background, may not be the best people to make those judgments.

The Delphi method is well suited to the task of gaining such an overview. This method is a consensus-seeking activity that relies on the independent judgment of various experts on matters affecting the demand for products or services in the forecast period. This estimate of level of demand then helps to estimate the demand for labour. Delphi has the advantage of combining the expert opinion of people with knowledge of areas likely to affect a company, such as economics, the legal environment, international management and so on.

Delphi is a five-step process that avoids face-to-face meetings. The method proceeds as follows:

- an issue or a problem is identified (in this case forecasting demand);
- a small group of experts is selected;
- independent judgments are obtained from each expert through a questionnaire or structured interview;
- an intermediary or facilitator collects, analyses and feeds back information on the question or issue to each expert;
- steps 3 and 4 are repeated until a reasonable consensus is reached.

Delphi avoids face-to-face contact in order to eliminate factors that can contaminate meetings such as dominant personalities, status differences, hidden agendas and so forth. Delphi has been shown to give quite accurate demand forecasts (Cascio, 2006). The strength of a Delphi is that it provides an external overview of the bigger picture. However, in our view, it is more powerful when combined with unit forecasting. The combination of the two approaches draws on both internal and external expertise to provide a more complete picture than either approach on its own. The combination is also fairly easy to use and is relatively inexpensive. Delphi has been improved recently by advances in ICT, which can provide quick turnaround times and eliminate problems of distance.

Scenarios are another qualitative approach that can provide useful insights for the forecasting process. Scenarios are descriptive scenes that allow planners to consider several factors in combination in order to forecast human resource needs for each set of circumstances.

For example, a scenario might assume environmental conditions for the next three years that would include a recession, the entrance of a new competitor and technological changes that require some modification to the production process.

Another scenario for the same period might assume the entrance of a new competitor, modification to the production system but no recession, and so on. Using this method, forecasts and contingency plans could be developed for each set of scenarios and judgments made as to the likelihood of each scenario occurring. If the Delphi method is used, the results could help in constructing the scenarios.

It is likely, in light of the compressed time cycles in the current global environment, that scenarios will be increasingly used to give a quick reading of the competitive situation facing a company. Again, this method, like the previous two, is relatively easy to use, is inexpensive and can be used in combinations. These methods are, essentially, aids to collective judgment.

Computer simulation is one of the most sophisticated methods of forecasting HR needs. It is basically a mathematical simulation of an organization's policies, processes and human movement through an organization over time. Computer simulations typically include the topics that are included in scenarios, but they can handle additional factors that would be difficult in a scenario approach. Examples include the:

- minimum and maximum number of people in each job
- minimum length of time before promotion can occur
- average rates of recruiting for new employees
- turnover and termination data
- data concerning costs and productivity rates.

Computer simulations can provide infinitely detailed scenarios based on an infinite number of assumptions. Thus, human resource needs can be pinpointed for any combination of organizational and environmental variables. The downside to computer simulations, for many companies, is the level of expertise, cost and time required by this method.

Replacement and succession planning

Replacement and succession planning are internal activities that feed into the planning process. They take the form of internal status reports on the availability and capability of the managerial stock of human resources in an organization. Table 7.1 contrasts the two methods (a team is different).

Replacement planning is basically a static process that is designed to identify the most likely replacement(s) for key managerial positions should the incumbents leave for any reason. In contrast, succession planning is a dynamic process that identifies possible successors, and is also concerned with the identification and future development of a pool of managerial talent within an organization. This includes preparing managers for higher-level assignments as well as future development plans.

Therefore, succession planning has a direct link to management training and career planning for an organization's development of its managerial talent pool.

TABLE 7.1 Contrasts between replacement and succession planning

Variable	Replacement planning	Succession planning
Timeframe	0–12 months	12–36 months
Focus of planning	Vertical lines of succession within units or functions	A pool of candidates with capability for any of several assignments
Development planning	Usually informal, a status report on strengths and weaknesses	Specific plans and goals for the individual
Flexibility	Limited by the structure of the plans, but in practice a great deal of flexibility	Plans conceived as flexible, intended to promote development and thinking about alternatives
Basis of plans	Each manager's best judgment based on observation and experience	Result of inputs and discussion between several managers
Evaluation	Observation of performance on the job over time; demonstrated competence; progress through unit	Multiple evaluations by different managers on different assignments; testing and broadening early in careers. Managers who are initially stretched go farther

This helps the company to focus on the developmental needs of key managerial talent and to plan accordingly. This type of succession planning obviates the need for replacement planning as it effectively encompasses the latter. The error that many companies commit is to assume that simple replacement planning is the same as succession planning. It isn't!

Study guide

Review questions

Identify three reasons why a job analysis is important. Describe six ways the job analysis can be undertaken. What are some of the criticisms of traditional approaches to job analysis?

1. What are some of the limitations of job analysis information in regard to translating this into usable data? Explain the use of the Delphi technique and its benefits for HR forecasting.
2. How does job analysis relate to human resource planning and forecasting?
3. Compare and contrast three ways of undertaking human resource forecasting. Describe three aims of human resource planning.

Discussion questions

1. What is the difference between job analysis and work role analysis? Why might this distinction be important?

2. Compare the different strategies you might take if you were to conduct a job analysis for a policeman, a hotel receptionist and a taxi driver.
3. One of the criticisms of conducting a job analysis is that there are some components of some jobs that cannot be quantified and therefore a job analysis might not be useful. What do you think?
4. Drawing on your own experiences and taking into account the lack of predictability in the external environment, how far into the future should organizations plan for?
5. How relevant and useful are the approaches to job analysis discussed in this chapter when dealing with knowledge workers?
6. Consider that you are the newly appointed manager of a small engineering operation in the southern suburbs of your city. You supervise 23 employees, who are a mixture of blue collar and professional workers. While some members of each group seem to be extremely busy, others do not appear to have sufficient work. You have examined some job descriptions and identified that the job specifications are out of date and do not match descriptions of what employees are actually doing. How would you set about addressing this problem?

Case study: Biometrics Consulting Group

Bruce Bennett is a consultant with Biometrics, a firm that specializes in human resource management applications and solutions. His current assignment is with Automotive Accessories in Johannesburg, South Africa, a company that manufactures rubber and plastic automotive parts such as pedals for brakes and accelerators, windscreen wipers, seals and belts and plastic fittings for interiors. The production process consists of four machine-based production lines which stamp out, cure and finish the various products.

The workers are semi-skilled and can handle most of the processes on a line. Their pay is based on volume and quality produced and on supervisors' assessment of individual performance. Bruce has been called in to assess a problem that management has been concerned with over the last few years: high turnover and complaints about supervisor assessment.

Bruce decided to review a sample of performance assessments from various supervisors to get an idea as to why workers were dissatisfied with their assessments and why turnover was high. The assessment form was a one-page report that rated workers on traits such as:

1. initiative
2. adaptability
3. responsibility
4. productivity

5.   cooperation
6.   communication

Supervisors rated workers on descriptors such as unsatisfactory to excellent and most of the ratings were average or below. The traits used were not defined, so supervisors could not provide any meaningful feedback to workers to justify their ratings. Since this affected their pay, they complained or sometimes quit.

Bruce felt that the solution was to use a form of job or work analysis that linked defined roles and performance criteria to the remuneration system.

Questions

1.   What would be an appropriate form of job/work analysis for Bruce to recommend in his report?
2.   Is the system of pay and performance assessment appropriate for what is essentially a batch production system? Why, or why not?
3.   Briefly describe a more appropriate system based on information in the chapter.

Exercise: Understanding your job, role, responsibilities and outcomes (job analysis) – Guidelines

The purpose of this is to understand the activities, responsibilities and outcomes of your job.

Think of the most important functions you undertake in your job – not everything you do, but the key functions of the job. List in numerical order, e.g.

1.   Supervise 8 staff
2.   Plan and monitor annual budget

Then describe HOW each of these tasks is accomplished. What do you do to complete each aspect of all jobs/tasks? For example, using point 1 above:

1.   Supervise 8 staff:
     a.   ensure availability of job descriptions for each staff member;
     b.   plan with each staff member priority goals and identify performance indicators against each for the provision of feedback;
     c.   spend time with each staff member on a weekly basis to communicate regarding problems, achievements and plans.

What competencies, as in skills and abilities, and experience are necessary to do each component of the task well? How do you know whether each function or part of the job (as described above) has been done well? What performance indicators would be useful? For example, should the performance be evaluated in terms of volume, quality, timeliness or customer or employee satisfaction? Use the following job analysis questionnaire to guide you through this process.

Job description

Consider including:

Job responsibilities and duties

1. List the job title.
2. Department or area title.
3. Title of immediate supervisor.
4. Description of duties (Describe the duties in enough detail to provide a complete and accurate description of the work).
5. Provide a general overall summary of the purpose of your job.
6. What are the major results or outputs of your job?
7. Describe the duties and tasks you perform daily or weekly. Which are the most important?
8. List the instruments, tools, equipment, materials and work aids and how often they are used.
9. How is your work reviewed, checked or verified?
10. Give examples of the types of decision you make in this job.

Reporting relationships

1. Describe the nature and frequency of supervision received.
2. How many employees are directly under your supervision? What are their roles?

TABLE 7.2 Job description

Job title
Job summary
Typical duties in your job.(Use action words)
What are the outcomes expected of your job?
How is success in your job measured?
Physical requirements
Working conditions
Equipment and machines used
Reporting relationships
Qualifications
Job knowledge/skills required
Is there any additional information?

3. What contacts are required with departments or persons other than your immediate department in performing your job? Describe the nature and extent of these contacts.

Working conditions

1. Describe the working conditions present in the location and environment of your work such as cold/heat, noise, fumes, dust, etc. Indicate frequency and degree of exposure.
2. Describe any hazards present in your job.

Job qualifications

1. Describe the kind of previous work experience necessary for satisfactory performance of this job.
2. What kinds of knowledge, skills, and abilities (KSAs) are needed to perform the job?
3. What is the minimal level of education required?
4. Are any special physical skills and/or manual dexterity skills required to perform the job?

Conducting a job analysis

Working in pairs, interview your partner to identify the features of his/her job. As you speak with your partner, record your results on the job analysis questionnaire. When you have finished interviewing each other, write a job description for your partner's job. Show it to him/her to see how closely it matches the real position.

Job analysis questionnaire

A. *Job responsibilities and duties*
Job title

1.   Department title and/or division title

2.   Title of immediate supervisor

3.   Description of duties (describe the duties in enough detail to provide a com-
     plete and accurate description of the work).
a)   Provide a general overall summary of the purpose of your job.
b)   What are the major results or outputs of your job?
c)   Describe the duties and tasks you perform daily or weekly.
d)   Which are the most important?

4.   List any machines, instruments, tools, equipment, materials and work aids used
     in your job. How often do you use them?

5.   Describe the nature and frequency of supervision received.

6.   How is your work reviewed, checked or verified?

7.   Give examples of the types of decisions you make in this job.

B.   *Reporting relationships*
8.   How many employees are directly under your supervision? What are their roles?

9. What contacts are required with departments or persons other than your immediate department in performing your job? Describe the nature and extent of these contacts.

C. *Working conditions*

10. Describe the working conditions present in the location and environment of your work such as cold/heat, noise, fumes, dust, etc. Indicate frequency and degree of exposure.

---

11. Describe any dangers or hazards present in your job.

D. *Job qualifications*

12. Describe the kind of previous work experience necessary for satisfactory performance of this job.

---

13. What kinds of knowledge, skills and abilities (KSAs) are needed to perform the job?

---

14. What is the minimal level of education required?

---

15. Are any special physical skills and/or manual dexterity skills required to perform the job?

16. Are there any special certification, registration, licence or training requirements?

17. Consider how else you might have collected data on this position. How effective do you think these alternative strategies would be.

18. What are some of the limitations of analysing positions through job interviews?

Job description

TABLE 7.3 Job description

Job title
Job summary

Describe the typical job duties - (Use action words)

Physical requirements

Working conditions

Equipment and machines used

Reporting relationships

Qualifications

Job knowledge/skills required

Demand analyses

Your company is a long-established and well-reputed supplier of computer parts. You have a 20 per cent market share, and have 60 staff in the production division, 20 in the administrative division, and a further 15 sales staff.

The company is concerned at the increasing number of new computer part producers from overseas and is also viewing the emerging mini-notebook market with interest. It wishes to consider likely changes to its demand environment.

Complete Table 7.4 below. Show the changes in staffing from the current level, as shown in the first column, if the market share altered by the percentages indicated in the following columns.

TABLE 7.4 Changes in staffing

Staffing	Current	7% drop	2.5% raise
Managing director	1		
Senior managers	3		
Finance	4		
Clerical/Reception	12		
Senior sales consultants	5		
Sales consultants	10		
Engineers	2		
Technical assistants	12		
Assembly line workers	26		
Supervisors	4		
Quality control	7		
Technicians	8		
Robotics expert	1		
Total staffing	95		

Case study: Time for a change

ABC Company manufactures and distributes homeware products and started selling these products directly on line four years ago; however, competition has increased and ABC is now facing a decline in profit margin and market share. Household linens and cotton items, such as sheets and towel sales, which are produced locally, have taken a hit, but no worse than imported tableware and cookery products. ABC's products are of excellent quality, but are 15–30 per cent more expensive than the cheaper imported products they are competing with online. The General Manager has called a meeting of the senior management team to discuss the options; she wants to review the options for downsizing, organizational restructuring, or a strategic refocus and expansion, particularly of the warehousing facility, to increase the distribution network.

Using the information provided in Tables 7.5 and 7.6, identify the issues and strategies which should be considered for each of these three options.

TABLE 7.5 ABC Company staff profile

Total staff:	1645
Senior management	32
Call centre	320
Production	755
Marketing and sales	25
Packaging	150
Warehousing and dispatch	68
Catering	20
Gardeners	10
Clerical support	120
Information technology	14
Research and development	15
Health and safety staff	12
Human resources	25
Maintenance staff	27
Cleaners	30
Security staff	22

TABLE 7.6 Performance measures

	Call centre, packaging and warehousing	Production
Number of workers	508	755
Average worker age	26 years	49 years
Turnover per year	25%	5%
Injuries and sickness – Average hours lost per month	5200	1000
Net profit from sales	$17 million	$16 million
Age of facility	4 years	22 years

Note: the Research and Development team have recently developed a new microfibre product that has the look and feel of linen or a high-quality cotton, but has the durability and ease of use of microfibre. Preliminary market research suggests this innovation has high sales potential and the company estimates it will attract 15–30 per cent of the market for that type of product when it is released into the market next year.

Option 1: Downsizing

1. If you were required to downsize, how would you do this?

2. What issues might arise?

3. What impact might downsizing have on the company?

Option 2: Restructuring

1. What areas could benefit from review and restructuring?

2. Consider likely ways you could change the way the organization functions. How would you achieve these?

3. How could the restructuring process help the company?

4. What issues might arise in the restructuring process?

Option 3: Expansion

What planning and preparation needs to take place? How would this effect staffing?

Demand forecasting

Forecasting staffing patterns usually relies on four methods:

*   Extrapolation – from past experience of trends
*   Projected production or sales information
*   Employee analysis – models the profile of employees, i.e. age skills, training needs, succession
*   Scenario building – speculating on future trends and needs

Questions that need to be answered:

Why are staffing patterns reviewed?
Who manages manpower planning in your organization?
Does this work well? Why?

Which of the following DEMAND factors are affecting your firms staffing needs?	*Which of the following SUPPLY problems is your firm currently experiencing?*
Turnover	Lack of trained internal staff
Changing skills required of workers	Lack of available candidates locally
New markets	High-level skills required
New products	Cost of suitable candidates
New services	Inadequate identification of skills required
Information technology improvements	Lack of forward planning
System developments	Are there others?
Change in sales	
Are there others?	

From your reading in this area, how could manpower planning be improved in your organization?

Further reading

Eggers, K. (2012) Ten ways to lose top performers. *Dow Jones http://it-jobs.fins.com/Articles/SBB0000872396390443991704577579670822064102/Ten-Ways-to-Lose-Top-Performers.*

Lähteenmäki, S. and Laiho, M. (2011) Global HRM and the dilemma of competing stakeholder interests. *Social Responsibility Journal,* 7(2): 166–180.

Wood, S., Van Veldhoven, M., Croon, M. and de Menezes, L.M. (2012) Enriched job design, high involvement management and organizational performance: The mediating roles of job satisfaction and well-being. *Human Relations,* 65: 419–445.

8

RECRUITMENT AND SELECTION

Historically, although HRM and personnel were middle-level functions, they still had responsibility for staffing companies. This reflected the lack of importance that was attached to this critical function between the 1940s and the 1970s.

Essentially, recruitment and selection are the opposite extremes of the same process. It follows, therefore, that the quality of selected applicants can be no better than the quality of the pool of candidates who are presented for the selection process. The purpose and importance of recruitment are reflected in the following points. Recruitment makes it possible for the firm to:

- determine its present and future staff needs in conjunction with HR planning and work/job analysis;
- increase the pool of job applicants at minimum cost;
- increase the success rate of the selection process by reducing the number of obviously under-qualified or over-qualified job applicants;
- reduce the probability that new hires will leave the organization after only a short period of time;
- meet its responsibility for equal opportunity programmes and other social obligations regarding the composition of the workforce;
- evaluate the effectiveness of various techniques and services for sourcing job applicants.

Unlike the previous era, current labour conditions are varied and volatile. Despite the downturn caused by the global financial crisis, there are widespread skill shortages in the developed world. For example, Microsoft expects that Cloud technology-related jobs will grow to 7 million by 2015, and estimates that in 2012 an existing 1.7 million positions related to the technology could not be filled because of insufficient numbers of trained and accredited staff (Microsoft.com,

2012). Before the current financial crisis, many developed countries were struggling to fill professional positions, and even with the current downturn, this is still a problem in areas like health care, education and engineering. In 2008, Australian company Worklife Solutions estimated that 50 per cent of staff turn over every two years, one in four leaves within six months of being recruited, and 70 per cent of companies report turnover has a negative effect (Roth, 2008). Employee turnover, whether voluntary or company initiated, is frequently the result of a poor recruitment/selection match. It is worth considering examples of these costs to illustrate the importance of getting it right.

Merck & Co., a pharmaceutical company, have estimated that the costs associated with turnover are between 150 and 250 per cent of an employee's annual income (Cascio, 2006). It is hard to predict actual costs, but tracking of turnover and pay rates in the United Arab Emirates, where, particularly among expatriates, these must be reported to the Ministry of Labour, estimates turnover at approximately 21 per cent per annum with a base cost of US$2.7 billion (Anon., 2008). On the other hand, retention of staff as in the earlier example of KPMG means their skills are retained. The additional benefit is that it promotes loyalty and commitment among staff, which maintains productivity. Given the significance of these costs, it is worth taking a closer look at them. The following example (Exhibit 8.1) represents the potential cost of a poor selection decision at middle manager level.

Exhibit 8.1   Potential costs of a poor selection decision at middle management level

1. **Costs of initial recruitment**
    * advertising;
    * employment agency/executive search;
    * screening applicants/correspondence;
    * travel expenses to attend interview(s);
    * executive time.
2. **On-the-job costs**
    * induction, learning the ropes;
    * low productivity of function/group managed, due to poor job match;
    * low morale, stress of staff managed;
    * other costs, i.e. absenteeism, disputes, turnover.
3. **Correcting the mistake**
    * buying out remaining contract;
    * severance costs;
    * costs of relocating into an appropriate position;
    * morale of remaining staff.

4. **Replacement recruitment costs**
   - as for (1) above;
   - period of lower productivity/effectiveness while settling in.

Turnover costs can range between 50 and 150 per cent of the annual salary range (Work Life Solutions, 2008). At middle-management level, these costs can amount to A\$75,000 to A\$250,000 per mismatch, or above. Although the costs themselves are highly significant, particularly if they occur quite frequently, the insidious fact is that most companies are not aware of them. Cascio (2006) suggests that companies often fail to take into account that employees who are in a learning period can have reduced productivity. It can take up to six months for managers to settle in and really get to know the ropes, and their productivity deficit can range from 75 per cent at the time of their appointment to a 40 per cent deficit after two months and a 15 per cent deficit after four months. These losses do not appear on financial statements in a form that would highlight the costs.

The discussion of organizational architecture by Lepak and Snell (1999) suggested that companies are moving towards a two-tier workforce, employees in the top tier being the 'core' employees, with extra workers being employed on a temporary or ad hoc basis. The company depends on the effective recruitment, selection and maintenance of core staff as there is already strong competition for people talented enough to be part of the core and this is likely to intensify (Hewlett, 2009). In order to attract and retain core people, firms will need to be seen as high-performance work practice organizations. This means that they have to offer job security, scope for personal and professional development, and above-average compensation.

On the other hand, recruits are recognizing that they need to continuously acquire knowledge and skills and be proactive. A study of recent MBA graduates in the US by Deloitte identified that 95 per cent agreed they needed skills that distinguish them from others (PR Newswire, 2012). To help them gain traction in the jobs market, 100 per cent attended networking events, 69 per cent attended industry or job-specific career fairs, 88 per cent linked into social media groups and 51 per cent into professional business societies; 72 per cent participated in mock interviews.

Another report by Deloitte highlights the difficulty that organizations face; despite the current high levels of unemployment, there is a shortage of talented and skilled workers. For example, there was a shortfall of 3.2 million workers in the US in 2011 (Erickson et al., 2011). They blamed this in part on high turnover rates where employers poach from each other, which in turn drives up the cost of these workers. They cite one company that is paying US\$20,000 per annum more for their engineers than they were six months previously. Further, Deloitte research suggests that only 35 per cent of employees expect to stay with their current employer.

This suggests that employers need to do more to develop and grow skills and talent within their own organizations, which can be a powerful recruitment incentive. Placing a greater focus on the broader attributes identified through work analysis, job role descriptions and competency profiling, rather than the more specific knowledge, skills and abilities derived through job analysis, might be a more productive way for companies. Although a detailed discussion of how the above attributes are measured is beyond the scope of this study, some observations are offered below.

In a review of thousands of validity studies, Schmidt and Hunter (1997) concluded that cognitive ability is the single best predictor of job performance, performance in training programmes, and the acquisition of job-related knowledge for virtually all jobs. There are valid and reliable tests for this, known as 'mental ability tests'. Cascio (2006) cites the meta-analysis findings of the study by Schmidt and Hunter, which illustrates that the predictive accuracy of various tests is in most cases no more than 50 per cent or less. Tests on general ability, work samples, job knowledge, peer ratings and structured employee interviews are about 50 per cent accurate, whereas assessment centre testing, unstructured interviews and biographical details are about 30 per cent accurate and reference checks are rated as 26 per cent accurate, with job experience being an even lower predictor at 18 per cent.

Given the above finding, multiple predictors are preferable to using single measures in the selection process. Some selection devices are discussed below. The purpose of the discussion here, in reference to recruitment, is to illustrate the importance of identifying the attributes that best describe the job role or competency profile to be included in the recruitment message. This helps to better target the recruitment audience and allows for self-elimination of under- and over-qualified applicants; in addition, it helps to create accurate expectations from prospective employees, which is important as part of forming the psychological contract that we discussed in Chapter 6.

Online recruiting

A rapidly expanding and changing aspect of staffing is the accelerated use of online recruiting. Thousands of companies, small and large, are using this medium to access more potential recruits more quickly than ever before. In the United Kingdom, the government site Jobcentre Plus claims it handles 39 per cent of jobs and these, plus another 14 per cent of advertisements, appear on line (M2 Presswire, 2006). Similar services are provided by governments in other countries. Freeman identified in 2000 that nine out of ten UK college leavers used the internet to find their first job, and the number of employers recruiting graduates online had doubled in the preceding year; in the intervening years this has increased. For example, SEEK Limited, an Australian internet employment company, claims its revenue grew 34 to 37 per cent from 2007 to 2008 and the company attracts two-thirds of online advertisements, handling 66 per cent of the Australian job market, with approximately 200,000 jobs posted per month (SEEK, 2008). By January 2013 this had jumped to 14 million visits per month. With 83 per cent capture of the time spent online searching for jobs; the average return on investment was 26 per cent over the past four years and this is expected to average 36 per cent over the next five years (Shadforth, 2013).

Online recruiting is less suitable for locating executive talent as applicants run the risk of being recognized as being in the job market. Many would be recognizable even if their contact details were removed. Furthermore, executives job-hunting on the internet run the risk of sending their CV to their own employer due to the growing trade in the sale and purchase of data among websites.

Some of the problems related to internet recruiting have to do with the relevance and volume of CVs retrieved via the net and an organization's ability to process that information in time to make competitive offers to top candidates. Cascio (2006) also highlights the risk of online résumés being duplicated or stolen, or used by current employers to scan for those seeking work elsewhere. Many HR managers we deal with tell us that the ease of submitting applications means they receive many irrelevant or low-quality applicants; however, the increased numbers also give a bigger pool to choose from.

Companies that use the net for recruiting need to build in screening devices and to adapt their internal processes to the real-time environment of the cyber world. There is very little advantage to be gained from the speed and reach of the internet if the recruitment message is not targeted sufficiently to eliminate under- and over-qualified people or to emphasize the attributes that fit the organizational and job roles on offer. A recent interview with Chirag Nangia, the CEO of Reppify, a San Francisco-based company that helps companies recruit using integrated social media, gives some tips on how to deal with this. Use technology to streamline the process, leverage through internal connections to seek out high calibre employees (Quast, 2012). Nangia acknowledges that gathering data can be very time consuming and it can be difficult to compare candidates because there is so much information. In addition, some available information may be protected by equal opportunity or antidiscrimination legislation and this should not be used. His advice for people wanting to get the best out of social media from the perspective of both the employer and prospective employee is to keep professional profiles up-to-date, engage with communities that reflect your interests so it is obvious to an employer when you have a passion about a topic, and network with other professionals (Quast, 2012).

The other side of the coin is the capacity of companies' internal processes to deal with applications and CVs quickly enough to be first in offering employment to the best candidates. Some companies are putting ability tests on the net for use as a screening device. This practice also avoids the need to go through the same exercise at a later stage in the selection process (Davis, 2000). Other problems relate to the currency of information and the availability of applicants, particularly where online recruiters are trading information among themselves. Finally, companies need to be cautious about the accuracy of information received via the net.

For example, there is still a need for validation of information, such as whether the person taking an online test is in fact the applicant; it is also necessary to check that qualifications and experience are genuine.

A Workspan 2000 report, cited in ILO (2001), suggests that companies recruiting on the net consider the 'FUD factor'– fear, uncertainty and doubt. Possible questions include the following:

- What commercial job boards and Usenets cater to which jobs and candidates?
- Which résumé databases are best?
- What sources are working, and where are the advertising dollars best spent?
- How does one manage arrangements with individual job boards?
- How does one get past the same candidate pool that everyone else is using?
- How can a résumé be processed quickly to avoid bottlenecks?

Selection processes and alternative procedures

Most companies use selection procedures that follow on from recruitment. The process has various steps between initial screening and final placement. Although the process is not standardized among companies, it typically covers the eight steps shown in Figure 8.1.

Certain aspects of the process depicted in Figure 8.1 may be more or less automated, particularly where a company uses online recruitment. Initial screening, an application form and, possibly, employment tests could be done with information obtained on line. Although teleconferencing could replace a face-to-face

Reception of applicants	Verdict	Decision choice
Step 1: Initial screening	No	Reject: Inadequate essential minimum requirements
Yes Go to Step 2: Application form	No	Reject: Unfavourable personal data
Yes Go to Step 3: Preliminary interview	No	Reject: Unfavourable personality factors and/or unfavourable general impression
Yes Go to Step 4: Employment tests	No	Reject: Unfavourable test score
Yes Go to Step 5: Second interview	No	Reject: Unfavourable second impression
Yes Go to Step 6: Reference checks	No	Reject: Unfavourable previous work history
Yes Go to Step 7: Final selection decisions	No	Reject: Unsuitable applicant
Yes Go to Step 8: Medical examination	No	Reject: Medically unfit
Yes PLACEMENT		

FIGURE 8.1 Decision flow in a typical selection process

interview and would be feasible and cost effective for preliminary interviews, most companies insist on interviewing in person for core positions. Despite the low predictive validity of interviews (more about this later), most organizations still see the interview as central to the selection process.

Steps 3, 4, 6 and 8 may even be eliminated for non-core, short-term contract employees. There are two broad approaches to selection that may be used according to the type of employee sought.

The first and most common is the 'hurdle approach'. The steps in the selection process are the hurdles to be cleared: when a hurdle is not cleared the process ends. The hurdle approach is essentially a screening device that would be employed when many candidates are likely to meet the selection criteria and there is a large pool of applicants. This would generally apply to lower-level, lower-skilled jobs.

The second method is the 'comprehensive approach' and it takes all, or most of the applicants through the entire selection process. This approach is used if there are few candidates who meet all the selection criteria and there is a small applicant pool. This would generally apply to higher-level managerial, technical and professional jobs or the core positions in a company. The comprehensive approach serves two important purposes. First, it preserves a sufficiently large applicant pool for the company to choose from a number of people with different strengths and weaknesses. Second, it allows the company to trade off strengths and weaknesses as, for example, accepting less experience than may be desired because of excellent technical and interpersonal skills.

Alternative selection procedures

Selection should encompass many predictors to increase the validity of the process and therefore the likelihood of choosing a candidate who will succeed on the job when appointed. A combination of procedures is generally used to increase the overall accuracy of the process. For example, we know from Figure 8.1 that the interview by itself has fairly low predictive validity. However, used in combination, the interview can be an effective part of the selection process. A list of the commonly used procedures is presented and will be discussed in turn.

1. Application forms
2. Pencil & paper tests; such as Aptitude tests
3. Personality tests
4. Bio data: Such as Education and or Experience
5. Reference reports
6. On-the-job tests
7. Interviews

Application forms

Application forms and interviews are probably the most commonly used selection procedures. The application form obtains basic data and also screens applicants on variables such as education, experience, previous employment and so on. An important requirement of application forms is that they should ask only for information that is valid and fair with respect to the job.

Cascio (2006) identifies some questions that should not be asked:

- any question that might adversely affect the employment of members of groups protected under civil rights law;
- any question that does not relate to the job or that does not concern an occupational qualification;
- any question that might constitute an invasion of privacy, for example, marital status.

Some questions may be asked after appointment. For example, the number of family members would have to be declared for medical insurance. Application blanks may be used to assign different weights to different items. These items can be used to establish cut-off scores for the purpose of screening.

Application blanks give companies a standardized set of data on all applicants, including information they wish to have before making an appointment. This contrasts with a curriculum vitae, which may be highly selective in terms of the information that the applicant wishes to convey. Application forms have followed the trend of computerization, particularly for companies recruiting online. Not only are there electronic formats, but they are also frequently accompanied by a screening test so that applicants can eliminate themselves. These online procedures can speed up processing and cut down quite substantially on the amount of paper that must be handled.

Tests

Before the 1970s, testing was commonly used for selection purposes. After a number of legal rulings that they were either discriminatory or misleading, companies largely abandoned tests with psychometric properties. Tests are once again being used for selection purposes, but more selectively and in combination with other procedures.

The major question in deciding whether a test should be used for selection purposes is the concept of job relatedness. One of the legal issues with the use of psychological tests was not the question of whether they measured something, but whether that something was job-related or might discriminate against protected groups. The validity of the test relates to its adequacy as a measure of the job that will be undertaken. Generally, tests with psychometric properties should be administered and evaluated only by qualified persons, or industrial or organizational psychologists.

Although these tests are still in use, they do not tell the whole story. More recently, there has been a greater emphasis on soft skills and a focus on getting on with others, personal interest and engagement with work. Christian et al. (2011) make the point that engagement is about a state of mind rather than an individual trait, and includes concepts related to the job characteristics model as well as working conditions, leadership that encourages engagement and participation, individual conscientiousness and positive affect. Trust in the relationship has also gained considerable credence as an influential factor for work and team performance (Martinez-Miranda and Pavon, 2012), and building trust starts with the shaping of the psychological contract prior to employment. Another topic that has gained attention in the developed world is the need for work–life balance; however, this should apply in any situation, as is evident from a study of 425 workers in Korea which identified that work–family enrichment had a significant positive effect on work–life satisfaction as well as job performance (Doo et al., 2012).

Reference checks

Reference checks have a mixed track record and a reputation for not being trustworthy. This is based on the belief that applicants would only nominate referees whom they expected to make positive statements. Therefore, there is more than a 'grain of salt' attached to personal references. As the result of several well-publicized lawsuits for slander in the United States, with some huge awards to plaintiffs, companies are reluctant to provide detailed information about former employees. Frequently, they will only provide the dates of employment and indicate whether the person left voluntarily or was asked to leave.

Despite the doubtful reliability of information from some reference sources, it is still necessary to check references as some items on a résumé may be validated through this procedure. Cascio (2006) reports that a study of 2.6 million résumés in the USA identified that 44 per cent exaggerated at least some details, 23 per cent claimed credentials they did not have and 41 per cent claimed to have fictitious degrees. In addition, in countries such as the United States employers can be held liable for negligence if they fail to check closely enough on an employee who subsequently commits a crime while on the job. Subsequently, many large firms such as Citigroup, IBM and Wal-Mart check applicants for criminal records. The following points show the kind of information most often checked:

- inclusive dates of employment in most recent job
- reason for leaving most recent job
- information about prior jobs
- salary and position of most recent job
- professional references
- current supervisor's evaluation (if applicant permits)
- worker's compensation record (if the company will release this).

Employment interviews

The employment interview is a problematic issue for managers and HR professionals and can be a poor predictor of job performance. Then why do we insist on using it? Probably because almost all managers, HR professionals and applicants feel the selection process is not complete without a face-to-face meeting, at least for core employees. The interview can be useful when it is part of a larger set of selection procedures and when it is carried out in a manner that overcomes some of its weaknesses. Some of the disadvantages and remedies are discussed below.

Weaknesses in common interviewing practice

Serial interviews. This is where an applicant goes through a series of one-on-one interviews with managers, HR staff or future workmates. Weaknesses and biases can arise when the different interviewers ask different questions and may focus on different aspects such as personality, job history and so on. This makes a discussion among the interviewers quite difficult, as they may not be talking about the same things. The lack of consistency is seen as a lack of reliability.

Solution. Work from a common script, that is, an interview schedule that asks the same questions in the same order for each candidate. Base the questions on a job or work analysis of the position to be filled to ensure work relatedness. This isn't a straightjacket for interviewers, as behavioural data such as ability to work in a team can be incorporated into the interview schedule and things that are unique to an individual can be followed up at the end of the interview.

A better solution would be to consider using a panel of interviewers rather than serial interviews. The strength of a panel lies mainly in the common understanding of process, the ability to debrief directly after the interview and the capacity to question widely divergent views. As above, the interview questions are derived through job or work analysis. Interviews are most useful for evaluating communication and interpersonal skills and the ability to project oneself in a clear, confident manner in a sometimes stressful situation. These qualities would be required in most managerial positions.

In a recent article in the *Harvard Business Review* Fernández-Hráoz et al. (2009) argued that periods of economic uncertainty and downsizing provide an opportunity for organizations to capture new talent which will aid them during the recovery phase to follow, particularly for senior executives. They recommend companies follow the standard steps of recruiting, which is to assess needs for the future, ensure jobs and roles are defined, identify a pool of suitable candidates, induct new employees into the organization, then review the effectiveness of the process to identify needed changes or streamlining. To check what is happening in practice, these researchers conducted a study of the processes and approaches used to hire senior executives based on information from consultants in relation to approximately 500 companies, and they surveyed 50 CEOs of global organizations.

To their surprise, they found that in practice the organizations relied on subjective rather than objective processes. There was no consensus about which assessment tools or retention strategies being practised were effective. As many as 43 per cent tended to favour work experience as a favourable indicator, whereas only 11 per cent considered their ability or readiness to learn. Half of the respondents said that they relied on their 'gut feel' in the interview process and there was little emphasis on reference checks. On the basis of these findings, they recommend recruiters:

- be as clear as possible about what the company will need for the future;
- be clear about the specific demands and skills needed for the job;
- develop a pool of talent to allow for movement and succession planning;
- carefully assess candidates with high calibre, well trained interviewers;
- specify what the entitlements and expectations are;
- effectively integrate and continue to support the newcomer, regardless of how well they are doing;
- review the process regularly to deal with problems, remove poor performance and recognize and reward high performers.

Study guide

Discussion questions

1. Explain the advantages of having effective recruitment policies and practices.
2. Explain what is meant by a two-tiered workforce. Is this happening in your region and if so, why?
3. Explain the competencies that will be required by a core workforce.
4. Identify two reasons why on-line recruiting may not be suitable for some employees.
5. What is meant by the successive hurdles approach to recruitment? How does this compare to the comprehensive recruitment approach?
6. Explain why it is important to conduct reference checks and describe the risks associated with reference checking.
7. What are some of the problems that can arise when interviewing prospective employees, and what strategies can be used to minimize these risks?
8. Confirm and compare the benefits and risks of two types of pre-employment testing that are used in the selection process.

Case study: Carter Sporting Goods Pty, Ltd

Carter Sporting Goods is a medium to large-size wholesale supplier of a wide range of sports equipment located in Auckland, New Zealand. Carter's major markets are largely in the Asia Pacific region, which includes New Zealand and Australia and most of the ASEAN (South East Asian Nations) Group of trading countries.

The product line is quite large to accommodate the range of sports played in the region, both amateur and professional. It consists of balls, bats, gloves, protective gear such as pads and headwear, shoes and uniforms for the various sports. The range would cover all of the forms of football such as soccer, rugby, Australian rules, together with basketball, netball, cricket, field hockey, athletics, baseball, bowls and some golf equipment.

Carter has decided to create a new senior management position of Regional Relations Manager that is designed to facilitate better working relationships with major suppliers as well as major retail customers. As such, the position will require a high-level knowledge of retail marketing and procurement as well as the ability to travel frequently.

The human resource manager, Chris Chan, has been delegated the responsibility by the CEO to develop appropriate recruitment and selection criteria to begin the search for a suitable pool of candidates. This is a challenging assignment for several reasons. First, the position of regional relations manager has never existed before and needs to combine high-level skills from different disciplines. In addition, there is a need for sensitivity as the position needs to fit comfortably with the positions of marketing manager and logistics manager, which are at the same level and could feel uneasy about the appointment.

Questions

1. List five personal attributes and five professional ones that you would include in the recruitment and selection criteria for this position.
2. What educational qualifications would you require?
3. What recruitment channels would be appropriate to attract candidates to apply for this position?
4. Using information in the chapter, what selection techniques would be appropriate to include in the selection process?
5. Is there an alternative title that would better suit this position?

During the course of discussion about the type of person that might be most appropriate for this type of position, several of Chris's HR team raised some of the following questions with regard to acceptance in the ASEAN region:

1. Explain why a younger person, regardless of how well qualified, might not be accepted in this role.
2. Explain why a woman may or may not be accepted in this role.
3. Explain why a person of Asian descent may or may not be more acceptable in this role.

Discussion question

Given the rapid rise in online recruitment, do you think that online recruitment has the potential to replace conventional recruitment methods? What are the advantages and disadvantages of online recruitment from both the employer's and employee's perspective?

Recruitment and placement exercise

The following job application form and interview schedule are for a clerical position. Please evaluate the job application form and amend it to comply with guidelines in your country. Use the prompts below to help you improve the job application form and develop questions for an interview.

1. Identify questions that are:
   a) not job related
   b) likely to cause selection bias
   c) an invasion of personal privacy
   d) difficult to verify.
2. Identify other questions you might ask of applicants which are *not* listed.

_____

_____

_____

_____

_____

Job Application Form

UNITED HOLY RADIO NETWORK – APPLICATION FOR EMPLOYMENT

Name: _____

Address: _____

_____

(Street)   (City)

Telephone No. (__) _____   Email address:

Gender: Male ☐   Female ☐   Age:: _____

PHOTO

Do you: Own your home: Yes ☐   No ☐   For how long?_____

Rent: Yes ☐   No ☐   For how long?_____

Marital status: Married ☐   Divorced ☐

Never Married   ☐   Widowed   ☐

If married, indicate name of spouse: _____

Citizenship: _____

Indicate languages spoken fluently: _____

List all physical disabilities: _____

Religion: _____

Church membership: _____

How often do you attend Church? _____

List church activities: _____

Do you smoke tobacco?   Yes   No

Do you consume alcoholic beverages?   Yes   No

Military experience: _____ Type of discharge: _____

Personal hobbies: _____

EDUCATION

Final year of school: _____

Date of graduation: _____

Post-school qualifications: _____

Where obtained: _____ Date of graduation: _____

WORK EXPERIENCE

List your three previous employers:

Name of employer _____ Job title: _____

No. of years employed: _____

Reason for leaving: _____

Name of employer: _____:Job title: _____

No. of years: _____

Reason for leaving:_____

Name of employer: _____ Job title: _____

No. of years:_____

Reason for leaving:_____

I certify that all the information which I have given in this application is true, accurate, and complete. I understand that any misstatement or omission of a material fact may be a cause for dismissal.

Date: _____ Signature: _____

The selection interview

Consider the job requirements listed in Table 8.1. Design interview questions that would help to evaluate a candidate's capacity to fulfil these expectations.

TABLE 8.1 Job requirements

Job requirements	*Your selection interview question*
High-level skills in developing organizational policies	
Demonstrated ability to work with others	
Good communication skills	
Demonstrated skills in meeting a customer needs	
Skill in managing a crisis on the assembly line	
Completes administrative tasks efficiently.	

Share your questions with others in your group, and identify the best example. Develop a *situational* question, a *job-knowledge* question and a *willingness* question, which could be asked of applicants for your own position.

**Situational
question:**_____
_____
_____
_____

Job-knowledge
*question:*_____

_____

_____

_____

Willingness
*question:*_____

_____

_____

_____

Further reading

Armitage, A. and Keeble-Ramsay, D. (2009) High performance working – what are the perceptions as a new form of employer–worker relationship? *International Journal of Employment Studies*, 17(1): 57(33).

Barrick, M.R. and Zimmerman, R.D. (2009) Hiring for retention and performance. *Human Resource Management*, March–April, 48(2): 183–206.

Breaugh, J.A. and Starke, M. (2000) Research on employee recruitment: So many studies, so many remaining questions. *Journal of Management*, 26(3): 405–434.

9

PERFORMANCE MANAGEMENT AND PERFORMANCE APPRAISAL

The literature on performance appraisal and performance management is, perhaps, the most extensive in HRM research. It is also the most problematic, with organizations continually adapting, modifying and re-inventing schemes to try and find one that works. The measurement and/or judgment of performance are inevitable in any organization. There are certain decisions which must be made, and which require an assessment of performance, whether on a subjective or objective basis.

Even in the high work performance environment, performance management can be a double-edged sword. On the one hand, involving employees in decisions and giving greater autonomy can motivate, but, as Wood et al. (2012) found in analysing data from the UK's Workplace Employment Relations Survey of 2004, the downside can be that employees feel stressed and anxious, which compromises job satisfaction. So one of the keys to an effective performance management system is to maintain the balance between employee and organizational needs.

In practice, the following decisions are usually based on a perception about performance. Managers have to decide whether an employee:

- should gain permanency after a trial period;
- should be promoted;
- should be given a merit raise in pay or a bonus;
- should be made redundant;
- should receive training and development to facilitate further advancement.

These are all decisions that are personally important to individuals and affect their motivation, self-worth, security and livelihood. It is a truism that a decision can be no better than the quality of the information on which it is based. It follows that if the quality of information about performance is poor, then the decisions made about performance will be poor and will engender resentment, lowered morale and a sense of injustice, all of which are dysfunctional. It also follows that in poorly designed systems or informal systems, where dysfunctional consequences are most likely to occur; there will be no useful feedback to help employees improve their performance, because no useful performance information is generated. This is a classic 'Catch-22' situation!

Because performance appraisal has a long history, most of the theory and practice underpinning it was developed in a period of relative stability, when employees expected long, secure tenure and regular promotion. In this era, the primary means of organizing work was through functional departments with strong boundaries and individual task assignments based on job analysis.

The goals of performance appraisal were mostly related to the individual, and the focus on individuals is still relevant for many organizations. These goals were concerned either with evaluation and judgment or with coaching and developing individuals. Even in companies where teams featured, performance appraisal still focused mainly on individual evaluation. The following points summarize these two types of goals:

Evaluation goals (judgmental)

- validating selection techniques;
- giving feedback so that people know where they stand;
- developing valid data for pay and promotion decisions, and communicating these;
- assessing individual productivity and contribution;
- guiding the managers in discharge and retention decisions and warning subordinates about unsatisfactory performance.

Coaching and developmental goals

- counselling and coaching subordinates so they will improve performance and develop future potential;
- developing commitment to the organization through career opportunities and career planning;
- motivating subordinates through recognition and support;
- strengthening supervisor–subordinate relations;
- diagnosing individual and organizational problems;
- identifying training needs.

Although there were, and still are, many variations of performance system measures, there are three main approaches to performance measurement which are outlined in Figure 9.1

What people are describes the oldest approach to performance evaluation, which was based on personal characteristics (traits) and perceived competencies. Terms like initiative, energy and drive, adaptability, responsibility, leadership and productivity were common on forms known as 'trait rating scales'. Managers and supervisors

What people are	What people achieve	What people do
↓ Characteristics Competencies	↓ Results/outputs	↓ Behaviour/processes
↓ Competencies	↓ MBO	↓ BARS

FIGURE 9.1 Choices in system measures

were required to rate employees on a numeric scale (there are other types) from low to high or on broad descriptors, such as unsatisfactory to excellent. There were a number of problems with this approach.

First, none of the descriptors of the traits were defined, and hence there was no common understanding of what they meant. This resulted in highly subjective reviews which were neither reliable nor valid. Second, because of the subjectivity and lack of descriptors that defined meaning, raters could not provide meaningful feedback to employees to help them improve perceived deficiencies in performance. This made both supervisors and subordinates distrust and basically resent the process.

What people achieve was popularized by the term 'management by objectives' (MBO), coined by Peter Drucker in 1954. MBO is a results-oriented system that measures employees' performance by what they achieve. This system is used extensively with sales representatives, workers on piece-rate systems and others whose output can be measured individually. This includes managers if they have specific goals. A results-oriented system is probably the most objective form of performance measurement where it is appropriate. However, a results-only performance measurement system has a number of potential problems. First, and most important, is that many jobs do not have discrete, measurable outcomes. They have a high level of task interdependency, which means that more than one individual is responsible for an outcome. This is also true for groups and teams.

Second, results-focused performance measurement tends to recognize and reward outcomes at the expense of process. In many cases, the way that a job is done is just as important as the outcome. For instance, after-sales service may be just as important as selling in terms of building and retaining a customer base, but service may be ignored in a system that only rewards sales.

A third potential weakness is that results-focused performance measurement does not always provide useful feedback if results are not good. Processes, which are about how things get done, are better described by behaviours than by results. For these reasons, if a results-based system is to be used, it is wise to build in behavioural measures as well, which is always possible.

What people do refers to performance appraisal systems that are based mainly on behavioural criteria. These are derived through some form of job, work or role analysis that describes and defines desirable behaviours for how work is performed. As such, in its pure form, performance measurement based on behaviour is concerned with processes rather than end results. However, the two concepts are not mutually exclusive and should be combined in an appraisal system where results can be clearly identified and measured. The strength of behavioural measures is that they are defined in sufficient detail to provide a common understanding to both raters and ratees as to what is meant by a measure and what represents poor or good performance. On this basis, feedback can recognize good performance and help to correct inadequacies. In essence, behaviours are anchored by descriptions of behaviour.

For example, the job of a university professor is usually assessed on the criteria of teaching, research, university and community service. One important aspect of teaching is classroom presentation. The following points could be used to evaluate classroom presentation:

- speaks in a clear expressive manner that avoids a dull monotone;
- delivers lectures at a pace students can follow;
- explains complex ideas clearly with appropriate illustrations;
- invites questions and feedback from the audience;
- maintains eye contact with the audience;
- uses attractive audio-visuals to introduce subject matter;
- provides class notes/handouts to supplement lectures.

All the above points are measurable by student evaluations, observation and examination of materials.

Some form of performance measurement is inevitable in all organizations because decisions have to be made that require some judgment about performance. In the absence of a formal system, subjective judgments will be made because there is no common understanding about what constitutes performance. This practice will not only produce unjust and inequitable decisions, but is also wide open to legal challenge. We have discussed three broad approaches to current and past practice. Trait-based systems with undefined criteria have largely disappeared, partly because of their dismal record in courts of law on questions of unfair dismissal and other forms of disciplinary action.

The traditional approach to performance assessment is to use the job analysis as the basis for assessing worker outcomes. Once a task is broken down into its behavioural components of what an individual needs to do, then the assessment evaluates how well each of these components is performed (Banks and May, 1999), either by comparison with others or by rating the outcome on a scale that rates or ranks the level of effectiveness; i.e. whether good performance or poor performance is demonstrated by the person being evaluated, so that they either do not meet, meet or exceed expectations. The appraiser's role is to give feedback to the worker, with the aim of discussing how performance can be improved or rewarded. Rewards can be additional pay, promotion or benefits; penalties can be demotion, or a reduction in pay if a lower level job is allocated, or the person could receive additional training to help them achieve the desired standard.

There are two reasons why performance management systems were often less effective than hoped for. Firstly, because of the focus on the individual through job analysis, traditional performance measurement rarely included broader organizational criteria (Banks and May, 1999). Performance measurement was linked to a downward cascade, where strategic planning decisions at the corporate level flowed down to operating units, sub-units and the individual. The first problem was that performance measurement was usually static rather than dynamic; that is, it captured, at one point in time, a summary of a whole year's work in terms of behaviours and outcomes.

The second issue is that because of their focus on the individual, rather than the organization, performance interviews tend to concentrate on reaching agreement about individual performance and where improvement may be needed (Cascio, 2006), rather than on the overall needs of the organization. This was often exacerbated by strong departmental boundaries, in which departmental goals predominated over organizational goals. The practices of the past are even less effective in the twenty-first century, for the reasons listed below:

- In the past, the environment was stable, jobs were more clearly defined and work practices were often procedural and observable, but this is no longer the case. The business environment is now much more turbulent, skills sets are broader and require multi-tasking.
- Managers had a narrow span of control; this is now much wider and because of interdisciplinary roles managers are often not able to observe or fully understand what their subordinates actually do.
- Large bureaucratic organizations are too slow to respond, so organizations are flatter with devolved decision-making.
- Work arrangements have changed; from individual to team based. In addition, flexible work practices mean an increase in telecommuting, home-based workers, short-term contract workers and/or part-time workers. Contingent workers are less familiar to management and may have little or no commitment to the organization, or even not care about performance improvement (Banks and May, 1999).
- Flatter structures and less job security have also reduced the opportunities for motivating and rewarding performance through a promotions system.

New ways need to be found to realign employees' focus to the factors that produce business success in the new era! Advice from Kondrasuk's (2012) article highlights that the appraisal should be about process; he eloquently sums up what other researchers and our own experiences show. Effective appraisals focus on understanding what is happening, they are not just about holding people accountable. Kondrasuk's (2012) study deconstructed 76 performance appraisal problems and suggests these can be allocated into four categories that can be addressed by jointly clarifying the goals, focusing on both performance and behaviour, involving those being appraised and managing the timing. In addition, leading firms tend to ensure that both tactical and strategic goals are clearly communicated to employees as part of a signalling process about the importance of performance; goals need to be clearly understood, raters need to be trained, staff and managers need to be involved (Biron et al., 2011).

Performance appraisal practices clearly demand a re-think and adaptation of the traditional approaches to performance assessment. The demands on HRM to do this are both challenging and paradoxical. On the one hand, we ask fewer employees to do more with fewer resources, to do it faster and at a higher level of quality. On the other hand, we ask them to accept less job security, to manage their own career and be principally responsible for their own professional development.

One of the main strategies to accomplish this transition is to move from performance measurement to performance management. Performance management includes a broader set of management practices than traditional performance appraisal. It moves from the individual management of an employee's performance over the last year to an approach that connects individual performance with organizational performance.

Performance measurement thus becomes something more than just a personal report card made once or twice a year. Rather, it becomes a continuous dialogue that provides feedback about performance issues, accomplishments and how the individual contributes to organizational goals. Two things differentiate performance management from performance measurement. The focus shifts from static, individual tasks that are measured at fixed points in time, to a continuous assessment of individual employees' roles and how they relate to goal accomplishment. Thus, performance assessment is transformed from a tool of evaluation and review to one that moulds performance through continuous feedback. The job description is still important in that individuals need to know what it is they are expected to do, but feedback on how well they perform can come from anyone who has the opportunity to observe the individual's or group's effectiveness; this can include peers, subordinates, clients and managers. The outcome is still aimed at assisting performance alignment and achievement, but in partnership with the worker, so the aspirations of the individual and the organization are kept in alignment.

The essence of performance management is that it is a broader approach to managing performance in a dynamic environment towards the accomplishment of organizational goals. The idea is to help employees see the connection between their personal performance and organizational success. This concept is an integral part of the notion of 'goal alignment' and MBO. The concept behind those approaches was a cascade effect where strategic goals were translated into more specific operational goals for units, subunits and individuals. This was supposed to connect individuals with the strategic goals of the organization so that they could see the impact of their own behaviours. This generally did not work, for the reasons discussed above.

In this era, organizations were fairly tall and work was largely organized by function. The translation through several levels of hierarchy tended to lose any real meaning for individuals, who could only remotely relate to distant goals. The functional unit in this instance was the more immediate focus. Within the functional unit individuals pursued static tasks, defined through job analysis, that had more immediacy for individuals as this was the basis of their rewards. The lack of frequent feedback also contributed to this disconnectedness, with one or two meetings a year being more like a ritual to be endured, rather than a continuous dialogue focused on performance. The actual goals were very much the same, that is, to connect individual performance with organizational performance in such a way that individuals could understand the impact of their actions.

How does performance management connect individual performance with organizational performance so that individuals can understand the impact of their actions? The following points summarize the discussion:

- organization structures are flatter, bringing the top and bottom much closer together;
- organizational goals are now much more visible to individuals;
- work is organized around interacting processes where the consequences of an individual's actions are more visible;
- work is defined dynamically in terms of processes rather than discrete, static tasks;
- rewards are more of a by-product of effective work than the focus of appraisal;
- managers see performance management as the focal point of their job rather than an administrative add-on that interrupts their work.

Study guide

Review questions

1. Explain the purpose of a performance management system.
2. Explain the difference between performance appraisal and performance management.
3. Identify three different approaches to performance management.
4. Explain the difference between evaluation goals and coaching and development goals.
5. Performance measures can be based on competency, achievement or behaviour; compare and contrast the benefits and disadvantages of each type of measure.
6. Explain the organizational factors that affect performance management.

Case study: A change in performance

XL warehousing holds goods for online sellers and the company has rapidly expanded over the last three years. Growth in the volume of products moved through the warehouse and increased need for storage space had necessitated the move to larger premises on the outskirts of the city. Jack Collins has been employed by the company for the last eight years. He started with the company as a labourer in the dispatch section and now works as a forklift driver. His role includes moving and stacking goods with the forklift for loading and unloading trucks that bring in or take out products; helping to maintain the stores' inventories by keeping accurate records of goods that are moved or dispatched; maintaining equipment that he uses in working order; and other duties as directed. The warehouse employs 12 staff to ensure the efficient day-to-day running of the facility: there is one supervisor, three administrative staff, two forklift drivers and five dispatch packers.

Jack has always believed it is his right to use up his sick leave and so he usually takes one day off a month, but apart from this, he has always been reliable and taken pride in his work. Recently Alan Roberts, the stores foreman, had reason to confront Jack over a number of minor incidents and performance problems. Firstly, there were several complaints from truck drivers about his abrupt and unhelpful manner. Last week, an altercation with another storeman arose when Jack refused to refuel the forklift, saying, "it's not my job". When the other worker remonstrated with him, Jack raised his fist to physically threaten the other man. Roberts had also noted Jack Collins had arrived to work late on a number of other occasions, but the final straw occurred yesterday when Roberts observed Jack Collins was not wearing a safety harness when working on an elevated load. This was against the company's new safety policy. When Roberts spoke to Jack about his lack of attention to safety procedures that were, after all, for his own protection, Jack responded in an aggressive and abusive manner, and said that he didn't need to be told how to do his job and the store foreman should mind his own business and let him get on with it. "If you want the volume through the warehouse, then don't put in place rules that slow the job down!" Jack added.

The supervisor reported the matter to the human resources manager, who filled out a disciplinary notice and issued a 'first warning' notice to Jack Collins, for "insubordination and swearing as well as disobedience in failing to follow the safety procedure". Jack immediately contacted his union steward. The union steward argued that threatening disciplinary action that could lead to dismissal was "harsh and unjust", particularly as Jack Collins had explained to him it was quicker and more effective to get the job done if he wasn't wearing the harness. Collins had a good previous record with the company and that should count for something. Collins wasn't the only one who didn't comply with this policy and other workers who took shortcuts had not been reprimanded. Jack Collins will have the Union's support to pursue an unfair dismissal claim if the company were to proceed in taking any action against him.

Questions

This case raises a number of issues relevant to the role of HR.

1. Identify what you see as the key contributing factors in this case.
2. What are some of the possible organizational factors that could be contributing to this employee's performance problems?
3. What are the 'employee relations' implications of this case?
4. If you were in the position of the HR manager at XL, how would you deal with Jack Collins?

Exercise: Designing a performance appraisal process

For this exercise, you will work in groups of four.

In your groups, select one organization that would benefit from an improved appraisal process.

Design an appraisal system, using the following headings:

1. Identification of performance measures.

2. People to be involved in the design process.

3. How will people be taught about the system?

4. For what purpose will the results be used?

5. How will staff acceptance be gained?

6. Are there likely to be any problems in introducing an appraisal system? How would you solve them?

Developing a training orientation in the workplace

To be successful, the skills learnt in a training programme need to lead to changes in behaviour on the job. The following chart identifies some of the factors that need to be in place for training transfer to occur:

Factors needed to encourage transfer of learning to the workplace

Transfer factor	Problem no	Implementation/ change strategies
Opportunities to practice the skill learnt		
Encouragement of employees to learn/grow		
Encouragement of workers to identify gaps in knowledge or skills		
Encouragement of workers to seek more training		
Encouragement from supervision to apply new skills		
Rewarding employees for learning new skills and demonstrating them in the workplace.		
Providing access to training opportunities		
Integrating training and performance appraisal outcomes.		

1. From your experience, can you add to this list?
2. Identify whether the lack of any of these factors make training transfer difficult in your workplace. Consider how each of these difficulties could be overcome.
3. What types of change would be needed to encourage a stronger acceptance of learning?

Training in the workplace

One challenge facing organizations is to identify how workers can be assisted to learn and grow. This helps the organization increase its profitability, productivity and adaptability.

Companies select training methods on the basis of a number of criteria:

- Cost
- Ease of presentation
- Likely influence of the employee
- Availability of trainers

TABLE 9.1 Training in the workplace

Learning outcome	Best training methods	Suitability issues
First aid techniques		
Performance appraisal rater errors		
Solving mathematical problems		
Conducting performance appraisals		
Introducing new staff to work routines		

While these are all important factors, another issue is whether the training methods suit the desired training outcomes.

A number of methods are available, such as:

- Lecture (with questions)
- Group discussion
- Demonstration
- Video
- Computer package
- On the job training
- Simulations eg case studies, role playing.

Consider the following learning outcomes and identify:

1. the best types of training you might use (there may be several types);
2. how these might work in your own organization.

Further reading

Albrecht, S.L. (2012) The influence of job, team and organizational level resources on employee well-being, engagement, commitment and extra-role performance. *International Journal of Manpower*, 33(7): 840–853.

Appelbaum, S.H., Roy, M. and Gilliland, T. (2011) Globalization of performance appraisals: Theory and applications. *Management Decision*, 49(4): 570–585.

Biron, M., Farndale, E. and Paauwe, J. (2011) Performance management effectiveness: Lessons from world-leading firms. *International Journal of Human Resource Management*, 22(6): 1294–1311.

Farndale, E., Hope-Hailey, V. and Kelliher, C. (2011) High commitment performance management: The roles of justice and trust. *Personnel Review*, 40(1): 5–23.

10

REMUNERATION AND REWARDS

Remuneration is a complex area of HRM that is constantly shifting as business conditions change and companies strive to create a competitive advantage through their remuneration systems. A detailed consideration of the wide variety of alternatives available is beyond the scope of this book, as there are many good resources devoted solely to this subject. We will therefore examine the reasoning behind the different approaches and look at some of the broader alternatives in current practice. We will consider how they complement or undermine the emerging organizational forms in a global environment.

Different types of reward can be grouped as financial or non-financial, and contingent or non-contingent. Non-contingent rewards are attached to the job or position, and do not depend on performance within that job. There is still controversy over which are the best rewards on offer, because different rewards can have greater appeal at different life and career stages. It depends on needs and wants! Nonetheless, a recent study by Zhou et al. (2011) in China reinforces what has long been accepted: money does motivate initially and to a point, but there is a point where this is no longer effective and intrinsic drivers become much more important for both performance and innovation.

As shown in Table 10.1, non-contingent financial rewards have a specific monetary value, whereas non-contingent, non-financial rewards have intrinsic value, such as job security. Both types of reward are important in attracting and retaining people. Both types of non-contingent reward are a permanent cost to the organization.

The contingent rewards shown in Table 10.1 depend on performance and are therefore not a permanent cost to the organization. Contingent financial rewards have a monetary value that is said to be variable and can range from zero to a limit fixed by the scheme and the level of performance. Contingent non-financial rewards generally have some intrinsic value but they could have monetary value in

TABLE 10.1 Types of reward

	Non-contingent	Contingent
Financial	Health care benefits	Merit pay
	Retirement benefits	Incentives/bonuses
	Employee stock ownership	Achievement awards
	Base salary	Promotion
	Child care supplement	Profit sharing (contingent on profitability)
Non-financial	Perquisites	Advancement
	Vacation	Responsibility
	Job security	Challenging work
	Sense of family or belonging	Autonomy
	Titles	Recognition of achievements
		Personal growth
	Permanent cost to the organization	Not permanent, earned every time

the case of promotion. The contingent rewards are described as being 'at risk' because they are only realized when specified levels of performance are achieved.

Lawler and Worley (2006) suggest that there is strong evidence that merit-based pay alone does little to motivate employees. This is because of the comparability across employees and the small changes that are made. On the other hand, bonus systems, stock options and individually priced strategies are far more successful because they put the emphasis on outcomes rather than the jobs people do.

There are various ways of paying for performance. The broadest distinctions among these are between plans that distinguish between individuals, groups and teams and the organization as a whole. Individual plans, such as merit pay and individual incentives, are contingent on individual performance and are generally short term, at risk type plans. They are appropriate where work is individually based, has discrete, measurable outcomes and where the individual has enough control over the factors of production. They are less appropriate where team-based, interdependent outcomes, are the norm. When used in a team setting, individually targeted plans can foster dysfunctional competition and discourage necessary cooperation as employees strive to outdo one another.

Team and unit incentive plans are targeted at interdependent groups of employees who can identify with each other and have common goals and objectives. The incentives are structured so that they can be achieved only through coordination and cooperative effort. Peer pressure can be a powerful means of ensuring that everyone contributes to achieving team targets and thus extra rewards. Again, teams need enough control over the factors of production to achieve positive outcomes. Team and unit incentive plans are useful for distinguishing between performance levels in different parts of the same organization, where a high performing team or unit can be differentially rewarded from a poor one.

Profit sharing, stock ownership and other organization-wide plans have a some-what different purpose. They encourage employees to identify with the organization as a whole and give them a share in the organization's success, which Lawler and Worley (2006) argue is a successful strategy. Well-designed plans that consistently produce positive results for employees can increase commitment and loyalty to an organization over time.

However, the more remote a plan is from individual performance, the less likely it is to affect personal motivation. As noted, different types of plans have different objectives and organization-wide plans can be quite powerful in attracting and keeping top talent. Nor are different plans mutually exclusive. Many companies run multiple plans to achieve multiple objectives, which can have overall synergistic effects.

Features of different plans

How pay and recognition schemes allocate rewards is more or less appropriate to the particular context. Piecework systems are one of the oldest forms of remuneration, stemming from the era of 'scientific management'. Piecework is still appropriate where individual tasks with tangible outputs are the norm. Payment is made close to the time output is completed, usually on a daily or weekly basis. These systems are less common today, but they are still fairly prevalent in industries such as apparel where a significant amount of subcontracting occurs. This is particularly true where supply chains extend into developing countries and become disaggregated into suppliers, subcontractors and private homes.

- Commissions are another traditional form of remuneration, usually associated with sales work. They may be the sole basis of payment, as in insurance, or more generally, a combination of base salary and commission, with the base salary representing a living wage and the commission representing the incentive. As with piece-rates, commissions are largely at risk as they depend on measurable output as the basis for payment.
- Merit pay is an individual plan where past performance is rewarded in future pay. Individuals usually have to requalify periodically to continue to receive the reward, which is over and above the base remuneration, thus placing this portion of pay at risk.
- Divisional or unit pay is a means of differentiating between units in relation to the allocation of rewards. This is appropriate where the performance of one unit is unrelated to that of another unit.
- Bonus schemes differ from profit sharing, gainsharing and company share plans, in that they are generally not permanent ongoing plans and they operate at the discretion of management. They are designed to reward corporate performance and share good results with employees.
- Profit sharing is an ongoing programme that is also designed to spread the benefits of good results by sharing a predetermined portion of profits. It is usually

based on corporate or divisional performance and reflects the organization's capacity to pay. In other words, a predetermined profit has to be achieved in order for profit sharing to occur.

- Gainsharing is not based on a final outcome, but on an agreed measure of productivity that produces savings, which can be shared. Such plans have existed for a long time and they have the advantage of directly rewarding something that employees directly cause to happen. In other words, employees have control, which is not the case with the more remote company-wide plans. Gainsharing has the capacity to work well in developing countries, where improvements in working conditions and wages can be funded by gains in productivity as they occur. This is particularly useful in developing country enterprises that are frequently short of cash to invest in improvements.

Company share schemes frequently operate at two levels. One level is stock options, given to executives at a discounted rate to be exercised at some future date when the stock has appreciated. These can operate as a 'golden handcuff' for top people who realize the greatest rewards by remaining in the company. Ordinary employees are usually allowed to buy stock at a discounted rate through payroll deductions. More recently, a number of internet start-up companies were trying to attract top talent by the allocation of shares as a sign-on bonus in lieu of cash, which in most cases was in short supply. A summary of these different approaches to pay is provided in.

Plan design

There are a number of points to consider before implementing variable pay plans. The most important factors are discussed below.

Plan objectives are concerned with what the plan is designed to accomplish. Too frequently companies implement plans because they are fashionable or because competitors have them; they fail to think about what they wish to achieve with a plan.

Some common objectives are to:

- facilitate the achievement of business objectives
- motivate employees
- attract and retain top talent
- increase competitiveness
- reinforce management/team culture.

Eligibility is concerned with who should participate in the plan. The points to consider include:

- the measurability of each participant's contribution
- the impact of job/role on results
- competitive market practice.

TABLE 10.2 Significant features of each plan type

Piecework	**Bonus**
• Simple to administer	• Reward based on company performance
• Fits single tasks with tangible outputs	• Paid quarterly, six-monthly or annually
• Reward relates to individual performance	• Discretion required on eligibility and amount to be paid
• Paid daily/weekly, or on completion	**Profit share**
Commission	• Payment on six-monthly or annual basis
• Simple to administer	• Eligibility and payment criteria established in advance
• Reward relates to individual or team performance above target	• Reward based on corporate/divisional performance
• Motivates achievement beyond target	• Reflects corporate/divisional teamwork
• Requires flexible target setting to accommodate seasonal fluctuations	• Reward directly related to organization's capacity to pay
• Payment on weekly/monthly basis	**Gainsharing**
Divisional performance pay	• Paid monthly
• Paid six monthly or annually	• Industrial democracy and participative management
• Payment criteria established in advance	• Rewards based on universal measure of group performance
• Paid for business unit performance and teamwork	• Pay linked to capacity to pay
• Pay not affected by performance of unrelated units	**Share scheme**
Merit	• Shares offered as part of reward
• Past performance rewarded	• Offered on discount of 10–20%
• Opportunity to appraise achievements	• Can be used to bind workers to the organization
• Rewards based on individual merit	• As part owner, engenders commitment

Performance criteria are concerned with measures that should:

• relate to important business objectives
• be quantifiable in advance and be measurable
• be consistent with the overall plan direction.

Reward determination is concerned with the reward formula and the extent of discretion to ensure:

• the threshold
• cost effectiveness
• fair reward for achievement.

Reward level should ensure that the:

- level of reward is appropriate at different levels of performance
- performance criteria are linked to reward levels
- mix of reward and fixed pay is fair
- incentive payment is competitive.

Payment methods need to consider:

- cash/non-cash mix
- frequency of payment
- lump sum or regular pay
- deferment strategy – mandatory or voluntary
- separations.

Managers need to think seriously about their choice of incentive plan. They need to be clear about what they hope to accomplish through that plan. If they cannot answer the questions posed above, they probably should not proceed until they can.

Pfeffer (1998a) points out that allocating labour costs is not always straight-forward and there are some common myths that create problems for managers when allocating pay. The first of these is that labour costs include productivity while labour rates do not, so therefore they are not equal. A higher pay rate among a very proficient workforce could lead to lower labour costs through greater productivity. Similarly, a lower-paid workforce that was less productive would mean higher labour costs. Thus, cutting the costs of labour, through seeking reductions in remuneration, employing lower skilled workers or laying off staff, may hamper productivity to a greater extent than the cost savings. Another of Pfeffer's (1998a) points worth mentioning is that employees are motivated to work for money and that money is the way to gain performance. Many studies show this is not the case, and even where money does motivate, it often does so only to a certain point. Of more interest often are the intrinsic benefits that individuals gain from the job. This does not mean money is not important; it is! A number of consulting studies in the US during the past decade consistently show that pay and benefits are important inducements to attract people to jobs; the findings suggest that other benefits such as challenge, growth, promotion and peer-relationships motivate because they engage people in the workplace (Giancola, 2012).

Money helps individuals achieve instrumental goals, such as paying for a home, or for a holiday; these serve the endpoint of quality of life and family needs. If the money can be gained elsewhere it will not engender loyalty and will not improve an individual's desire to stay in a job. Financial incentives can be appropriate, but it depends on how work is organized. Independent work such as sales or piece-rate production that is measurable and does not affect other people or groups may be perfectly appropriate. Where cooperating groups or teams are involved, individual rewards and incentives can be problematic, particularly if workers have the perception that these are not allocated fairly.

Conclusion

This book has explored where HRM has come from, the forces that are shaping a new business environment, the adequacy of current HRM practices and how they may need to be adapted or changed in that altered landscape. Much has been published recently about the changed environment of business, driven by the internet and advances in information and communication technology and, more recently, by the worldwide recession. Technology has transformed organizational structures so that they scarcely resemble structures from the not-too-distant past.

We talk in terms of B2C (business to consumer), B2B (business to business) transactions, virtual teams and businesses, process-based supply chains and so on. These do exist and will increasingly become a reality for many organizations. However, there is a danger that the 'hype' surrounding technology and globalization may outpace reality. Perhaps the majority of companies will make incremental, rather than radical, changes to adjust to the new environment.

The track record of many radical approaches, such as reengineering, delayering, outsourcing and downsizing has not been particularly successful, with firms reporting failure or little improvement more often than success. Indeed, the industry that has probably benefited most has been the management consulting industry.

The companies most affected by radical change in the past, either self-inflicted or forced upon them by the environment, were large companies involved in the global economy. There has been considerable growth in small to medium-sized organizations, and even micro organizations entering into global commerce, and recent figures from the USA Treasury Department suggest that approximately 57 million Americans work for companies engaged in global trade (Brutto, 2009). The reality is that America's global outreach is larger than others as the country still remains the world's largest manufacturer. Nonetheless, although many smaller companies are not directly involved, they feed into global supply chains. The exception is the small to medium-sized businesses in the service sectors. We have followed this caution throughout this chapter, so as to err on the side of contemporary practice rather than radical change, because we believe this is the reality for most businesses and managers.

Several trends are likely to require HRM attention in the near future:

- The Delta forces of change (demographic, economic, legal, technological and attitudinal) are largely outside company control, but they require careful monitoring from HRM because they predict critical skill shortages in the present and future, shorter periods for adjustment and changes in employment relationships. In this sense, globalization is redefining the way business will be conducted in the future even if a business is not directly affected by global trade.

- The trend towards outsourcing all but core activities has major implications for HRM as it is usually accompanied by major restructuring, which has profound effects on those who lose their jobs and those who remain. Socially responsible restructuring has not been a hallmark of this trend, and this in turn has an attitudinal effect on employment relationships.
- The HR practice of planning and forecasting has to adjust to much shorter cycle times to integrate with strategic planning. Strategic planning has moved towards an emergent-capacity building model to fit with a rapidly changing environment. Traditionally, cycle times for HR programmes have been longer term and will have to adjust to shorter timeframes to keep up with strategic planning cycles.
- Recruitment and selection programmes need to adjust their methods to the greater number of applications generated by the internet. At the same time they have to speed up the review process to screen out unwanted applicants and make offers before others do. The use of better and multiple predictors is a major challenge.
- As companies move to flatter, team-based structures, job analysis may need to focus more on work and role analysis to match people to broader roles rather than specific tasks. The focus here is on person–organization fit rather than person–job fit.
- The broader concept of performance management seems more appropriate than the traditional practice of performance appraisal, which has concentrated on the measurement of static tasks rather than the behaviours needed in a team environment. This also demands changes on the part of managers, whose new role requires more feedback and coaching and less control.
- The trend towards individually based incentive systems is inappropriate for team-based work arrangements that need to maximize cooperation and coordination. Developing team-based, unit and organization-wide incentive systems that are appropriate to work arrangements will be a major challenge in this complex field.

Overall, the above trends, and numerous others discussed throughout this book, suggest that managers and HRM professionals will face considerable challenges in adapting their HR practices to the changing circumstances of a business environment increasingly influenced by globalization. We have suggested that continuous adaptation, rather than radical change, will be the most prudent path for the majority of companies to follow. We have also presented considerable evidence that introducing high-performance work practices produces far better bottom-line results than radical restructuring approaches to a changed environment.

International Labour Standards also reflect many of these changes in management practice, and capture many of the best practices on a wide range of topics. Although addressed mainly to governments rather than enterprises, they can still be helpful for human resource managers seeking to understand international legal and attitudinal changes, which influence what constitutes an appropriate business strategy. The texts of ILO Conventions and Recommendations are available through the ILO website (http://www.ilo.org).

It is important to recognize that HRM programmes and processes need to be designed and implemented as an integrated package rather than isolated functions. For the purposes of this book, we have presented the topics in a logical sequence. In reality, HRM practices need to be integrated into larger processes that interact with other processes to achieve the speed and adaptation that are increasingly necessary in a rapidly evolving business environment.

The current global recession has added further complexity to HR's role in an already complex environment. On the one hand, HR has the role of protecting employee well-being, yet at the same time, it also needs to help the organization survive through these turbulent times. An example of this conflict can be seen in the negotiation between General Motors and their unions regarding unsustainable health-care and retirement benefits.

There is a risk that, in troubled times, organizations will sacrifice sound HR practices and programmes to cut costs, at the expense of losing valuable human capital, loyalty, community respect and sustainable competitive advantage. It is our view, shared by many, that you cannot downsize your way to prosperity. A more reasoned approach is to try to preserve human and social capital by looking for ways to reduce costs to sustainable levels through practices such as reduced hours, job sharing and reduced benefits. This will allow organizations to preserve their critical mass until such time as the demand and benefits are restored. It can take years of sound HR practice to build an effective organizational culture. This can be destroyed, almost overnight, by indiscriminate downsizing, which sends a highly negative message to employees and the wider community about your attractiveness as an employer.

Study guide

Review questions

1. Explain the difference between contingent and non-contingent rewards.
2. Explain why companies often use a combination of reward strategies.
3. Compare and contrast a profit-sharing pay scheme and a merit-based scheme.
4. Explain the purpose of a payplan.

Case study: Trouble with new recruits

Peter Harvey and several other software engineers, all of whom had been with Sunwrite Software for over five years, requested a grievance meeting with Dale Fisher, the human resources manager for Sunwrite. The men and women all held master's degrees in software engineering from prestigious universities and were considered to be very solid performers on the job.

Dale Fisher took this grievance complaint seriously as he knew well that well qualified software engineers are hard to come by and equally hard to retain. The average turnover rate in the software industry was known to be somewhere about 20 per cent per annum and engineers with good qualifications were a highly mobile group. Before the meeting, Dale reviewed the latest performance management reviews of each member of the grievance group and all reports were positive and each was considered to be promotable.

Peter Harvey acted as a spokesperson for the group and said the group wanted to discuss wage compression and equity in relation to parity with new recruits, with little on-the-job experience, who were getting about the same remuneration as the more experienced, proven performers.

Dale reflected on the fact that he had recently used substantial sign-on bonuses of around $20,000 in lieu of longer-term contracts to attract the talent Sunwrite needed. He also realized that these sign-on bonuses had not been available to the group that were complaining. Sign-on bonuses had become a fairly common method of recruitment in recent years in the intensively competitive software industry. Dale also realized that the pay secrecy policy he had introduced was not working. His dilemma now was to find a way to rectify the problem with his longer serving, high-performance group while still being competitive in the external recruitment market.

Questions

1. What are some alternatives that Dale Fisher could use to rectify the anomaly between the two groups?
2. Explain how wage compression occurs.
3. Do pay secrecy policies really work? if not, explain why.

Ethics and compensation

Compensation should apply rules, standards and principles that provide guidelines for morally correct behaviour and truthfulness in the remuneration and reward of employees. Many compensation issues contain ethical dilemmas. There are a number listed below.

Working in groups of three, identify and discuss the following in relation to each dilemma:

1. Is there an ethical issue?
2. Can the dilemma be resolved effectively and fairly?
3. How important is the issue?

Some questions you might find useful are:

- Does the action involve intentional deception?
- Does the action purposely benefit one party at the expense of another?
- Is the action fair and just for all concerned? The Golden Rule dictates that we "do unto others as we would have them do unto us".
- Would the manager feel comfortable if the action were made public, or must it remain a secret?
- Are managers justifying the action by telling themselves that they can get away with it or that they won't need to live with the decision's consequences?
- Would the decision-maker recommend the action to other managers or firms?
- Will the action build goodwill and better relationships?

In answering the questions, you also may want to consider three different schools of thought regarding ethical decision-making. The *utilitarian approach* argues that decision outcomes should result in the greatest good for the greatest number of people. The *moral rights approach* holds that decisions should be consistent with fundamental rights and privileges as set forth in the Bill of Rights or some other document such as the United Nations' Declaration on Human Rights. The *justice approach* stresses that decisions should be equitable and follow the distributive justice and fairness principle. Some argue that the ideal decision occurs when it is supported by the ethical standards of all three ethical approaches.

Ethical compensation dilemmas

On the basis of an evaluation of the knowledge, skills and abilities needed to do each of two jobs, XYZ Technology company has determined that jobs A and B are equal. However, there is a scarcity of applicants for job A, whereas there is an oversupply of applicants for job B. Should more money be offered to applicants for job A, or should pay be equal?

Assuming that there is a shortage of experienced receptionists, a five-star hotel hires four receptionists at $30 per hour. Two years later, the labour market has changed and there is an oversupply of receptionists, and the going rate is $25 per hour. Two receptionists have left and need to be replaced. Should the firm pay the two replacement staff the same as the existing two staff? If the firm's position was that wages are paid on supply and demand, should they try to lower the pay of the existing staff?

Yu Chin Lee was given a 6 per cent raise because of his excellent work performance over the past year. His current salary is $60,000 per annum, and other staff doing the same type of work are paid $54,000 per annum. Although Yu Chin's performance the following year is good, his performance is matched by a number of other workers. Should Yu Chin continue to earn more than his colleagues? What do you think would be an appropriate resolution of this dilemma?

Jenny and Mary both work for the same company. Jenny is 28 years of age and the mother of two young children. Her children attend the company childcare centre and Jenny receives a 40 per cent subsidy for childcare from the company to help maintain her in the workforce. Mary is 56 years of age and has asked for increased flexibility in hours so she can provide more elder care to her ageing father. The company's response was that she could take some time off, but she would not be paid for this. Do you agree with the company's decision? How else could this matter be dealt with?

One year, Matthew's performance as a building supervisor is outstanding. He has taken on more work than some of the other supervisors and always brings his construction projects to completion on time, and to a high quality. When he began his employment the company had told Matthew that bonuses of between 5 to 10 per cent would be paid annually. At the end of the year his manager tells Matthew that the company is struggling financially and will not be able to pay his bonus. Is this fair to Matthew? What advice would you give the company about managing Matthew's remuneration?

Chin and Moses work together in a local department store but in different departments. Chin believes that Moses is earning more money than her, even though their roles as sales consultants are the same. Chin complains to her boss and the compensation manager and has asked for a pay increase. Assuming that they are, in fact, being paid the same, what should the compensation manager say? If the company has a policy of not revealing individual employees' pay, how will this affect the compensation manager's response? Should information about pay be transparent?

When Indira was hired, her employer offered to pay the fees for the business degree that she was undertaking at a local university. However, she was told that payment would only be made on the successful completion of each course of study. She was also promised a raise of 5 per cent when she completed her degree, and accepted the job offer on the basis of this understanding. However, this past year, business has been slow and staff were asked to take a pay decrease of 8 per cent, or reduce their hours of work to four days a week. Indira chose to work four days a week to allow her to spend more time on her studies. She has now finished her study and taken the position that has more responsibility. Should the company still reimburse her fees? Should she receive a raise?

Two of the city's larger law firms have decided to merge. Junior lawyers at firm A have enjoyed higher than average pay and benefits, but now that firm A has been purchased by firm B there is talk of a pay cut as junior lawyers at firm B earn 6 per cent less. How should this be dealt with?

Further reading

De Waal, A. (2012) Bonuses don't matter in a high-performance organization. *Compensation & Benefits Review*, 44(3): 145–148.

Pfeffer, J. (1998) Six dangerous myths about pay. *Harvard Business Review*, May–June: 109–119.

Rynes, S.L., Gerhart, B. and Minette, K.A. (2004) The importance of pay in employee motivation: Discrepancies between what people say and what they do. *Human Resource Management*, 43(4): 381–394.

Whitaker, P. (2010) What non-financial rewards are successful motivators? *Strategic HR Review*, 9(1): 43–44.

REFERENCES

ABC (2009) Pacific Brands jobs head overseas. 26 February. http://www.abc.net.au/news/2009-02-26/pacific-brands-jobs-head-overseas/1601536. Accessed 3.1.2013.

Albrecht, S.L. (2012) The influence of job, team and organizational level resources on employee well-being, engagement, commitment and extra-role performance. *International Journal of Manpower*, 33(7): 840–853.

Aljazeera (2012) Spain unemployment hits record levels. http://www.aljazeera.com/news/europe/2012/12/2012124192857939301.html.

Anderlini, J. and Dyer, G. (2009) Downturn causes 20m job losses in China. *Financial Times*. 2 February. http://www.ft.com/cms/s/0/19c25aea-f0f5-11dd-8790-0000779fd2ac.html. Accessed 5.2.2009.

Anderson, D.L., Britt, F.E. and Favre, D.J. (1997) The seven principles of supply chain management. http://www.manufacturing.net/magazine/logistic/archives/1997/scmr/11princ.htm. Accessed 1.3.2001.

Anonymous (2008) Employee turnover remains regional business's invisible enemy, despite the global crisis says management expert. Al Bawaba, London. 13 December.

Anthes, G. (2006) Tapping employee brain power, IBM uses IT to solicit and test employee ideas. *Computer World*, 30 October. Accessed 1.5.2008.

Argyris, C. (1957) Personality and organization. New York: HarperCollins.

Argyris, C. and Schön, D. (1978) Organizational learning: A theory of action perspective. Reading, MA: Addison-Wesley.

Armenakis, A.A. and Harris, S.G. (2002) Crafting a change message to create transformational readiness. *Journal of Organizational Change Management*, 15(2): 169–183.

Armenakis, A.A., Harris, S.G. and Mossholder, K.W. (1993) Creating readiness for organizational change. *Human Relations*, 46(3): 1–23.

Armitage, A. and Keeble-Ramsay, D. (2009) High performance working – what are the perceptions as a new form of employer–worker relationship? *International Journal of Employment Studies*, 17(1): 57(33).

Arshad, A. and Scott-Ladd, B.D. (2008) Factors contributing to organizational learning in the hotel industry in malaysia. Issues on quality of work life: Book of Readings. pp. 191–209. Sintok: Iniveriti Utara Malaysia Press.

Aryee, S., Walumbwa, F.O., Seidu, E.Y. and Otaye, L.E. (2012) Impact of high-performance work systems on individual- and branch-level performance: Test of a multilevel model of intermediate linkages. *Journal of Applied Psychology*, 97(2): 287–300.

Auer, P., Berg, J. and Coulibaly, I. (2005) Is a stable workforce good for productivity? *International Labor Review*, 144(3): 319–343.

Australian Bureau of Statistics (ABS) (2012) Australian Social Trends, September 2012. Catalogue 4102.0. http://www.abs.gov.au/AUSSTATS/abs@.nsf/Lookup/4102.0Main+Features20Sep+2012. Accessed 3.1.2013.

Australian Financial Review (2012) Qantas looking at Emirates tie. 26 July. http://www.afr.com/p/national/qantas_looking_at_emirates_tie_GKZJYgOs7oRkwZIgeI6V QJ. Accessed 19.12.2012.

Badawi, I.M. (2003) Globalization of the B.O.T. System and its Taxation Problems. *Review of Business*, 24(2): 60–64.

Banks, C.G. and May, K.E. (1999) Performance management: The real glue in organizations, in Kraut, A.I. and Korman, A.K. (eds): Evolving practices in human resource management: Responses to a changing world of work, pp. 118–145.

Barnes, A. and Preston, A. (2008) Is Australia a working woman's paradise? On-line opinion 21.4.2008. http://www.onlineopinion.com.au/print.asp?article=7263. Accessed 1.2.2009.

Benjabutr, B. (2012) How world's leading companies manage supply chain? scm-operations.com. 2 December. http://bx.businessweek.com/china-manufacturing/view?url=http%3A%2F%2Fwww.scm-operations.com%2F2012%2F11%2Fsupply-chain-case-study-analysis.html.

Bird, A. (2009) McKinsey conversations with global leaders: Paul Polman of Unilever. *McKinsey Quarterly*. October. http://www.mckinseyquarterly.com/McKinsey_conversations_with_global_leaders_Paul_Polman_of_Unilever_2456.

Biron, M., Farndale, E. and Paauwe, J. (2011) Performance management effectiveness: Lessons from world-leading firms. *International Journal of Human Resource Management*, 22(6): 1294–1311.

Black, J.S. and Gregersen, H.B. (1997) Participative decision-making: An integration of multiple dimensions. *Human Relations*, 50(7): 859–879.

Brutto, D. (2009) Small business, big world. International clients can keep your company buoyant in tough times. 23 March. Forbes com. http://www.forbes.com/2009/03/23/small-business-international-opinions-contributors-trade-markets.html. Accessed 12.1.2013.

Bryant, C. (2012) VW–Porsche merger ends years of wrangles. FT.com, http://www.ft.com/cms/s/0/5baa9682-c69b-11e1-963a-00144feabdc0.html#axzz2GzdnLO4z. Accessed 2.1.2013.

Bureau of Labor Statistics, (2009) Employment situation for January 2009. http://www.bls.gov/schedule/news_release/200902_sched.htm. Accessed 16.2.2009.

Bureau of Labor Statistics (2012) Economic News Release Mass Layoffs. December 21. http://www.bls.gov//news.release/mmls.nr0.htm.

Burnes, B. (2004) Kurt Lewin and complexity theories: back to the future? *Journal of Change Management*, 14(4): 309–317.

Camps, J. and R. Luna-Arocas (2012) A matter of learning: how human resources affect organizational performance. *British Journal of Management*, 23(1): 1–21.

Cascio, W.F. (2006) Managing human resources: Productivity, quality of work life, profits, 7th ed. Boston, MA: McGraw-Hill.

Cascio, W.F. (2009) Sackings do not always deliver profit. *The Age*, 3 February. http://business.theage.com.au/business/sackings-do-not-always-deliver-profit-20090202-7vsg.html. Accessed 16.2.2009.

Casimir, G., Lee, K., and Loon, M. (2012) Knowledge sharing: influences of trust, commitment and cost. *Journal of Knowledge Management*, 16(5): 740–753.

Chan, C. and Scott-Ladd, B.D. (2004) Organisational learning: some considerations for human resource practitioners. *Asia Pacific Journal of Human Resources*, 42(13): 336–347.

Chandler, A. (1962) Strategy and structure: Chapters in the history of the industrial enterprise. Cambridge, MA: MIT Press.

Christian, M.S., Garza, A.S. and Slaughter, J.E. (2011) Work engagement: A quantitative review and test of its relations with task and contextual performance. *Personnel Psychology*, 64(1): 89–136.

CIA Factbook (2012) https://www.cia.gov/library/publications/the-world-factbook/geos/id.html. Accessed 2.1.2013.

CNN Money (2012) 100 Best companies to work for. http://money.cnn.com/magazines/fortune/best-companies/2012/snapshots/38.html. Accessed 3.7.2013.

Combs, J., Liu, Y., Hall, A. and Ketchen, D. (2006) How much do high performance work practices matter? A meta-analysis of their effects on organizational performance. *Personnel Psychology*, 59(3): 501–528.

Cope, R.F., Bass, A.N. and Syrdal, H.A. (2011) Innovative knowledge management at Disney: human capital and queuing solutions for services. *Journal of Service Science*, 4(1): 13–19.

Coupland, D. (1996) Generation X: tales for an accelerated culture. London. GB Abacus

Daft, R.L. (1998) Organization theory and design. Cincinnati, OH: South Western College Publishing.

Daft, R.L. (2007) Organization theory and design, 9th ed. Mason, OH: Thompson-South Western.

Davenport, T.H. (1995) Process innovation: reengineering work through information technology. Boston, MA: Harvard Business School Press.

Davis, R. (2000) New tests help to find the perfect match: graduate recruitment is improving all the time. *The Guardian*, 21 October.

de la Merced, M.J. (2008) Starbucks announces it will close 600 stores. *New York Times*. July 2. http://www.nytimes.com/2008/07/02/business/02sbux.html?_r=0 Accessed 10.1.2013.

Delden, E.Van. (1998) A clear vision: the task of the personnel administrator in the 1960s. *HR Magazine*, 43(3): pp. 161–170.

Dell.Com (2009) http://www1.ap.dell.com/content/topics/topic.aspx/ap/topics/storeinfo/en/deliverytime?c=my&cs=mybsd1&l=en&s=bsd. Accessed 16.02.2009.

Dessler, G. (2008): Human resource management, 11th ed. Upper Saddle River, NJ: Pearson Prentice Hall, 2008.

de Waal, A.A. (2007) The characteristics of a high performance organization. *Business Strategy Series*, 8(3): 179–185.

Doo, H.L., Ji, H.S. and Choi, M. (2012) Work–family interface: effect of enrichment and conflict on job performance of Korean workers. *Journal of Management and Organization*, 18(3): 383–397.

Downie, B. and Coates, M.L. (1994) Traditional and new approaches to human resource management. HRM Project Series. Kingston: IRC Press, Queen's University.

Drucker, P.F. (1968) Frontiers of management. New York: Truman Talley Books, p. 323.

Easterby-Smith, M. and Araujo, L. (1999) Organizational learning: current debates and opportunities, in Easterby-Smith, M., Burgoyne, J. and Araulo, L. (eds): Organizational learning and the learning organization. London: Sage.

Elmuti, D., Grunewald, J. and Abebe, D. (2010) Consequences of outsourcing strategies on employee quality of work life, attitudes, and performance. *Journal of Business Strategies*, 27(2): 177–203.

Entrekin, L. (2000) An exploration of how social performance objectives are achieved in supply chain driven MNCs. ILO Working Paper. Geneva: ILO.

Erickson, R., Schwartz, J. and Ensell, J. (2011) The talent paradox: critical skills, recession and the illusion of plenitude. Deloitte Review. http://www.deloitte.com/view/en_US/us/Insights/Browse-by-Content-Type/deloitte-review/eadd148c49305310VgnVCM1000001a56f00aRCRD.htm. Accessed 8.1.2013.

Ernst and Young (2010) Managing today's global workforce: elevating talent management to improve business. May. Accessed 5.1.2013. http://www.ey.com/Publication/vwLUAssets/Managing_Todays_Global_workforce/$FILE/Managing_Todays_Global_workforce.pdf

Espinosa, A. and Porter, T. (2011) Sustainability, complexity and learning: Insights from complex systems approaches. *The Learning Organization*, 18(1): 54–72.

Fernández-Hráoz, C., Groysberg, B. and Nitin, N. (2009) The definitive guide to recruiting in good times and bad. *Harvard Business Review Digital Edition*, May, pp. 74–84.

Foxnews (2013) US industries ranked by job growth in 2012, at a glance. 4 January. http://www.foxnews.com/us/2013/01/04/us-industries-ranked-by-job-growth-in-2012-at-glance/. Accessed 7.1.2013.

Freeman, M. (2000) When hiring the cream of the crop. *Printing World*, 16 October, p. 47.

Gandolfi, F. and Craig, R.L. (2012) Downsizing is dead; long live the downsizing phenomenon: conceptualizing the phases of cost-cutting. *Journal of Management and Organization*, 18(3): 334–345.

Giancola, F.L. (2012) The uncertain importance of pay. *Compensation and Benefits Review*, 44(1): 50–58.

Gluyas, R. (2009) Pacific Brands admits to backlash over jobs cuts. *The Australian*, 27 August. http://www.news.com.au/business/pacific-brands-admits-to-public-backlash-over-job-cuts/story-e6frfm1i-1225766632676. Accessed 3.1.2013.

Goleman, D. (1998) Guidelines for best practice: How to improve emotional intelligence (excerpt from 'Emotional Intelligence'). *Training & Development*, 52(10): 28–29.

Gore, W.L. and Associates (2012) Our culture. http://www.gore.com/en_xx/aboutus/culture/index.html. Accessed 19.12.2012.

Graduate Careers Australia (2006) Skilling Australia: Addressing the nation's skills shortages. *The Graduate Grapevine*, No. 5, September. http://www.graduatecareers.com.au/content/view/full/2616. Accessed 4.2.2009.

Hackman, J.R. (1987) The design of work teams, in Lorsch, J.W. (ed.), Handbook of organizational behavioral. Englewood Cliffs, NJ: Prentice-Hall, pp. 315–342.

Hackman, J.R. (2009) Why teams don't work. *Harvard Business Review Digital Edition*, May, pp. 99–105.

Hackman, J.R. and Oldham, G.R. (1980) Work redesign. Reading, MA: Addison Wesley.

Hamel, G. and Prahalad, C.K. (1990) The core competence of the corporation. *Harvard Business Review*, May–June, pp. 79–91.

Hammer, M. and Champy, J. (1993) Reengineering the corporation: a manifesto for business revolution. London: Brealey.

Handy, C. (1998) The hungry spirit. London, UK: Random House.

Harcourt, T. (2008) Australian small business is bullish in the china shop. Economists Corner, 4 August. http://www.austrade.gov.au/default.aspx?ArticleID=8424.

Harrison, J.S. and St John, C.H. (2009) Foundations of strategic management, 5th ed. Mason, OH: Cengage.

Herzberg, F., Mausner, F. and Snyderman, B. (1959) The motivation to work, 2nd ed. New York: Wiley.

Hewlett, S.A. (2009) Top talent: Keeping performance up when business is down (Memo to the CEO). Boston, USA: Harvard Business Press Books.

Hofstede, G. (1993) Cultures and organizations: Software of the mind. *Administrative Science Quarterly*, 38(1): 132–134.

Hooper, N. (2008) Interview with Matthew Quinn, CEO, property group, Stockland. http://www.afrboss.com.au/transcripts/transcript_18SEPTEMBER_2008.aspx Accessed 1.5.2009.

HR News (1998) September 1991 in flashback. *HR Magazine* (from the pages of SHRM publications). p. 61.

Humes, M. and Reilly, A.H. (2008) Managing intercultural teams: The eorganization exercise. *Journal of Management Education* (Thousand Oaks), 32(1): 118.

IBM Employee News and Links (2012) http://www.ibmemployee.com/Highlights121215.shtml. Accessed 13.1.2013.

IDC (2012) China to Overtake United States in Smartphone Shipments in 2012, According to IDC. 30 August. http://www.idc.com/getdoc.jsp?containerId=prUS23668012#.UNLQS6xtpBn). Accessed 14.1.2013.

ILO (1982) Termination of Employment Convention (No. 158). http://www.ilo.org/ilolex/english/reportforms/pdf/22e158.pdf. Accessed 1.5.2009.

ILO (1999) ILO and European Baha'i Business Forum: Socially responsible enterprise restructuring, Joint working paper. http://www.ebbf.org/business_human_rights.html. Accessed 1.5.2009.

ILO (2001) World employment report. Workspan Report 2000. http://www.ilo.org/public/english/employment/strat/wer2001.htm. Accessed 1.5.2009.

ILO (2006) 14th Asian regional meeting in South Korea. http://www.ilo.org/public/english/region/asro/bangkok/14arm/index.htm. Accessed 16.5.2009.

ILO (2007) Equality at work: Tackling the challenge. pp. 1–127. http://www.ilo.org/global/About_the_ILO/Media_and_public_information/Press_releases/lang—en/WCMS_101462/index.htm. Accessed 4.2.2009.

ILO (2012a) Global employment trends. Preventing a deeper jobs crisis. http://www.ilo.org/wcmsp5/groups/public/@dgreports/@dcomm/@publ/documents/publication/wcms_171571.pdf. Accessed 1.1.2013.

ILO (2012b) Gender pay gap drops, but not for the right reasons: Global Wage Report 2012/13. http://www.ilo.org/global/about-the-ilo/newsroom/news/WCMS_192901/lang—en/index.htm.

Jackson, S.E. and Schuler, R.S. (1990) Human resource planning: challenges for I/O psychologists. *American Psychologist*, 45: 223–239.

Jacobsen, J. (2008) Teamwork makes the difference. *The Journal for Quality and Participation*, 31(3): 30–38.

Johnson, G. and Scholes, K. (1997) Exploring corporate strategy. 4th Ed. Europe, London: Prentice-Hall.

Junco, R. and Mastrodicasa, J. (2007) Connecting to the net. Generation: What higher education professionals need to know about today's college students. NASPA.

Kampstra, R.P., Ashayeri, J. and Gattorna, J.L. (2006) Realities of supply chain collaboration. *International Journal of Logistics Management*, 17(3): 312–330.

Katou, A.A. (2012) Investigating reverse causality between human resource management policies and organizational performance in small firms. *Management Research Review*, 35(2): 134–156.

Keane, A.G. (2012) U.S. postal service to cut 35,000 jobs as plants are shut. Bloomberg, 20 February. http://www.bloomberg.com/news/2012-02-23/u-s-postal-service-to-cut-4-9-of-jobs-by-closing-almost-half-of-plants.html. Accessed 7.1.2013.

Klimoski, R. and Jones, R.G. (1995) Staffing for effective group decision making: key issues in matching people and teams, in Guzzo, R.A., Salas, E. et al. (eds): Team effectiveness and decision making in organizations. San Francisco, CA: Jossey-Bass, pp. 330–380.

Kling, J. (1995) High performance work systems and firm performance. *Monthly Labor Review*, May.

Kochan, T. (2006) Taking the High Road. *MIT Sloan Management Review*, 47(4): 16–19.

Kondrasuk, J.N. (2012) The ideal performance appraisal is a format, not a form. *Academy of Strategic Management Journal*, 11(1): 115–130.

Kotter, J.P. (1995) Leading change: Why transformation efforts fail. *Harvard Business Review*, 73(2): 59–67.

Kotter, J.P. and Cohen, D.S. (2002) Creative ways to empower action to change the organization: Cases in point. *Journal of Organizational Excellence*, 22(1): 73. ABI/INFORM Global.

Kotter, J.P. and Schlesinger, L.A. (2008) Choosing strategies for change. *Harvard Business Review*, 86(7, 8): 130–142.

Kraut, A.I. and Korman, A.K. (Eds), (1999) Evolving practices in human resource management: Responses to a changing world of work. San Francisco, CA: Jossey-Bass.

Kubler-Ross, E. (1993) Questions and answers on death and dying. Maxwell Macmillan International.

Kumar, Cdr, N. (2012) Relationship of personal and organizational values with job satisfaction. *Journal of Management Research*, 12(2): 75–82.

Latham, G.P., Winters, D.C. and Locke, E.A. (1994) Cognitive and motivational effects of participation: A mediator study. *Journal of Organizational Behaviour*, 1(15): 49–63.

Lawler III, E.E. and Worley, C.G. (2006) Winning support for organizational change: Designing employee reward systems that keep on working. Ivey Business Journal Online. pp. 1–5.

Lengnick-Hall, M.L., Lengnick-Hall, C.A., Andrade, L.S. and Drake, B. (2009) Strategic human resource management: The evolution of the field. *Human Resource Management Review*, 19(2): 64–85.

Lepak, D.P. and Snell S.A. (1999) The human resource architecture: Toward a theory of human capital allocation and development. *Academy of Management Review*, 24: 31–48.

Levine, E.L. and Baker, C.V. (1991) Team task analysis: a procedural guide and test of the methodology. Paper presented at the Sixth Annual Conference of the Society for Industrial and Organizational Psychology, St Louis, Missouri, April.

Levitt, B. and March, J. (1988) Organizational learning. *Annual Review of Sociology*, 14: 319–340.

Levy, S.M. (1996) Build, operate, transfer: Paving the way for tomorrow's infrastructure. New York: John Wiley & Sons.

Lewin, K. (1952) Frontiers in group dynamics, in Cartwright, D. (ed.): Field theory in social science. London, UK: Social Science Paperbacks.

Lievens, F., Sanchez, J.I. and De Corte, W. (2004) Easing the inferential leap in competency modelling: the effects of task related information and subject matter expertise. *Personnel Psychology*, 57(4): 881–904.

Life Work Solutions (2008) Beware of the Hidden Costs of Turnover. http://www.lifeworksolutions.com.au/news/beware-of-the-hidden-costs-of-turnover/. Accessed 9.9.2009.

Linke, A. and Zerfass, A. (2011) Internal communication and innovation culture: developing a change framework. *Journal of Communication Management*, 15(4): 332–348.

Liuibic, R.J. (1998) Corporate codes of conduct and product labelling schemes: the limits and possibilities of promoting international labor rights through private initiatives. *Law and Policy in International Business*, 30: 112–158.

Losey, M. (1998) HR comes of age. *HR Magazine*, 43(3): 40–53.

Lublin, J.S. and Karp, H. (2011) Avon replacing Andrea Jung as CEO. *The Wall Street Journal Asia edition*, 14 December. http://online.wsj.com/article/SB10001424052970203518404 577096901465046874.html. Accessed 5.1.2013.

M2 Presswire (2006) UK Government: one in four businesses looking to hire; Jobcentre Plus employer survey reveals buoyancy in recruitment market. Coventry, 24 August. p. 1. Accessed 27.2.2009.

McGregor, D. (1960) The human side of enterprise. New York: McGraw Hill.

McIntyre, D.A. (2012) Ten Brands that will disappear in 2013. *Fox Business*, 21 June. http://www.foxbusiness.com/industries/2012/06/21/ten-brands-that-will-disappear-in-2013/. Accessed 31.12.2012.

Markels, A. (2006) Turning the tide at P&G. *US News*. Posted 10/22/06. http://www.usnews.com/usnews/news/articles/061022/30lafley.htm. Accessed 4.1.2013.

Martin, A. (2012) Avon Chairwoman to quit earlier than expected. *New York Times* on-line. http://www.nytimes.com/2012/. Accessed 31.12.2012.

Martinez-Miranda, J. and Pavon, J. (2012) Modeling the influence of trust on work team performance. *Simulation*, 88(4): 408–436.

Messersmith, J.G. and Guthrie, J.P. (2010) High-performance work systems in urgent organizations: Implications for firm performance. *Human Resource Management*, 49(2): 241–264.

Metz, P.J. (1998) Demystifying supply chain management. *Supply Chain Management Review*, Winter. http://www.manufacturing.net/scl/scmr/archives/1998/04.myst.htm.

Microsoft.com (2012) Technology analysts predict widening cloud skills gap for IT. 19 December. http://www.microsoft.com/en-us/news/Press/2012/Dec12/12-19Cloud SkillsPR.aspx. Accessed 10.1.2013.

Milmo, D. (2011) Royal mail inundated with Christmas job applications. *The Guardian* (London), 29 October. http://www.guardian.co.uk/uk/2011/oct/29/royal-mail-job-applications-christmas. Accessed 2.1.2013.

Milne, R. and Saigol, L. (2008) Hedge funds take a pounding as Porsche drives for control of VW. *Financial Times* (London), 28 October, p. 1. Accessed 29.10.2008.

Muller, J. (2012) Leadership, not another bailout, will fix GM (and no, it is not going bankrupt). *Forbes*. http://www.forbes.com/sites/joannmuller/2012/08/16/leadership-not-another-bailout-will-fix-general-motors/. Accessed 4.1.2013.

NBC (2013) Fiscal cliff compromise leaves few satisfied. NBC Politics. http://nbcpolitics. nbcnews.com/_news/2013/01/02/16298460-fiscal-cliff-compromise-leaves-few-satisfied?lite. Accessed 7.1.2013.

Odlyzko, A. (2008) Threats to the internet: Too much or too little growth? *Internet Evolution*, 25 February. http://www.internetevolution.com/author.asp?doc_id=146747&section_id=592. Accessed 12.5.2009.

OECD (2000) Codes of corporate conduct: an expanded review of their contents. Working Party of the Trade Committee, TD/TC/WP (99) 56/FINAL, June.

OECD (2012) Trends in retirement and in working at older ages. http://www.oecd-ilibrary. org/docserver/download/8111011ec006.pdf?expires=1357100667&id=id&accname=guest &checksum=6050CE035C19E07CDDD27A9FE45E7BA3. Accessed 1.1.2012.

Office for National Statistics (2012) Population ageing in the United Kingdom, its constituent countries and the European Union. 2. March 2012. http://www.ons.gov.uk/ons/ dcp171776_258607.pdf. Accessed 7.1.2013.

Oman, C. (1999) Globalization and regionalization: The challenge for developing countries. Paris: OECD Development Center.

O'Toole, J. and Bennis, W. (2009) What's needed next – a culture of candor. *Harvard Business Review Digital Edition*, June, pp. 54–61.

Palpacuer, F. (1997) Development of core–periphery forms of organization: some lessons from the New York garment industry. Geneva: ILO, International Institute for Labor Studies.

Pasmore, W.A. (1995) Social science transformed: the social-technical perspective. *Human Relations*, 48: 1–21.

Patel, P.C. and Conklin, B. (2010) Perceived labor productivity in small firms – the effects of high-performance work systems and group culture through employee retention. *Entrepreneurship Theory and Practice*, March, pp. 1042–2587.

Pearson, C.A.L., Entrekin, L.V. and Safina, T.H. (2004) Managerial and organizational trends in a BOT treatment: a study in the Indonesian telecommunications sector. *Global Business Review*, 5(1): 97–111.

Pesqueux, Y. (2012) Social contract and psychological contract: a comparison. *Society and Business Review*, 7(1): 14–33.

Pfeffer, J. (1998a) Six dangerous myths about pay. *Harvard Business Review*, May–June, pp. 109–119.

Pfeffer, J. (1998b) The human equation: building profits by putting people first. Cambridge, MA: Harvard Business School Press.

Pfeffer, J. (2007) Human resources from an organizational behavior perspective: Some paradoxes explained. *Journal of Economic Perspectives*, 21(4): 115–134.

Pfeffer, J. and Sutton, R.I. (2006) Evidence based management. *Harvard Business Review*, 84(1): 62–74.

Piper, C.J., McLachlin, R. and Osborne, W. (2003) Blount Canada Ltd – Continuous improvement. Richard Ivey School of Business Case Collection. London: 24 January, pp. 1–10.

Popper, M. and Lipshitz, R. (2000) Organizational learning: mechanisms, culture, and feasibility. *Management Learning*, 31(2): 181–196.

Porter, M. (1980) Competitive Strategy. USA New York: The Free Press.

PR Newswire (2007) New analysis sees men failing to reach income levels of previous generation. New York, 25 May. Accessed 1.5.2009.

PR Newswire (2012) MBA students, employers find innovative ways to stand out in a tight job market: Deloitte poll. 24 October. http://www.prnewswire.com/news-releases/mba-students-employers-find-innovative-ways-to-stand-out-in-a-tight-job-market-deloitte-poll-175615761.html. Accessed 7.1.2013.

Prensky, M. (2006) Don't bother me mom – I'm learning! St Paul, MN: Paragon House.

Quast, L. (2012) Recruiting, reinvented: how companies are using social media in the hiring process. *Forbes*, 21 May. http://www.forbes.com/sites/lisaquast/2012/05/21/recruiting-reinvented-how-companies-are-using-social-media-in-the-hiring-process/. Accessed 20.1.2013.

Quinn, J.B. and Hilmer, F.G. (1994) Strategic outsourcing. *Sloan Management Review*, 35(4): 43–55.

Rampell, C. (2009) Layoffs spread to more sectors of the economy. *The New York Times*, 26 January. http://www.nytimes.com/2009/01/27/business/economy/27layoffs.htmlthe New York Times. Accessed 5.2.2009.

Razi, N. and More, E. (2012) Employee firm-specific knowledge and the acquisition of a high-performance work system organisation. *Accounting, Accountability & Performance*, 17(1): 79–93.

Ready, D. (2009) Forging the new talent compact. *Business Strategy Review*, 20(2): 4–7.

Rigby, D., Gruver, K. and Allen, J. (2009) Innovation in turbulent times. *Harvard Business Review Digital Edition*, pp. 79–86.

Right Vision News (Lahore) (2012) Pakistan: FDE inundated with job applications. 7 October. http://search.proquest.com/docview/1086969058?accountid=10382. Accessed 18.12.2012.

Robinson, G. (2009) Unions to block Pacific Brands offshore move. 27 February. http://www.smh.com.au/business/unions-to-block-pacific-brands-offshore-move-20090227-8jih.html. Accessed 3.1.2013.

Rogovsky, N. and Sims, E. (2002) Corporate success through people: Making international labour standards work for you. Geneva. Switzerland: ILO.

Roth, H. (2008) Interesting facts regarding staff turnover. *Lifework Solutions*. 1 February. http://www.lifeworksolutions.com.au/news/staff-turnover-facts/. Accessed 8.9.2009.

Rousseau, D.M. (1995) Psychological contracts in organizations: understanding written and unwritten agreements. Thousand Oaks, CA: Sage.

Sanburn, J. (2011) 5 Reasons borders went out of business (and what will take its place). *Time Business and Money*. http://business.time.com/2011/07/19/5-reasons-borders-went-out-of-business-and-what-will-take-its-place/. Accessed 2.1.2013.

Sanchez, J.I. (1994) From documentation to innovation: reshaping job analysis to meet emerging business needs. *Human Resource Management Review*, 4: 51–74.

Sanger Institute (2013) MalariaGEN – Malaria Genome Epidemiology Network. http://www.sanger.ac.uk/research/initiatives/globalhealth/partnerships/malariagen.html. Accessed 12.1.2013.

SBS World News (2009) Pacific faces mounting anger from unions. 27 Feb. http://www.sbs.com.au/news/article/1009910/Pacific-faces-mounting-anger-from-unions. Accessed 21.12.2012.

Schein, E.H. (1986) Organizational culture and leadership. San Francisco: Jossey-Bass.

Schmidt, F.L. and Hunter, J.E. (1997) The validity and utility of selection methods in personnel psychology: Implications of eighty-five years of research findings. Unpublished paper. Iowa City: University of Iowa.

Scott, C.D. and Jaffe, D.T. (1989) Managing organizational change. A practical guide for managers. Menlo Park, CA: Crisp Publications.

SEEK Limited (2008) Corporate summary 2008. http://www.seek.com.au/investor/keyfacts.ascx. Accessed 27.2.2009.

Senge, P.M. (1992) The Fifth discipline – the art and practice of the learning organization, 2nd ed. London: Century Business.

Shadforth Financial Group (2013) A closer look at Seek Holdings. 12 November. http://www.sfg.com.au/Knowledge-center/News/Articles/November-2012/seek.aspx. Accessed 20.1.2013.

Smith, J. (2009) Expert expects more job losses in 2009. Metro Canada, 16 February. http://www.metronews.ca/ottawa/local/article/182569. Accessed 16.2.2009.

Spector, B. (2007) Implementing organizational change: theory and practice. Upper Saddle River, NJ: Pearson Prentice Hall.

Standing, G. (2009) Work after globalization: Building occupational citizenship. Cheltenham, UK: Edward Elgar.

Stefanescu, L. and Stefanescu, A. (2008) Need of knowledge management strategy for the successful implementation of reengineering projects. MPRA, Munich Personal RePEc Archive. http://mpra.ub.uni-muenchen.de/7794/1/MPRA_paper_7794.pdf. Accessed 18.5.09.

Styhre, A. (2002) Non-linear change in organizations: organization change management informed by complexity theory. *Leadership and Organization Development Journal*, 23(5/6): 343–351.

Sutton, R.I. (2009) How to be a good boss in a bad economy. *Harvard Business Review Digital Edition*, June, pp. 42–50.

Syed, N., and Yan, L.X. (2012) Impact of high performance human resource management practices on employee job satisfaction: Empirical analysis. *Interdisciplinary Journal of Contemporary Research in Business*, 4(2): 318–342.

Taylor, P. (2009) Unions defer pay rises to blunt Alcoa axe. *The Australian*, 20 January. http://www.theaustralian.news.com.au/story/0,25197,24935554-5006789,00.html. Accessed 16.2.2009.

The World Bank (2008) Migration and development brief. 11 November. http://siteresources.worldbank.org/INTPROSPECTS/Resources/334934-1110315015165/MD_Brief8.pdf. Accessed 12.3.2009.

The World Bank (2012) Remittances to developing countries will surpass $400 billion in 2012. http://siteresources.worldbank.org/INTPROSPECTS/Resources/334934-1288990760745/MigrationDevelopmentBrief19.pdf. Accessed 1.1.2012.

Tombaugh, J.R. (2005) Positive leadership yields performance and profitability: effective organizations develop their strengths. *Development and Learning in Organizations*, 19(3): 15–17.

Traub, A., Draut, T. and Callahan, D. (2012) Level the playing field for American Manfacturing. *New York Times*, 4 September. http://www.nytimes.com/2012/02/03/business/economy/a-lure-to-keep-jobs-made-in-america.html?_r=0). Accessed 7.1.2013.

Trist, E.L. and Bamforth, K.W. (1951) Some social and psychological consequences of the long wall method of coal getting. *Human Relations*, 30: 201–236.

Truchon, M., Schmouth, M., Côté, D., Fillion, L., Rossignol, M. and Durand, M. (2012) Absenteeism screening questionnaire (ASQ): A new tool for predicting long-term absenteeism among workers with low back pain. *Journal of Occupational Rehabilitation*, 22(1): 27–50.

UN Global Compact (2013) Overview of the UN Global Compact. http://www.unglobalcompact.org/AboutTheGC/index.html. Accessed 6.1.2013.

United Airlines (2012) United Airlines Delivers Best 2012 Monthly Performance, to Pay Bonuses to Employees. http://finance.yahoo.com/news/united-airlines-delivers-best-2012-145000546.html. Accessed 4.1.2013. Press Release, United Continental Holdings, Inc., 3 December.

US Census Bureau (2010) Class of worker by sex and selected characteristic: 2010. Table 605. http://www.census.gov/compendia/statab/2012/tables/12s0605.pdf. Accessed 3.1.2013.

US Census Bureau (2012) Degrees earned by level and sex. Table 299. http://www.census.gov/compendia/statab/2012/tables/12s0299.pdf. Accessed 2.1.2013.

Vroom, V. (1964) Work and motivation. Malabar, FL: Krieger.

Waddell D.M, Cummings, T.G. and Worley, C.G. (2007) Organisation development and change. 3rd Asia Pacific ed. South Melbourne. Aus. Thompson.

Wang, M.K., Hwang, K.P. and Lin, S.R. (2011) An empirical study of the relationships among employees' perceptions of HR practice, human capital, and department performance: A case of AT&T Subordinate telecoms company in Taiwan. *Expert Systems with Applications*, 38(4): 3777–3783.

Whitaker, P. (2010) What non-financial rewards are successful motivators? *Strategic HR Review*, 9(1): 43–44.

Wikipedia (2012) IBM. http://en.wikipedia.org/wiki/IBM. Accessed 12.1.2013.

Williams, P., Khan, M.S. and Naumann, E. (2011) Customer dissatisfaction and defection: the hidden costs of downsizing. *Industrial Marketing Management*, V40(3): 405–413.

Winner, L. (1997) Autonomous technology: technics-out-of-Control as a theme in political thought. Cambridge, MA: MIT Press.

Witt, L.A., Andrews, M.C. and Kacmar, K.M. (2000) The role of participation in decision-making in the organisational politics – job satisfaction relationship. *Human Relations*, 53(3): 341–358.

Wood, S., Van Veldhoven, M., Croon, M. and de Menezes, L.M. (2012) Enriched job design, high involvement management and organizational performance: the mediating roles of job satisfaction and well-being. *Human Relations*, 65: 419–445.

Woodward, D. (2009) Generation next. *Director Magazine*, March. http://www.director.co.uk/magazine/2009/3%20March/generation_y_62_8.html. Accessed 7.1.2013.

Work Life Solutions (2008) Beware of the hidden costs of turnover. March 6. http://www.lifeworksolutions.com.au/news/beware-of-the-hidden-costs-of-turnover/.

Wray, R. (2009) Global recession costs 80,000 jobs a day. Guardian.co.uk, Tuesday 27 January. http://www.guardian.co.uk/business/2009/jan/26/job-losses-uk-europe-usa. Accessed 12.12.2012.

Wright, P.M. and Dyer, L. (1999) People in the e-business: new challenges, new solutions, in SHRM (Cornell University, Center for Advanced Human Resource Studies), November.

Zhou, Y., Zhang, Y. and Montoro-Sánchez, A. (2011) Utilitarianism or romanticism: The effect of rewards on employees. *International Journal of Manpower*, 32(1): 81–98.

INDEX